LETTERS
TO A FRIEND

Edward Field (on the right) and Neil Derrick
in New York in 2008

LETTERS
TO A FRIEND

DIANA ATHILL

W. W. Norton & Company • New York • London

For information about permission to reproduce selections from this book, write to
Permissions, W. W. Norton & Company, Inc., 500 Fifth Avenue, New York, NY 10110

For information about special discounts for bulk purchases, please contact W. W. Norton
Special Sales at specialsales@wwnorton.com or 800-233-4830

Manufacturing by RR Donnelley Harrisonburg
Production manager: Louise Mattarelliano

Library of Congress Cataloging-in-Publication Data

Athill, Diana.
Letters to a friend / Diana Athill. — 1st American ed.
p. cm.
ISBN 978-0-393-06295-3 (hardcover)
1. Athill, Diana—Correspondence. 2. Authors, English—20th century—Biography.
3. Women editors—Great Britain—Biography. 4. Field, Edward, 1924– —Friends and
associates. I. Title.
PR6051.T43Z46 2012
828'.91409—dc23
                                          2011044200

W. W. Norton & Company, Inc.,
500 Fifth Avenue, New York, N.Y. 10110
www.wwnorton.com

W. W. Norton & Company Ltd.,
Castle House, 75/76 Wells Street, London W1T 3QT

1 2 3 4 5 6 7 8 9 0

CONTENTS

INTRODUCTION

These letters belong to my dear friend Edward Field, to whom they were written. He kept them and decided that he would like to see them published. Usually when someone's letters are published the writer is dead. In this case there was a problem: Edward is six years younger than I am, but since I'm ninety-three that doesn't make him young. If he waited until I was dead he might be dead too.

From his point of view, therefore, the sooner the letters were published the better. From mine, once I had reread them I knew I would like them to be in print. This was because they record something precious to me: a friendship that has given me, and still gives me, much pleasure.

An important gain from being old is that one ceases to be a sexual being (though this may be less true of men than it is of women – indeed, in some ancient men a sort of freakish sexuality seems to intensify). For me, anyway, age has brought the end of it, so I have become free to love men without wanting to go to bed with them, which is surprisingly delightful. Having someone congenial to share experience with makes things more interesting, funnier, sometimes easier to bear. It is the essence of a friendship, and once past middle age one doesn't often find a new person to add warmth and colour to existence in this way. Getting to know Edward and his partner Neil Derrick in the early 1980s was an extraordinary piece of luck.

Edward is a poet who lives in New York with Neil, who writes prose. The nature of their life together is partly determined by the fact that in 1972 Neil was diagnosed with a brain tumour, the removal of which left him blind. Their friends marvel at the stoicism with which Neil endures his inevitable lack of independence and the generosity with which Edward makes light of being depended on. Between them they divest the situation of anything unusual or poignant, becoming just two people whose company is exceptionally enjoyable; but when one stands back and looks at them from a distance one sees two different kinds of heroism which happen by great good fortune to interlock, and the sight does one good.

I am a bad reader of poetry. When it is complex, greatly condensed and obscure I don't like it because I believe that the purpose of language is communication. If something which has to be expressed can only be put on paper to the satisfaction of the expresser in what amounts to code, I am prepared to take other people's word for it that it is beautiful but I don't want to read it. At the same time, however, no one can be quite unaffected by the surrounding intellectual climate, which means that often I find that poems I can understand leave me feeling that anything so easy can't be much good. It was therefore a wonderful surprise when I found that I loved Edward's poems. Their character can best be explained by one of his own accounts of his approach to poetry:

The main thing for me is that I've always wanted my poetry to be understood by anybody ... I don't see why poetry can't be as readable as prose. In fact, it seems to me that poetry should be easier to read than prose. A poem is short, usually, and the lines are broken up into nice little segments that clarify ideas. I make it even easier with my narrative style ... The whole point of poetry for me is subject matter, saying what I have to say, saying what has never been said before, what's not polite to say.

It is not surprising that he welcomes a recent development in American poetry which first emerged in California and has been labelled 'Neo Pop' – and which was influenced by his own work. 'Vulgar, funny, dirty, sassy, Neo Pop doesn't aim at tightness, though the expression is often succinct and precise. Nor is it obscure, it speaks right out, plainly and directly, in the language we use.'

That last sentence is an exact description of Edward's own poems, and I suppose I was drawn so quickly into friendship with him because he is a person who 'speaks right out', and is at the same time loveable (of course 'speaking right out' would not be a recommendation if the person were horrid!). An open nature invites an open response: right from the start I knew that to Edward I could say anything, and this it was that made these letters fun to write. It also makes them a true portrait of a happy relationship – from which, being still around, I have been able to remove things hurtful to other people (there were very few) and to which I could add explanations when it seemed necessary. For these reasons, although I know it may seem odd to allow this publication while I am still alive, I am happy to do so.

My interventions: when only a few words seemed necessary I have inserted them in the text enclosed in square brackets. When more is needed, it comes in italics after the letter concerned. I should also explain that neither Edward nor I can produce explanations for the long gaps between letters that sometimes occur. Too much time has passed. Every year Edward and Neil would come to Europe, usually to London, for long visits, during which – no letters. And in between those gaps we were both leading full lives, so that weeks and weeks could pass without our having time to write – although sometimes we would call each other. Also I suspect that occasionally – very occasionally – a letter has been lost. Looking at the correspondence from the outside, so to speak, as I can now do, I am struck by how little the gaps mattered. They never seem to have diminished the friendship.

When the question of this book's title arose, and someone remarked that it almost amounted to the story of my life during the years it covered, it occurred to me that perhaps, without realizing it, that was what I had been doing when I wrote these letters: because I hadn't got a book to write, my book-writing energy was going into them. Whereupon its title became evident. My first book, way back in 1962, was written (at least partly) to explain myself to someone I loved, so I called it *Instead of a Letter*. In England, these letters are *Instead of a Book*. In America, they are *Letters to a Friend*.

Diana Athill
London, 2011

EDWARD FIELD'S
INTRODUCTION

It wasn't until she was over ninety years old, with the success of her memoir of aging, *Somewhere Towards the End*, an unlikely international best seller, that Diana Athill became an icon of the British literary world – 'the doyenne of English letters', according to the *Guardian* newspaper. But her professional involvement with writing began fifty years before, at the end of World War II, when she and Hungarian émigré André Deutsch founded one of the liveliest of London publishing houses, André Deutsch Ltd, where she remained as senior editor until she retired in 1993.

But she also had a parallel career as a writer with a small, devoted following since the 1962 publication of *An Unavoidable Delay*, a book of crisp, poignant short stories, followed by her revealing memoir *Instead of a Letter*, in which she told about her first love, the awful betrayal, and recovery. This was followed by a novel, *Don't Look at Me Like That*, and full-length portraits of two of her authors – *After a Funeral*, about Waguih Ghali, an upper-class

Egyptian exile who committed suicide in her apartment, and *Make Believe*, which relates the disastrous trajectory of the Black Panther Hakim Jamal, whose lovers included the actress Jean Seberg and, briefly, his editor. Everything she's written demonstrates her famously beady eye, and an unusual – for a Brit of her class – openness about her intimate life. She's so frank about her sexuality, she does not hesitate to talk about giving up sex at the age of seventy.

After retirement from publishing she produced a further series of memoirs, of which *Stet*, a razor-sharp account of her years as an editor, marked the beginning of her post-retirement rise to fame as an author. This book included profiles of some of her more memorable, and difficult, authors, such as Jean Rhys and V.S. Naipaul, as well as her running battles with André Deutsch. But the most eccentric and colorful of them all was surely the American writer Alfred Chester, whose books invariably lost them money, but was for me the most important – for he was one of my closest friends, and it was he who drew Diana and me together.

Alfred Chester with his pudgy, eyebrow-less face, ratty red wig and manic energy was one of the inescapable figures on the literary scene of the Fifties and Sixties, the period of his brief but intense literary flowering, both in expatriate Paris and New York, when each thing he published was distinctive enough to cause a flurry of excitement. I had watched, helpless, as he slid into irrecoverable madness and, after his shadowy death at the age of forty-one in Jerusalem, in spite of his reputation, he was quickly forgotten. He was such a disturbing presence, it was as though the literary world was relieved to be rid of him.

But I was not about to let him disappear without a fight. As early as the Fifties, he had written me from Paris about Diana Athill, his devoted editor in London who had published him before any American publisher would risk it. He would never be a popular writer, but, even with the good reviews his books got, considering their minimal sales, Diana's sticking by him was proof to me of her courage and independence.

So in 1980, a decade after his death, the injustice of his literary wipeout provoked me to consult with her on how to revive his reputation. I never could have imagined that this would be the beginning of a thirty-year correspondence between us. And I couldn't have foreseen that she would become such a significant person in the lives of my partner, Neil Derrick, and me. Diana sympathized with my Alfred Project, and wrote a moving introduction to Alfred's novel *The Exquisite Corpse* when an American publisher reprinted it in 1987, an essay she later included in *Stet*, her memoir of her André Deutsch years.

It was shortly after our correspondence began that Neil and I went to London and met her. The impression I'd gotten from Alfred was an English spinster out of a Barbara Pym novel, though with an erotic life that thrived in Mediterranean climes. As it turned out, this wasn't totally wrong, as readers of her confessional memoirs well know. More crucial to the picture I had of her was that when Alfred went crazy, he turned to her for help, and she brought her sensible nature to bear on the problem of What to Do About Alfred. Though by then, little could be done to halt his downward slide.

The reality, when we finally climbed the dusty stairs to the shabby, cluttered offices of André Deutsch, was much more vivid – no twittery Barbara Pym character she! It was love at first sight. Or was it, on our part, Awe? Imposing the way she stood, the almost Roman head, the formidable jaw, the crisp diction – all spoke of a breed that built an empire. To the manor born. Neil immediately said 'county'. She is a handsome woman who, when young, had the kind of 'strong' face that is wasted on the young and has to be grown into.

To our American ears, the variety of accents in Britain is endlessly fascinating. Hers is one of those that to us evokes country houses, horsemanship and the ruling class – it's not heard much anymore, even in the House of Lords. Speaking with her, it became a challenge to me almost from the beginning to try to imitate not her accent but her composed sentences, the clarity of her speech. Having grown up with parents who spoke immigrant English and lacking her classical Oxford education, I can only approximate her syntax – it's just not built into me.

Her writing is equally structured. We Americans have to rewrite and rewrite to get there. If the rigors of writing poetry have given me an appreciation of her verbal discipline, I console myself with the thought that English is really their language, one that we Americans have adapted to a different world and mentality.

Our friendship coincided with a long period when, thanks to a helpful real estate agent who found us affordable flats, Neil and I were managing to spend several months at a time in London. From our downmarket neighborhood off

Bayswater, we would make the trek to decidedly posh Primrose Hill on the far side of Regent's Park, where Diana then lived with the late Jamaican playwright Barry Reckord. This upper-class woman openly having a black partner was, I believe, even in a country as tolerant as England, not everywhere accepted, and they seemed to live largely separate lives, which, however, squared with Barry's belief in open relationships. It also turned out that Barry had an abrasive social manner that made him somewhat difficult in company. But when Neil and I met him, it was a great relief that he approved of us.

During World War II, when I was stationed at an airfield in the Midlands, I had experienced the legendary damp and chill of the British Isles. So when I first returned to England in the Sixties, I arrived with long underwear and fur boots. But it soon became apparent that things had changed. Postwar austerity was gone and such precautions were no longer necessary – except on Primrose Hill. Diana's flat, on the top floor of her cousin's big house with a view over the greenery of the park, lacked central heating, and the sitting room where we had tea was heated by a measly gas log in the fireplace that barely sent out a few rays of warmth. [*Nonsense; it was a very efficient and superior gas-fire. DA*] For an American this was simply inconceivable.

But it was somehow tolerable for this sturdy daughter of Britain. For her Jamaican companion's room, however, there were blazing electric heaters and a luxurious duvet on the bed, where he spent a good deal of his time. Barry Reckord was a name in the theatre during the Fifties and Sixties, with an impressive series of productions at the

Royal Court Theatre and on television. But by the time we got to know him through Diana, his plays were no longer being produced, and as the years passed his solution was to give up writing and take to his bed.

In the early days, Barry came out of his room to have a cup of tea with us and preach his bohemian theories of free sex and society – unnecessary, since we were old Greenwich Villagers well-versed in Reichian lore. But later, impatient with our small talk, he'd disappear into his room. His relationship with Diana was never supposed to be a conventional man-and-wife arrangement, but as he had one health crisis after another through the years, as related in her letters, Diana was forced to become his carer – cook, nurse and mopper-up after. It was a role that did not suit her, and as she aged became too difficult, resulting in his return to Jamaica where he died in 2011.

Subsequent to Barry's departure and the success of *Somewhere Towards the End*, Diana left her Primrose Hill flat and moved into an old-age residence in the upscale community of Highgate in North London.

Grand as Diana appears, I quickly learned that she's about as unconventional as I am – well, almost. If living with a black man was violating the rules of her class, it soon became clear that 'unsuitable' relationships, often with her authors, were an important part of her life, not just lovers but friendships and orphan types she adopted – a notable example here was of course my friend Alfred Chester, though Jean Rhys was equally unbalanced. Her lovers, of course, ran the gamut.

Authors as a breed tend not to be sober, thrifty or wise,

and in this kind of crowd someone with good sense is a treasure. And this quality of Diana's was called upon alarmingly often, as her authors and friends leapt off cliffs of unreason – drugs, husbands, wives, boyfriends, girlfriends, extravagance and just plain craziness. She was always there to rescue, connect them to needed help, or simply keep them from rocking the boat too wildly. But, ultimately, they were her material and she wrote about them.

In one important area she joins her authors in being extremely reckless by revealing in her writings personal details of her life that people of her sort in England Don't Do. Perhaps that is why she doesn't disapprove of my poetry, which is nothing but self-revelation.

Another rule of English life is never to talk about your health, but Diana actually talks about her ailments, not as much as New Yorkers do – New Yorkers of our age talk about little else – but more than any of our other English friends.

When Diana's long, marvellous letters arrived, I'd read them aloud to Neil – they were an Event! It felt flattering to be the recipients of a kind of epistolary diary, and indeed they were full-blown literary works. No question of tossing them out. They soon had an ever-expanding accordion envelope of their own.

And as they accumulated, one day – it was in 2003 – we both said, *these must be published,* and started typing them up. Neil is blind, but he's an expert typist – in fact, we met in a typing pool when working as temps. So he sat at the keyboard and I dictated the letters to him, enjoying them all over again.

But when I informed Diana about what we were doing, she wrote back that publication of private correspondence wasn't appropriate while she was still alive. Still, it was such fun to read the letters again that we kept going back to typing them up when there was time between our other literary projects. In any case, it was clear that these letters were an intimate portrait of Diana's life that would ultimately have to be published.

It was a huge job. There were a lot of them, and many were so long – pages of tiny script. Diana had improved her handwriting, she told me, by practicing the discipline of calligraphy. But I couldn't help noticing how the writing loosened considerably on the second page, and by the end of the final page revealed a schoolgirl enthusiasm in the large, loopy letters. Evidence of a certain recklessness under that sensible exterior!

Many friends of my own generation resist computers, no matter how I argue their benefits. But about this time Diana found it almost impossible to find ribbons for her electric typewriter, and since Neil and I were in London for a couple of months, I set out to convince her to switch to a computer, which, admittedly, can be traumatic – I remember my own early digital days when poems vanished in the middle of writing them. But I would be there to help her with the transition, initially at least.

I located a 'learner model' (meaning a cheap clunker) in a secondhand market, and taught her the rudiments – then heartlessly decamped to New York, leaving her to struggle on her own. She managed, though, and became one of my two success stories teaching oldies to use a computer. Although some handwritten letters still occasionally arrived, when she was in her country cottage in Norfolk or when that old computer died on her, our correspondence was by e-mail.

Finally, in 2010, it was finished. And this time, when we sent the transcribed manuscript to her, Diana, now reading with her editor's eye, saw it as a book and agreed that it could be published.

As a literary work, the letters chart the voyage from her final years at André Deutsch, and how she recovered from the chrysalis of retirement and emerged like a butterfly as a famous writer at the age of ninety. And with that, honors – the Costa Prize and an OBE (Order of the British Empire), among others. Neil and I listen regularly to the BBC over the Internet and often hear her distinctive voice commenting on her life. In fact, her retirement home received a flood of applicants after she spoke about it on the air! She has even had a television documentary about her, and is the subject of numerous interviews in magazines and newspapers, as well as being photographed by top photographers. Being famous is a role that suits her admirably – fame coming late in life, she accepts it calmly and remains herself. If she now has trouble walking and travelling is difficult, she still manages to appear in literary festivals around the country – at the age of ninety she discovered she can perform effectively before an audience. She is undoubtedly an inspiration to many, though she confessed that she was nonplussed when a man at her car wash – she drove a car until the age of ninety-four! – fell to his knees, took her hand and declared, 'You are my inspiration!'

My 'conversation' with Diana Athill, as revealed in the letters, has lasted thirty years. But since Neil and I finished typing them up and sent her the full manuscript to edit, it feels like our major correspondence phase has finished – with publication, 'completion' hangs over it. But it's not that our friendship with her is any different, although, sadly, with age our trips to London are less frequent.

But I still rely on her stability and good sense. The older we get – and she is always six years ahead of me – I have come to depend on her, not exactly for inspiration, but for the kind of advice that only someone older than you can provide. I think this is the function she has come to serve the British public, as the Chief Guide to Old Age, a reassurance that it need not necessarily be dire. Or if it usually is, she is a vast exception to the rule.

But when I was in my late seventies, still struggling with my old Freudian problems that Jewish New Yorkers never seem to escape, Diana told me that at eighty, I would wake up one morning with a flash of happiness, and this would be a foretaste of a happier old age. It had happened to her. And, indeed, in my eightieth year, I woke up on a February morning and there was a heavenly smell of spring in the air, brief but blissful. And in the following years her prediction came true.

Edward Field
New York, 2012

LETTERS
TO A FRIEND

23 JULY 1981

Dear Mr Field,

Alfred's letters arrived yesterday when, as it happened, I was spending a day at home so that I was able to read them straight away; then lie awake most of the night thinking about him. What an old cat among the pigeons of my quiet mind!

I shall wait until André Deutsch gets back from New York next week, before letting you have our decision, but straight away I can warn you: don't be hopeful. Alfred's work never made the mark it should have done in this country ... I guess it would be impossible to persuade booksellers to stock them. André may feel that we could get away with it, but I doubt it. So, as I say, don't expect anything good from my next letter. [*I was the editorial director of André Deustch Ltd from 1952 to my retirement in 1992.*]

They are marvellous letters – and thank god for you, being there for him to love and trust. In me they awoke the most painful feelings because I have always felt that I betrayed Alfred because I was frightened by madness. The first time he came to London after settling in Morocco – or the first important time – was when he brought Dris [*Alfred's boyfriend*] over to have his foot treated, and that was fine. How deeply I regretted that I couldn't afford Dris's brother, when he suggested

1

sending him over (because he was so shocked to see a friend of Alfred's washing her own dishes – in fact he took over and did them, bless him). I think that was the first time I saw Alfred without his wig – though there may have been another cheerful visit on which that happened. I thought he looked so much better without it. Should I, or should I not, mention it? Then I decided that naturally how people reacted to its absence must be of importance to him (I hadn't yet read his last writings so didn't know *how* important the presence or absence of that ghastly wig was) so I said how good it was to see him without it and that he looked very impressive – which he did – and he seemed to be quite pleased about that. After that occasion, I remember, it seemed to me that Morocco was a marvellous thing in Alfred's life. He had talked a good deal about the Moroccan attitude to sex, and it seemed that here was a place where he could be easy and happy sexually, and could let his wig go, so surely it would make him better (I didn't then know anything about his madness, but still I must have felt worried about him or why that feeling that he needed to be made better?).

And then came the day when I walked into the office and there was Alfred sitting in reception, and no sooner were we up in my room that he told me that he'd come to ask me to tell the prime minister to stop the voices. Then there was something about having attacked Dris because he was on 'their' side – he must have been, because he kept on denying 'they' were there when 'they' so clearly were – and then a reference to what I had said to him when I was in Marrakesh the other day. 'But Alfred, love,

I never was in Marrakesh,' whereupon he started to try to trap me into admitting that I knew what I had said on that occasion, and there was a little cold hint that whereas up to this point I was being seen by him more or less as a potential friend and helper, I might become one of 'them' at any moment. Anyway, we struck a sort of bargain. He said that if he could admit that he knew that I believed him to be mad, surely I could admit that I knew that he believed absolutely in the reality of what he was telling me – 'it's as real to me as a bus going down the street.' So if I would fix him up with a meeting with the prime minister, he would go see a doctor of my choice. OK I said.

I thought the best doctor to phone would be Ronald Laing – he would at least be kind, it seemed to me. He was away so they put me onto his buddy David Cooper. Cooper said he'd see him but I mustn't cheat, I must keep my side of the bargain. Luckily I'd told Alfred that I had no way in to the prime minister, but could get on to a member of parliament, if that would do, and he'd accepted that. So I called a member of parliament of my acquaintance who said 'God, no! Are you mad yourself? If you knew how many nuts we have after us about their bloody voices!' But by that time it had sunk through into my mind that Alfred would not have come to me if it were not that something in him was badly wanting to be taken to a doctor – probably I had seemed the right person to come to simply because of all of the people he knew I was probably the squarest and the most likely to think in terms of doctors. So I guessed that if I told him that I tried the MP, but that he wouldn't see him, he would probably choose to accept that, and go to the doctor anyway, and he did. He didn't like him, though – said he was like an Irish bookie. (I believe he was, rather – he collapsed not long after into alcoholism which is something many Irish bookies must do, or would, if they didn't have strong Irish heads.) But the doctor took some trouble and said that if I could arrange for payment he could arrange for a psychiatric social worker to go and talk to Alfred every day and try to help him through this crisis. So I called Alfred's brother – how did I get his number? Perhaps the doc had got it from Alfred? – and told him he must pay, and he agreed that he would (sounding less villainous than Alfred had led me to expect, so that it occurred to me that perhaps having Alfred as a brother was no joy-ride). And Alfred was lent a place by someone on the edge of London, and the young man started to visit him, and it seemed that their talks were going alright – the young man used to report back to me for lack of anyone else, and was soon tremendously on Alfred's side and most excited at having the privilege of knowing him. And I, apart from a couple of telephone calls, left it at that. I did not go to visit him, I did not ask him round to my place. In other words, my affection for him, though genuine as far as it went, only went so far – the strain of all this had exhausted me, and I felt scared of this unknown quantity of madness, so I kept thinking 'Well, I've done what I can in a practical way,' and putting off seeing him. And then, when the young man said he'd gone back to Morocco, I felt relieved. Very! And never again did I hear another word from Alfred.

Sometimes I've told myself 'Well, maybe he felt embarrassed . . .' But really I feel sure that he felt 'she's no true friend' and in that he was right. Not a really true friend. And I wish I had been. So you can see how sad those letters have made me feel.

Yours, Diana Athill

I never even heard from anyone how he died. I would like to know, if it wouldn't be too painful for you to tell me briefly. I don't, by the way, imagine that I could have made any real difference by being closer to him after fixing up the young man's visits. Just selfish disappointment, really, at finding myself a less generously loving person than I would have liked to be!!

13 AUGUST 1981

Dear Edward (if I may?),

Thank you very much for your letter – Oh, I was so glad to get it. [*Because it told me not to feel bad – none of Alfred's friends were able to cope with his madness.*]

You'll be less glad to get this one, because it has to say the 'no' I warned you of. But André Deutsch points out that Harpers have a big organization in this country, so if you let them have the British rights as well as the US rights, they could – well, to make you flinch by quoting André exactly: 'the forty-five copies we could sell in this country, they could sell.' It's worth considering, I think.

Your comparison with [*J. R.*] Ackerley ought to be true, but in this country Ackerley has two things going for him which Alfred lacked. Ackerley's *Hindoo Holiday* benefits from the special possessive feeling the English have for India – a feeling with large accretions of nostalgia accumulating on it daily; and Ackerley didn't just have a dog, he fell in love with it and wrote about it at length [*in* My Dog Tulip], and even though his passion did rather raise the eyebrows of your average English dog lover – well, you Can't Go Wrong with Books About Dogs. Whereas Alfred's only asset is that he's a marvellous writer (far better than dear Ackerley), and it's terrifying how being a marvellous writer has diminished in weight as a reason for buying books during my long career in publishing. Of course André was exaggerating when he said 'forty-five' – but he wasn't exaggerating enormously.

How lovely to have a Prix de Rome – I am glad for you. Please don't fail to get in touch when you are in London. I think I'd remember if we met in Sullivan St. – I'd liked your poems so much – but then again, my head is full of holes these days, so you might have fallen through one of them. All I can clearly remember is feet coming up that dangerous stairway as Alfred and I sat eating mushrooms in sour cream, and Alfred whispering Oh my God – sssshhhh!, and us having to pretend we weren't there, because the feet belonged to a boy Alfred was trying to get rid of – a recent pickup I gathered, about whom he'd thought better. (But perhaps someone he was testing?) It wasn't long after Arthur's departure – I remember how I wished he were still there, not because

I liked him (didn't know him at all well, but took against him fairly strongly) but because of poor Alfred's forlornness. Oh yes – and then I said: 'But Alfred, dear heart, what on earth makes you suppose that it's likely that someone you pick up in a urinal will suddenly become your true love?' And he was condescending to me for being so lacking in romanticism.

Good luck with your huge popular novel – how clever you and Neil must be – and I do look forward to meeting you both sometime in your Roman year. Sincerely, Diana

[*The 'huge popular novel': Edward had never written fiction, but Neil had, and now because Neil needed to defy his blindness, they had decided to collaborate on a novel – a straightforward 'good story' novel, not an egghead one, because it must please a readership wide enough to bring them in some money. They chose to make it a family saga illustrating the history of New York's Greenwich Village, a subject in which they were both genuinely interested. The collaboration was far from easy, but it was successful.* Village, *by Bruce Elliot, was published by Avon Books, publisher of original paperbacks, and sold 220,000 copies. Their attempts to follow up this dizzying success have not so far come to anything, perhaps because none of their many ideas have interested them as much as that first one. They have, however, given* Village *a second life, reissued as* The Villagers; *and neither of them appears to be much distressed at Bruce Elliot's demise.*

Alfred's Arthur: his great love. He'd smuggled him from Paris to New York by sending him a girl to marry, and then Arthur went hetero on him – and ended up, I believe, with six children.]

17 AUGUST 1981

Dear Edward,

Alfred's 'Letter From The Wandering Jew' arrived today and I read it straight away. Heartbreaking. [*This was something he'd sent Edward not long before his death in Israel, hoping Edward could sell it to a newspaper for him.*] I'm glad his poor heart broke (if he didn't give himself an o.d. of tranquillizers etc. – and if he did, he was right to do so). What is so terrible is the thought that perhaps before too long the scientists who are working on the assumption that mental and emotional disturbances are caused by various kinds of chemical imbalance will prove to be right – I feel almost sure they are – and it will become possible to see that the hell lived through by Alfred, and all the other hells lived through by a great many other mad people, come from some quite simple mechanical defect ('simple' compared with the kinds of solution proposed by psychiatrists). There was a time when I veered towards being impressed by the Laing school of thought (that the mad were really sane etc.) – but now I suspect that the only good thing about that school was the rejection of the violence done by conventional psychiatrists to the insane; and that they were heaping a great load of exhausting theory onto the helpless patients and doing them no good at all – as though they had said to patients with enteritis 'you're quite right to vomit, the food you are being served is disgusting – go on, eat and vomit, eat and vomit, that's what everyone ought to do with such food' instead of giving the poor things a soothing medicine. I think of that young psychiatric social worker finding tremendous significance in the wisdom of Alfred's madness – and now I think 'what nonsense!' The wisdom, the brilliance, was poor darling Alfred surviving being mad, reappearing in fits and starts as himself in spite of his madness. Since no one has yet found out how the chemistry of the brain operates or how to remedy its malfunctions, nothing else could be done, I suppose, but attempt psychiatric methods – and tranquillizers – but how dreadful to think that there is quite likely a method of curing madness such as Alfred's waiting to be produced by some laboratory, and that if it comes, he won't be here.

I remembered the other day how the very first time I met him – soon after the publication of *Jamie*, I think, when he was living in Paris with Arthur [Jamie Is My Heart's Desire, *his first novel, was published by André Deutsch in 1956*] – he began to talk about identity: did I feel that I knew who 'I' was? Yes, I said, rather apologetically – it seemed a bit crude and simple-minded to admit to it! and he said I was lucky, he didn't, he felt he was just whatever he happened to be behaving as at the moment – and I thought at the time, and for a long time afterwards, that this preoccupation of his was purely philosophical. Still – nothing would have been gained by recognizing it as the maggot stirring in the brain, since there was no way in which anyone could get at the vile thing. But how I wished, reading this sad sad piece, that some accident could have carried him off before all the joy had been leeched out of him. Compared to you, I was only a slight acquaintance of his – so if contemplating his plight at the end makes my heart ache so badly, I can't bear to think what it must have done to yours. Diana

[*There was a first meeting sometime between this letter and the next, at which I saw how much I liked them both; but it was not until their next visit to London that the friendship became established.*]

6 FEBRUARY 1983

Dear Edward –

Lovely to get your letter – and of course I don't mind your sending my Alfred piece out. [*It was used as introduction to a reissue of his novel* The Exquisite Corpse in America *by Carroll & Graf.*]

The very name of Norman [*Glass – a friend of Alfred's*] fills me with alarm . . . but why should one feel looming a terrible sense of obligation towards a person who deliberately chooses to live a perilous existence? Will he end murdered? Or a toothless and decrepit old nut huddled in a corner of some monastery or whatever? I suppose it could be argued that in either case he wouldn't be much worse off than those of us who cautiously end up in a hospital bed, because after all that's no fun either . . . But I do think you're right to advise him against Mexico.

Barry [*on a visit to Jamaica*] sounds rather cheerful on

the telephone. At the moment he's got some darling friends of ours staying with him – a couple much younger, so that to me she seems almost like a daughter. To Barry too, by now I think, tho' to start with, when she was acting in a play of his, she was a girlfriend. Friends used to be astonished – and I think rather disapproving – at our all three getting on so well, but Sal didn't turn up till after B and I had already turned into something nearer Family than Lovers. The great luck is that this lovely and amazing girl, when she decided to marry someone her own age, hit on a lovely and amazing boy, and her Henry fits in as naturally and unjealously as possible. She has now become a farmer, as her parents have always been, and has just started her first pregnancy and they are taking a heavily deserved two-week hol in Jamaica staying on the edge of the sea with Barry. B's brother Lloyd owns a studio apartment in a condominium in Montego Bay – a very approximate and wobbly attempt at the kind of thing which, I imagine, exists in Miami. B cheerfully contemplated having Sal and Henry and his mother there all at once, saying 'But why not? There is a separate bedroom'. His mother is a very querulous (tho' strong) 85, who specializes in being Displeased – and, if one happens to be around, Barry is wholly unscrupulous, saying 'Go and sit with Mama and chat with her for a bit' and then vanishing for the day . . . which, luckily for Sal and Henry, Sal already knew. B was astonished when she said she thought she would expire if she had to spend her hard-won vacation closeted with Mama – but when we had acted out a few little scenes for him, of what would happen, he had to agree that we were quite right, so he has put the old lady off until Sal and Henry have left. And is therefore having a nice easy rum-and-sun-soaked time, which he needed. But I bet Mama manages to make him rue it before he is through!

I'm quite pleased with myself, because I haven't once woken up in the night and heard thieves and rapists creaking up the stairs – and that in spite of being home for a week with some kind of throat infection – not a bad one. It is really strange how subjective that kind of nervousness is, depending entirely on one's mood or chemistry, not on objective fact. I've gone through my Ritual Fury at the filthy condition in which B leaves his room – it is my contention that if an able-bodied adult doesn't choose to keep him/her self clean, that's his/her business, so it's understood that while I have a full-time office job and he's working at home, I do not clean up after Barry, or wash for him. But regularly, once a year or so, when he hops off to see his Ma, he wins – simply because it's not possible to leave that room to Suppurate for three months – people want to come and stay in it from time to time, when it's available. So I storm through it, swearing and spluttering – and end up feeling rather pleased and soothed at its clean and fresh appearance. Once I wrote Barry a letter while at Storm-pitch, saying 'An old man you can't help becoming, I know, but a dirty old man – a filthy, stinking old man . . . that you can help and it's *too much*.' (Marginal Note: all it actually is, is a fair number of unwashed socks stuffed into shopping bags, and half an inch or so of cigarette ash on all flat surfaces.) And oh the horror of what happened. He was staying with Lloyd and Lloyd's boyfriend Colin, and just before that letter arrived he had a spat with them and left – and Colin had staying a pretty boy of dubious morals who Lloyd threw out – and the pretty boy in a fit of pique stole all the mail that came in one day, which included that letter, and read it, and later showed it to Colin ... Which all goes to show that my father wasn't far out when he used to say: 'Never write a letter which you would blush to see published in the correspondence columns of *The Times*.'

Well now, I wonder about this one ...

Anyway, it brings you both the Season's Greetings as well as much love, Diana.

21 JULY 1983

Dear Edward,

I was so very glad that you will be in London for a while. This is to confirm what I fixed with Neil on the phone – that you will come and have supper with me on Saturday, July 30, at about 7.30. It won't be a dinner party. My friend Barry's sister is staying with us – her first visit to England from Jamaica in sixty years, which is fun because she is loving it – and I'm too lazy to make a meal for more than five people.

Map enclosed – which you may need even if you come by taxi because sometimes they don't know it.

It will be lovely to see you both again. Diana

24 AUGUST 1983

Dear Edward,

I enclose my Alfred memories [*he had asked for a descriptive piece, which I included eventually in my book* Stet]. I don't think they'd be of much interest to anyone who didn't know him – for one thing I'm not sure that I could be bothered to put in whatever 'explaining' might be necessary, or to pin down dates (something I can never do even to recent ones – how on earth can people even *begin* to answer when a lawyer asks them in court 'Where were you on Tuesday the 10th of November two years ago?' I couldn't tell them where I was at 8.30 last Tuesday!).

You once said something about Alfred being dreadful when he put Dris out of the car in Spain. Can that have been on the journey when they had the accident? [*Described in my book* Stet.] There must have been something wrong about that story as I heard it – altho' Dris did a lot of the telling . . . probably your story is something quite different. But I'm sure the bits of Alfred I was allowed to see were edited – not with the intention of deceiving, but for stylistic reasons.

I loved our evening with you, and so – this is a marvel – did Barry. It's a marvel because he's becoming more unsociable every day. When people come to us he feels safe because he can say will they please forgive him but he has to get a piece of work finished (and then hope they don't hear that he's listening to football on the telly). But going out he often jibs at, because once out there's no escape. So you and Neil should feel flattered that a) he looked forward to our evening with you, and b) enjoyed it.

Love to you both, Diana

4 OCTOBER 1983

Dear Edward,

I'll get round to xeroxing some of Alfred's letters when I get back from a spell of holiday I'm just about to embark on. After five weeks running without a weekend off (usually I manage to stay in London for one weekend in three, but my ma's helpers were away) I collapsed into a state of very heavy exhaustion and couldn't drag myself out of bed one morning. So I called my doctor who couldn't see me for a week, and by the time the appointment came round was feeling better enough to contemplate cancelling it – but I'm glad I didn't, because she found that my blood pressure was a good deal too high and ordered me to take a couple of weeks' rest at once, after which, if the b.p. has gone down hurrah and if it hasn't we will start medication.

I think it's worry rather than physical fatigue. My mother doesn't often have 'turns' (angina attacks, or a wretched vertigo which is very distressing) but she does sometimes, and when I'm there I go to bed listening for the bell which I've had rigged up between her room and mine; and if in the morning I wake up and don't hear her shuffling along to the bathroom at exactly her usual time, I go along to her room quite expecting to find her dead. How I admire the innumerable people who live all the time with their ancient parents. The way it abolishes one's own life and substitutes a half-bored, half-pitying anxiety over someone else's is pretty grim. I know what you mean about 'nothing to keep you from dying' once the parents have gone. I see my mother as a sort of breakwater between me and the sea – an increasingly frail and worm-eaten one, but still something to prevent the direct impact of the breakers on my own crumbling sand. I'd love to read your poem for your ma.

Yes, it was amazing to find Venice still so possible. You wouldn't have thought it was if you had gone straight to St Mark's Square and the shopping streets between there and the Rialto Bridge – unbelievable, the turmoil of tourism around there. But one benefit of package tourism is that it can't let its members stray: they've got to be conveyed from A to B within a certain time or the whole thing will collapse. The Pensione Accademia, where I stayed, is literally only inches off the beaten track, but was still very serene, and the flat rented by my nephew was yards off it and might have been in a city without tourism! We spent most of our time marvelling at what a secret, silent town it is. I'd love to go back there now, but think taking it easy in my own pad for half the hol, and a spell in a luxurious fat farm for the other half, makes more sense in the circumstances. I have a faiblesse for fat farms (though my favourite one, which is in a very distinguished Georgian house with a magical garden, hasn't a vacancy,

and the one I'm actually going to is composed of rather
suburban-looking architecture – I only hope that it's
being a good deal more expensive than my favourite
means it's even more comfortable). People who've never
been to such places suppose them to be fiercely austere
and say 'But imagine paying all that money to be fed on
lettuce!' But in fact the whole secret of a good one is that
it is infinitely cosseting, from the snugness of its electric
blankets to the soft yet firm hands of its masseurs, and
such starving as one does is done on very pretty and
tasty morsels of this and that – little bowls of fresh
yogurt mixed with honey and adorned with grapes. I
think there's fierce competition between them, and the
ones which make the punters feel most cherished are the
ones which win.

What a treat if you come in November. Diana

17 OCTOBER 1983 (FROM SHRUBLAND HALL,
CODDENHAM, SUFFOLK)

[*In the end, my favourite fat farm did have a place for me.*]

Dearest Edward –

This is an incongruous place to be thanking you for
your poems from. More about it later. First – I've read
The Crier only once, so far – the earlier collection twice –
so I'm not really familiar with the new poems, except
that I am very familiar with the subject of many of them:
getting old! Those poems don't just touch a nerve, they

play arpeggios on it. I expect I'll like *The Crier* as much
as I do *Full Heart* when I know it as well. It's a bit
heretical for an English person to love poems so direct,
so surely aimed at the quickest route to the naked truth
about feelings. I can think of several English critics who
would shrink from them. But I felt I was hearing you talk
only more so, which I enjoy very very very much.
(Except when I get steamed up over the ridiculousness of
someone so handsome and so easily able to charm
suffering all those torments.) The poems about you and
Neil are scary and marvellous. Bless you for sending me
this wonderful package.

The above palatial surroundings are for losing weight
in. It's not a good drawing [*I think it was on a letter
heading*]. At the top of those steps is a dear little temple,
through which you reach a lush lawn, and then a terrace
(draped, in season, with roses) and then a stately front of
an enormous Country House. Behind the viewer is
another little temple, slightly larger and very elegant, and
behind that, splendid pretend-wild woods fall gracefully
away. The house's noble owners have very sensibly
moved into a much smaller place and have turned the
big house into a Fat Farm, which enables them to keep
the garden, park and farmlands in sleekly prosperous
condition. Being – rather surprisingly – Buddhists, they
disapprove of huge profits, so it's simultaneously the
lushest and least expensive fat farm in England, and I
adore it. Every year I say to myself 'This is the *last time* –
it's too corrupt and shocking in this starving world . . .'
And every next year I reach a point of exhaustion where
I say 'If I don't have a week at Shrubland I shall

collapse.' It's so beautiful, and the rooms are so charming (mostly furnished with their original stuff). And being expertly massaged every day is such bliss, and the country is so delicious to walk in, and the staff is so kind, and losing about ten pounds in a week makes you feel so good (even tho' you do quickly put it on again). Above all, it's total relaxation. Most of the other fat ladies are very boring, and the fat gentlemen worse, but you can easily avoid them – and each time I've been here there have been one or two congenial spirits to go sight-seeing with in the afternoons or whatever. But mostly I read, sleep, listen to music and think my own thoughts. Heaven! And oddly enough you don't feel hungry when eating almost nothing, if everyone else is doing the same and you are making the ritual act of acceptance – i.e. paying for it.

It's the poems about shitting which seem the most splendidly out of place here, not just because on such an empty belly one hardly does, but because (apart from the rare congenial ones) people at a place like this talk the most tinkling-tea-spoons kind of small talk imaginable. I think it's defence against the alarming intimacy of everyone being in dressing gowns most of the time not to mention naked some of the time – if they let their guard down, where would it end? Even if one or both of you were quite fat, I still don't think you or Neil can be imagined here so actually to have you here (in a sense) is piquant.

Love to you both, Diana

[*Here is one of Edward's poems, to give a taste of them:*]

TO LOVE

Away from home on a tour in the West
I worried about you constantly, my dearest,
until I had a dream one night where you
were a large plant I was chopping down with a shovel.

First I slashed off your feet
and then battered your head in, that head
that has already been attacked
by scalpel, drill, and saw
and is always blindly thumping things,
making my heart ache.

I woke in a sweat of course
but after the shock wore away that I
could do such a thing to you, my angel, even in a dream,
I saw how absolutely necessary it was.
Your needs had pursued me across a continent
and this was the only way of getting free, of
    renouncing
even for a week the relentless care of you,
the concern of my days and nights: how to keep you,
an exotic, delicate plant, alive in an arctic clime
though in my dream, I must admit,
you were a vigorous weed, bigger than me.

And then, my leafy, my green one,
whom I water daily and put in the sun,
after chopping you down and shovelling you away
I could leave you in God's hands

and loving you not the less for being free,
went almost light-hearted on with my journey.

I I NOVEMBER I983

Dear Edward,
For the last week or so I've made *The Crier* my bedside
reading, with great enjoyment. And great interest. You
are such a different kind of person from me, and how
rarely does someone open his sensibility so wide that one
is able to enter into a different way of feeling.

Is it temperamental or cultural (a mixture of both, I
expect) – your impulse to open, unloose, let flow, mine
to control? You turned my mind anew to age and death,
and I was visited by a poem (I am not a poet, of course,
but from time to time – like most people I suppose – am
moved to some kind of poem-like statement, particularly
after reading something which has woken me up). It
made me laugh, it was so different from your getting-old
poems. I send it herewith [*'Familiarity'*] for you to see.
One thing – you are much braver than I am. I guess it is
one of my deepest instincts, to control by being beady-
eyed; while you have this wonderful strong instinct to
feel – to risk yourself on the flood of feelings. I like it very
much. Perhaps you would say you have had to learn it,
and painfully at that. But encounter groups and so on are
available in this country as well as in yours, and not only
have I never felt tempted to try such an exercise, but I've

known (or felt that I've known) that I mustn't: it would be 'not me' to the extent of doing me a damage. Whereas you must have felt something quite different to venture out into these explorations. Just braver, I guess.

Barry likes your poems, too – and he's a great one for not liking poems. Any kind of 'poetical' rhetoric turns him off (even when it's fine of its kind, as I suppose it can be). So he sniffed at your books most dubiously, like a dog at an unfamiliar smell, then ventured on a small taste, then thought, 'But I like that!' and took another . . . it was quite funny to watch.

He's off to Jamaica in a week or so, to spend a couple of months with his mother. She's old enough for him to feel threatened by the possibility – each time he does this – that it will be the last time. She's a tough old nut, in fact – but one of the signs of being raised in a poor country is that when people get poorly you expect them to die. The Reckords are middle-class Jamaicans (tho' poor ones since Barry's father died, when B was ten years old, so Mrs R had a struggle to give her sons their middle-class education which she would have died rather than not done) – but their attitudes about medicine and health are so different from those of middle-class English people that I never cease being surprised by them. In our childhoods B and I read the same books, learnt the same nursery rhymes – at first blush it seems that the Englishness of the education and habits bestowed on the island by its then 'owners' was absolute. But he only has to start running a slight temperature for it to become apparent that whereas I was raised with a wide, secure safety net of medical knowledge spread under me, which

was taken wholly for granted as being accessible to me
whenever I needed it, he wasn't. In his parents' youth
probably, in his grandparents' youth certainly, all that
would have been available to a black person was herbs
and obeah; and now that they haven't got herbs and
obeah anymore, but haven't yet learnt to take medical
science for granted (no wonder! It's pretty lousy in
Jamaica) they've got nothing. Except a sort of wobbly
fatalism.

An annoying thing is that I sometimes feel scared,
now, when I'm alone in the flat. I never used to. I'd miss
him when he was away, but didn't lie awake listening to
the house creaking. Now, after all the stories I've heard
of breakings-in etc., I can't help doing so at times.
Luckily the two little music students to whom my cousin
has let the bottom part of the house [*her work took her to
Washington for six years*] are even more nervous, and
make a point of leaving lights on when they are out, etc.,
so it usually looks pretty well populated (which doesn't
always help). Poor André Deutsch was sleeping in his old
girlfriend's house to ease her nervousness when a burglar
broke in, tied her up, raped her, and made off with all
her jewellery, and André never even woke up! It's a very
big place – she's wildly rich – and the man's first words
to her were 'my mate is in your husband's room with a
knife, and he'll slit his throat if you so much as squeak'.
Which, naturally, the poor woman believed. She said the
man moved absolutely silently – she couldn't tell whether
he'd left the room or not, after he'd blindfolded her – so
it was not surprising that A wasn't woken. She, who is
over 70, had a most terrible time after the man had

finished with her, trying to decide whether it was safe to wriggle free (he hadn't bound her very tight) and make her way to André's room – and wondering what she'd find there. There now. I've written that down so I needn't think of it again!

The fall is being magical here. Luckily London has so many tree-filled spaces that the seasons can be felt in it and this one is being a super-technicolour spectacular. And warm, too. I wish you and Neil were still here. It seemed very right that you should be around (altho' I know now that your feelings about being in this country aren't exactly those of rightness!). Let me know when/if you move back to Holland because one can get 'Bargain Breaks' to Amsterdam very reasonably, and I like the place anyway, so it would be fun to dart across and see you.

Love from Diana

FAMILIARITY

I have learnt to recognize the plain white vans with
  painted-out black windows
and the black ones, equally discreet, standing at those
  back-street doors
which have a never-opened look (misleading)
so that people going by fail to notice them.

The white vans carry dead junkies picked up in alleys;
  old women
found frozen when the neighbours began to wonder
  and called the cops;

the man who stayed late at his office to hang himself;
   the boy
stabbed in a sudden brawl outside a discotheque.

The black vans, early every morning, deliver coffins to
   mortuaries.

Men who handle corpses despise people who don't.
Why? How? What? Where? cry the hearts of the
   bereaved,
and the men who handle corpses lower their eyelids over
looks of secret but impatient ribaldry.
A few of them are necrophiliacs onto a good thing, but
   most
are normal men who have learnt from handling death
that it tells nothing because it has nothing to tell, there
   is nothing to it.

When I first recognized those vans I waited for my
   skin to crawl.
I am still surprised that they cheer me up.
'There goes death' I think when I see one. 'There it
   goes about its daily work
and they think I don't see it. They think they are the
   only ones
with the nerve to know how ordinary it is.'

Recognition of a van: no more familiarity than that,
and already the look I give my unrecognizing friend
has in it, I suspect, a touch of secret but impatient
   ribaldry.

31 AUGUST 1984

Dearest Edward,

By the oddest coincidence, last night I was reading some of Alfred's Tangier letters. I was so *exhausted* from a feverish stint of gardening (because the evenings are getting shorter it has to start the minute I get back from the office without even time out for a drink) that when I went to bed a book seemed too big – and there was a bit of typescript sticking out from under a pile of something, and I pulled it out in an idle way, and it was a letter of A's, so I thought 'Good – a couple of those would be just the thing' . . . As a result, I do rather wonder whether you and Neil would be wholly Wise to pick Tangier for the winter? One can't avoid the impression that it wasn't only Alfred who went mad there.

It's good to hear of your productive industry, and that after its painful beginnings the novel is now giving you pleasure. Also that John Gross spoke up for *Variety Photoplays*. Perhaps that's the start of the Tide's turning. [Variety Photoplays: *Edward's cinema-based poems. He felt that he'd 'gone out of fashion'. The tide did turn.*]

If I hear of a house or flat I'll quickly let you know – how much can you afford to pay?

For all of this month a niece of Barry's, her economist husband and her two little boys have been based in our flat. They've trotted off on little jaunts from time to time, and Richard has mostly been at Sussex University where he's attending some sort of seminar, but on the whole Barry's been working in my sitting room and sleeping on its floor, while they have taken over his room. We've been having an uncharacteristic heatwave – positively New Yorkish at times – and I decided I was too old to go back to sharing a bed in a heatwave, particularly since B has got even fatter during the last few months (not to mention my own increasing portliness). But he quite likes sleeping on the floor, luckily. To start with I did a good deal of Inward Muttering about this invasion (particularly as for the first four days it also included another niece of Barry's and *her* economist husband – tho' luckily *they* left their two children in Washington where her husband, an American, is personal assistant to a congressman on the Committee of Ways and Means. (Part of the muttering went 'Don't tell me that a personal assistant to a congressman on the Committee of Ways and Means couldn't afford a hotel for four nights.') However, I'm very fond of both young women, and their husbands are charming – it's a mystery to me how Richard manages to be charming, and cheerful as well, considering that he's an Expert on International Debt – which certainly ensures continual employment in Jamaica, but which surely must be a bit debilitating? And now that they are packing in order to leave tomorrow, I find that I shall be sorry to see them go. The boys, 12 and 7, are models of their kind, lively and responsive, but they do what they are told! I'm used to it now, but to start with I could hardly believe it. Margaret says that having observed the disastrous consequences of permissiveness in the families of her friends, she has decided to be an Old-Fashioned Jamaican Mother – and so she is. But as she's also a very loving and sympathetic person she manages to do it without harshness – in fact they're an exceptionally warm and communicating family. No doubt the boys will start to fight their way out before too long – but perhaps without too much blood, given such a comfortable beginning. I hope so.

Much love to you both, Diana

27 SEPTEMBER 1985

Dearest Edward –

What *marvellous* news! Kent Carroll [*of the publishers Carroll & Graf*] was temporarily out of my good books because, in a flash of uncharacteristic common sense, he declined to publish my book about my poor suicide [After A Funeral] on the grounds that his sales people don't think etc. ... But now he is back in my very best of books *for good*. [*Carroll had agreed to reissue Alfred Chester's novel* Exquisite Corpse.]

I shall write at once, and congratulate him. I expect I have a copy of my piece somewhere – tho' he might be shrewd enough to prefer some distinguished American Name ... Anyway, I'll offer it [*Edward had proposed my Alfred piece as an introduction*]. After all, I was quoted in a *New York Times* leader (on censorship) the other day, without reference to *Instead of a Letter* – simply 'as Diana Athill has said' as tho' I were Somerset Maugham or someone!!!! Wow!

I'm glad your book is going well. I've been rambling

through *Village* and do think you're clever – because while it's the sort of thing lots of people like, it's not a cynically cooked up nonsense. It's a most craftsmanlike job, and there's every reason to be interested in how the people and their relationships develop. Barry didn't get on very well with it because he's (to a fault) without any 'so what happened then?' feelings – he says he doesn't despise people who respond to story-telling just as story-telling, but in fact he can't help feeling that they are a bit infantile, which cuts him off from a lot of fun. He says he feels embarrassed about not having read *Village* but that he still loves you both.

I was only in Berlin once, for a few days, just before the war. One could feel Armageddon looming – indeed, when leaning over a balcony in the Rhine valley, revelling in the view as I waited for my breakfast, I saw a group of cheerful boys and girls marching by, led by a sort of scout master and singing a stirring song, and I can still vividly recall a cold sinking feeling that struck as I realized that the words they were singing were '*Wir gehen nach England*' or whatever 'we are marching against England' is in German. 'Yes,' said my father, 'I'm afraid that is what it means. I think it's probably lucky that we are on our way home.' So I didn't take to Berlin . . . another memory has just this moment returned: getting the curse and having to buy some sanitary diapers and the chambermaid in the hotel saying that I could get them downstairs in the barbershop and having to stammer out my request to the fat insolent looking barber while watched with even more insolent amusement by his three even fatter customers, all with two rolls of fat at the backs of their shaven necks, like the tritest caricatures of Germans ... horrid Berlin! But I'm very glad to know that it is giving you comfortable and convenient shelter.

Went last night to rejoin my beloved sewing class and found that I'd left it too late and it's over-full for this coming semester, so ended up in a life-drawing class instead – which was marvellous. Lovely solid pink model and about twelve earnest students, all but one of them with much less idea of how to draw than me!!! I'd forgotten that years ago I used to long to go to a life class and have a naked body there, immobile, for as long as I needed to look at it, in order to get it on to paper ... God knows why – I certainly shan't suddenly turn into a painter – but it was *madly* absorbing.

My cousin who owns the house and lives downstairs but who is now in Washington until after the next American election, for the *Economist*, has decided that she can't after all afford not to let the two bottom floors of the house for a realistic rent. [*The music students had moved on.*] She is no nest-builder, so it has always been fairly scruffy down there, and by the time she left for Washington it was a slum, more or less, so it has to be decorated before I can let it. And carpeted. And furnished. And – this has only just transpired – cured of very bad damp in one bedroom. And – an even later discovery – the other bedroom's ceiling to be stripped off and replaced before it actually falls off which it will do any minute now ... Partly I shudder with horror as what I have undertaken to do, and partly I get a mad kick out of playing at being a real house-owner but I expect the horror will prevail before too long. At the moment I am able to repose in a condition of imbecile trust on the (metaphorical) bosom of my builder, who is really a Nigerian potter (his pots are good), because he is very tall and very handsome and has a divine black-velvet voice and loves gardening – I only have to amble around the garden with Cornelius, talking about propagating lilies, to feel that All Must Be Well. But whether in fact that assortment of elderly Irish alcoholics and teen-age Rastafarians that he employs ... Ah, let's not cross bridges until we come to them.

I'm now going to write to Kent Carroll – I shall even address him by his first name, which I have never done before! – and tell him how much honour he brings to American publishing.

Much love, Diana ooxxooxxoo. Do Americans write hugs and kisses like we do?

10 APRIL 1986

Dear Ed,

Sorry to hear that you've had such a terrible winter, and that your poor mother is in this ruined state. What a nightmare! Of course it's not heartless to 'flee abroad' when there's nothing you could possibly do if you stayed ... but of course you are going to feel guilty about doing it. One goes on stubbornly feeling that all situations must have 'right' answers which, if hit on,

would leave one feeling good about them – but it's almost
always a choice of evils; and certainly you're choosing by
far the lesser evil in this case, since only you will be made
uncomfortable by pangs of needless guilt – your sisters
would have to be there anyway.

Listen – I shall be coming to Washington on May 15
for a three week vacation spent mostly staying with my
cousin – but no doubt I'll visit NY anyway, and *certainly*
I shall if you are still there.

Congratulations on finishing the book [*a successor to*
Village, *but less successful*]. Oh what a heroic and
industrious pair you are!

Much love, Diana

Would a one room flat do you? With small kitchen,
bathroom and separate john? Because, having done up
my cousin's part of the house for her, I'm now doing up
her son's flat, the floor beneath mine. He wants to keep
one room 'in case' – he'll rarely be there – and a tiny
room to store things in, and I'm planning to let the
remaining sitting room as a bed-sitter. It won't be smart,
but it will be clean and not disagreeable. But I feel that it
would almost certainly be too claustrophobic for two
people. If Adam wasn't around, his room could be
overflowed into for sleeping – but it would be full of his
things . . . I reckon I can charge 50 a week for the bed-
sitter plus kitchen etc. (it's all on Barbara's, my cousin's,
behalf) – you'd probably be more comfortable
elsewhere, but I could keep this for you if you wished.
xx D

9 JUNE 1986

Dearest Edward,
   Of course I didn't mind learning that Alfred bad-mouthed me! [*To his friend Harriet Sohmers who told me about it when I was in New York and Edward had us to dinner together.*] I was lucky that he never went for me – he easily might have done, considering what a perilous relationship with him being his publisher was. I enjoyed Harriet enormously – just thought 'The old bastard!' at the bad-mouthing bit, and forgot it. It's dear of you to have worried.
   I loved visiting you in your cave – your exotic, snug, oriental cave. I've been wondering ever since, on and off, how that impossible space can possibly have been so attractive and welcoming ... clever you!
   Kent Carroll has written offering me 'a token fee' of $100 [*for my piece about Alfred*] – OK by me – and sending me a copy of their jacket, which I think is very good.
   Enjoy the Getty. Stern Neil! I expect he's right, and staying put is the thing if you want to get that wretched synopsis done.
   Much love to you, Diana

10 SEPTEMBER 1986

Dearest Edward,
   Just as I was getting around to feeling really *bad* for not

having answered your last letter, here comes another one – and such a treat of a letter. It's not possible to imagine more delicious words than 'absolutely spectacular'!!!! Barry likes the piece [*the Alfred memories*] too – he said 'exciting' . . . and I know why it has worked so well: it's thanks to you and Neil.

Because I was, in the first place, writing it down for you two and not thinking of it in print. I've often said to people here who have written a disastrous blurb – 'Look, imagine you're writing a letter to a friend telling them what a lovely book you've just read. That'll get it going.' And it does – which this little introduction is a proof of. I must say I'm a bit cross with Kent – something like half a dozen glaring typos, no me on the title page, and not copyrighted! That really is very amateurish. I hope he's ashamed of himself. I didn't have the nerve to complain about the title page (why the hell not? I don't know a single writer who wouldn't have, and quite right too . . . it's some ridiculous residue from An English Upbringing) but I did about the copyrighting, because that's really shocking.

What wonderful work you've put in. I wish I could think there's some kind of Alfred-consciousness still floating around, to know. Of course, there may be, since what I think or don't think has nothing to do with it.

My dears – if Elaine says your book's going to be Money I'd be very surprised if it isn't. Oh how clever you are. Having never written anything that didn't bubble out of an Impulse, I'm stunned with admiration for the kind of constructive effort that goes into thinking out a book.

It must, of course, bring the impulses in its wake – once you've rough-hewn your characters you must find lots of things about them beginning to dictate themselves ... I'm not surprised that you are beginning to enjoy teaching yourselves how to write novels, but I am a bit awestruck that you can do it.

How extraordinary people are! There are you, going around with an aura of such assurance and poise ... I truly find it hard to believe that you aren't pretending when you say you're not like that. Is it not rather comforting to know that the efforts you have made to appear what you don't feel like have been so very successful? And as for old – you're very lucky to have Such Good Bones, dear! Eyelashes don't matter all that much when the features are Truly Distinguished. When you get to be really old it will be possible to say of you what a cleaning lady I once had wanted to be able to say about her wildly irresponsible Polish husband: 'Oh God,' she said to him, 'I wish you'd hurry up and be eighty, because then I'll be able to enjoy you as a work of art.'

I've decided that it's a waste of precious time to think about getting old. We'll have to think about creeping and wheezing when we're actually doing same, but to hell with letting such miseries cast their shadows before them; while things like not looking pretty anymore, getting fat (me), losing eyelashes (you), hair getting terribly thin (me) ... it's amazing how little they matter if you forget about them. I reckon my looks were more of a worry to me in the days when they could aspire to being good than they are now – Jesus, the anxious hours I used to spend painting absurd Thirties faces onto my faultless 19-year-old skin!

It's lovely that your travels are now in sight again, so to speak. It'll be such a delight to see you again. Much love, Diana. xxoo from B.

13 JANUARY 1987

Dearest Ed –

How I bless you both for laughing at *After A Funeral*, because I thought that lots of it was funny in spite of the misery of it all at the end – but most people seem to be too oppressed by the sadness to feel that. As for me in the role of psychiatrist – on showing to date I'd have a dismal record, since nothing but the Worst seems to happen to the nuts who come my way!

Alas – the flat downstairs has now been claimed by my cousin's son. My feelings about Barry's absences follow a well-worn path: first, pangs of loss; second, when I set about cleaning his room, Black Rage (God, what an old shit he is!); third, a nice, serene time of enjoying being on my own; fourth, fairly mild but genuine pleasure at the thought that he'll be back next week ... Ah me, look at what becomes of Passion!

Writing about sex – I enjoy it while I'm doing it, but yes – I do feel quite embarrassed when it's done. I try to avoid thinking of people reading it! When I said that to Barry he said once, 'Well, why don't you cut the bit when

you went to bed with Waguih?' But it seemed to me it
had to be there.

Much love and longing to see you. Diana

20 JANUARY 1987

Barry's gone off to Jamaica for two months – the first
time since his mother died. He sounds glad to be there.
He's worried about his eldest brother Carol, whom he
hasn't seen for years, because he thinks he may have
Parkinson's; and his sister Cynthia has just had to
employ three men armed with cutlasses to catch her
mad son, who had taken to living wild in the bush, and
reported this to him 'in precisely the same voice as she
used when she talked about everything else!' Poor
Cynthia – I guess she's so accustomed to the
tribulations of having a mad son that she feels she *is*
talking about 'everything else'. A foolish woman of my
acquaintance who loves to drop little seeds of
discomfort into her friends' lives, has just written me a
long letter condoling with me for having to spend a
dreary Christmas with my ancient ma while Barry 'is
off to all that sun and family warmth in the Caribbean'.
Little does she know! Fortunately I don't have to pay
good money to keep out of that simmering little plague
spot of an island, but if I did, I would! However, B does
love his family, so it does him good to see them from
time to time.

I'm feeling very happy at the moment because I've just had a New Year's card from New York addressed in a hand I didn't recognize, and it turned out to be from the cousin of the man I wrote *After A Funeral* about – the cousin appears briefly in the book, called Mémé – and he says he's just read it: 'tears, laughter, tears – you've written a lovely thing'. *Such* a relief to know that a member of 'Didi's' family was able to like it – I've secretly been dreading what their reaction might be if they came across it. (I think I've been failing to allow for how very much of the stuff about them I cut at the last moment.)

I never got a note from Kent to say he was sorry he'd left my name off the E.C. Isn't he horrid!

Much love to you both, my dears. Diana

[*Waguih Ghali (whose nickname in his family was Tou-Tou but I changed it to Didi in my book), author of* Beer in the Snooker Club, *killed himself in my flat after a long battle with depression.* After A Funeral *is my account of our relationship, in which some members of his family figured.*]

9 SEPTEMBER 1987

Dearest Edward,

Oh what torture that tax business must have been – I'm sure I would have expired from stress. The sensations of guilt inspired by the very word! That you got off so lightly in the end ought to inspire the beginnings of confidence that they won't actually eat you up if they catch you – but of course one will go on cowering and squeaking at the sight of brown envelopes.

Have just buried poor old George Mikes, whose rather unfunny funny books (largely written – hush! – by me) [*a gross exaggeration!*] we've been publishing for forty years and who was the last of André's Hungarian childhood friends. Funeral strictly family (memorial due later) – so who was the very elegant and rather insane-looking Hungarian lady hovering on the outskirts? I went over to be hospitable and she clutched me by the wrist (hers tintinnabulating with gold bangles and chains) and hissed: 'I vas zee first fiancée – zee werry first. He did not leaff me – I leaf him. He vas not man who show feelings – you know him, you know zat? – but ven his sister tell him I marry somevun else – *he faint.*' There must be a great difference between the way little Hungarian girls and little English girls are brought up, when it comes to Boasting. I'd have died rather than tell anyone at the funeral how much the lazy old so-and-so used to expect me to do to his books – and only tell you because you are far away and never knew him. But perhaps if there had been as many editors in George's life as there were women, I too would have felt the need to proclaim my standing among them.

Love to you and Neil, Diana

19 JANUARY 1988

Dearest Edward –

What a disappointment – the collapse of your plans for the winter. I'll certainly let you know if I bump into any likely prospects in the way of 'exchangers' – and you must be inventing seeing my face fall as I first saw your exotic lair, because I liked it at once. It seemed to me beautifully un-New Yorkish.

I've had to decide on four days in the country looking after my ma to every three days at home in London. On first reaching that decision I came home to London and instantly went down with a violent flu – which proved to be psychosomatic, since once it was over my despair at the prospect was purged. It does mean frantically hard work during my three London days, because I can get very little done in the country – a couple of hours a day if I'm lucky; but fortunately I love my ma, and my sister has lent me an old car to keep down there so I don't have an exhausting drive twice a week but come and go by rail, which is quick and comfortable and can be read on . . . it isn't too bad, and I've learnt not to waste nervous energy when there by waking up at night and brooding on the fact that sooner or later I'll have to cope with ma's dying. Of course, she may become ill beyond my nursing abilities and die in a hospital, but I do really hope for her sake that she's carried off by a heart attack while still at home. Mentally she's fine – reads avidly, knits and embroiders the most dashing objects considered madly trendy by her great-grandchildren, and we share a passion for her garden . . . and Barry and the flat give me very intense pleasure now they are no longer every-day, so there are blessings to count.

Had my 70th birthday just before Christmas. A tremendous to-do was made about André's, in November – profiles in the newspapers, subscription raised for a portrait etc. I was given a sweet little party by the office and lots of lovely little presents in addition to a very splendid official one – the most superb sound system complete with compact disc player and all – but the difference of emphasis was very marked. It is true that I would never have started a publishing firm on my own, as he did, and if I hadn't existed some other person without-whom-it-couldn't-have-existed would have turned up; so some difference of emphasis was justified – but I think a good deal of it was the difference between what a man gets and what a woman gets. Pondering it, I reckon that distribution of honours – and of money! – could have been more equitable if I'd rolled up my sleeves and fought for it; but I can't decide whether my not ever doing so was a matter of gender or of temperament – or even of class? I was raised in a setting where fussing about money was considered pretty vulgar. I suppose any individual is so inextricable a tangle of all those elements that the question is an unreal one . . . Anyway, the difference was quite funny, but I admit that my appreciation of the funniness was distinctly *wry*! If there were any way of measuring the amount put into something (as opposed to window-dressing) I'm quite sure my contribution would outweigh his [*Nonsense! – I was in a bad temper because of the celebrations*].

Ah well! I guess I enjoyed not bothering to roll up my sleeves and fight!

Love from Diana

23 MARCH 1988

Darling Edward,

My split winter hasn't gone too badly – I get a bit exhausted in the London part because so much work piles up, but otherwise it has been OK. Your favourite interpretation of my calling my mother Ma was undeserved. As children we called her, always, Mummy or Mum – words which sound so silly on adult lips that we all three felt we ought to change them. My brother tried to change to Mother, but it never sounded convincing and now he's slipped back to Mum. My sister and I both adopted Ma, which seems to have to English ears a faintly jokey sound which makes it sound less embarrassing than Mummy (which we will still use, sometimes, between us). Quite often we call her Gran, that having been established by the grandchildren. She doesn't mind what we call her. When she was a young, modern mother I remember her taking it into her head that we ought to call her and Dad by their first names ... 'What a flighty and ridiculous notion' we all three thought in a disapproving way, so poor Ma's bid to be dashing came to nothing. (She also thought it would be nice if we all, children and adults, felt natural about seeing each other naked – a daring notion for the time, I wonder what she had been reading? – which we squelched even more firmly. What boring brats!)

Love from Diana

7 JUNE 1988

Dearest Edward,

Do send me copies of new poems – they'll make up for not seeing you.

My ma is doing well. While I was in Venice she had a heart attack – not a big one, but still there was discussion about telephoning me, which she forbad (and the doctor, too, said to my brother that it probably wasn't necessary, so they didn't). Naturally I expressed concern when I got back – and a few days later she said: 'Come here – sit down – there's something I want to say to you. I want you to understand that *I am not afraid of dying alone.* Dying will not be much fun, but it won't be more fun for having someone here, and I've had a long life and a good one, so don't fuss.' Altho' I know quite well, of course, that she would hate to be alone when it becomes apparent that this is it (who wouldn't!) I still found that a weight-lifting moment. Also, I like to know that my old ma is brave and generous.

Venice was heaven – I can't wait to get back there. I'd

never before really got the feel of it . . . strange, silent, secretive place, when it isn't flashing and sparkling with sun on water. And the wild hordes of tourists (a bit less thick in May than they will be later, but still alarming) are mercifully conservative in their habits. On their main runs and stamping grounds you feel that you might well be trampled under foot at any minute, but you only have to go three yards down a side street, and they might not exist. Luckily the trend is towards more and more package tours, and people organizing them have to keep them to set routes, while the solo tourist like me becomes increasingly rare.

Barry sends his love, and we both wish you luck with the new novel – three families and a hundred years to pilot them through, my God! Rather you than me!!!

Hugs, Diana

17 AUGUST 1988

Dearest Ed –

I wonder where you've got to for the summer. It doesn't seem likely that you are in New York, but I suppose you'll find a letter sent there sooner or later.

I'm writing simply to let off steam about feeling terrible about Norman. Out of the blue there comes a phone call – 'It's Norman here – Norman Glass. I'm at Heathrow. Can you come and fetch me' . . . This is at 7 in the morning of a day on which I'm about to drive up

to my mother's – which also happens to be the day after
a Trinidadian friend and her daughter have arrived to
stay for three weeks and revealed that they have brought
with them a) No warm clothes, not so much as a
cardigan, and b) No money. Poor Norman, he couldn't
have hit a worse moment. 'No,' I said, 'I'm afraid I can't.'
The fact that I only ever met him three times (twice he
turned up to be taken to lunch, and once Alfred was
staying in a flat he was living in, and N came in just as I
was leaving) and that those meetings were about twenty
years ago, rises up within me and injects an hysterical
tone in my voice. 'Then what am I going to do? I'm in a
very bad position.' – 'I'm really very sorry, Norman, but
I truly can't.' – 'But you were always so strong and
reliable.' – 'Well, I'm not strong and reliable now – I can't
imagine why you thought I would be when we haven't
even set eyes on each other for twenty years – I'm far
from being strong' – hysteria increasing – 'I'm old,
dammit.' – 'Well, I'm not all that young myself, and I'm
not at all well, and I've got no money.' – 'Norman, I'm
very sorry but I simply cannot do anything about it and
that's that. Goodbye.' And I hung up, literally shaking,
half with rage at his nerve and half with shame – because
he must really have reached the bottom of the barrel, to
be calling me, since our only link was that distant fact
that we both knew Alfred. But to take him on in my
present circumstances would be impossible . . . to tell the
truth to take Norman on in any circumstances would be
impossible . . . Oh dear! I think he said he'd come in from
Athens – he must have run completely out of resources
there (perhaps he'd been thrown out). I keep on having

to suppress pangs of thinking 'what in God's name happened to him after I said no?' Fuck Norman! But oh dear . . .

Otherwise things are OK, though I have little time to myself. Last week I was inveigled by her special do-gooders into visiting in prison the most famous murderer in Britain. Did you ever hear of The Moors Murders, some twenty-four years ago – a young man and his girl who were caught for the murder of an adult and then it turned out that they'd been debauching and murdering children and burying them up on a Yorkshire moor. It was a crime – or series of crimes – so cold-blooded and appalling that it became in the whole nation's mind a sort of epitome of evil. The man has gone round the bend in gaol. The woman (who never actually did the killing, but who lured the children into his hands and was at his side throughout the whole of each unspeakable murder) has spent her years in prison educating herself, has worked with a counsellor, and is now being urged to write the truth about it all. She is dismayingly impressive. What we do about it will depend on what she finally manages to write. What was creepy was that in spite of keeping the utmost secrecy about this visit, I was still there in the prison when the phone rang in the office and it was one of the most disreputable of the daily newspapers calling to ask 'Are you doing a book about Myra Hindley?' – one of the prison officers must be in their pay and must have run to the phone the moment I was signed in! She (Myra) has become a sort of legendary figure of Evil, much treasured by the press. I was violently against the whole idea to start with, because of that – and still am against it, I think – but couldn't help feeling that anyone who is so startlingly much her own woman after twenty-four years locked up, with all that on her conscience, will be interesting to listen to – if she can really do it. As they used to say in the *Publishers Weekly*, 'You Meet Such Interesting People'.

Much love to you both, Diana

P.S. Simultaneously the most infuriating and the most comic thing about Norman's call was his imperious tone of voice, which changed to Stern Disapproval as I let him down.

[One of Myra Hindley's 'do-gooders', a Methodist minister, believed that if she plumbed the darkest depth of her guilt by 'writing it out' it would save her soul, while the other thought we could learn from it something useful about the nature of evil. After a long talk with her I concluded that probably, if she forced herself to abandon the few flimsy defences she had contrived against being totally submerged in guilt (which she never denied, only tried slightly to mitigate), she would go mad rather than be 'saved'; and that knowing more than we already knew about her crimes would not be of the smallest use. One way and another, the world has been told an immense amount about evil, without ever becoming better at dealing with it. Helping her to write the book they wanted from her, so that André Deutsch could publish it, would therefore be profiting from the public's greed for horrors, as disreputable as the worst kind of cheap journalism. So I had to tell the 'do-gooders' that we could have no part in it, and that was that.]

5 FEBRUARY 1989

Darling Edward,

Barbara has given her son Adam instructions to start decorating the flat, including redesigning the kitchen – she has been corrupted, she says, by her lovely Bethesda kitchen and can't face anything less efficient and handsome – ditto the washing-machine room, that hell-hole next to the bedroom you were in. Cornelius has surfaced to the point of saying over the phone that he's sorry, and he'll see what he can do – which seems still to be nothing. [*Cornelius, the charming builder who knew about propagating lilies, had eventually faded out on us. Reclining on his bosom had been – alas – a mistake.*] However, as Adam too, seems to be doing nothing, there's no great sense of urgency and my guess is that everything will hang fire until I suddenly wake up and think 'Oh my God, she'll be back next month' and have to do everything myself.

I've started going to Tai Chi classes. The theory, I have to admit, suggested to me that the ancient Chinese were fairly simple-minded, but the series of movements (terribly hard to learn) is very beautiful when done by our serene and elegant teacher, and I would like to master the whole ritual, breathing included – I feel it would be good for one's balance, and calming. I guess it's not unlike acupuncture – something which works, although the reasons why, as given by Ancient Chinese Science, are entirely unconvincing. At one point we had to lie on our backs and do 'bone breathing' – slow deep

breathing imagining that we were drawing in the air
through little holes in the tips of our toes, and that it ran
up through the hollow tubes of one's bones as far as the
pelvis, then across and down the hollow tubes of the
other leg and out through the holes in the toes of that
foot. Can they, I wondered, really have had such a rum
idea of anatomy? But squelched the thought and went on
imagining as well as I could – and the fact was that it was
an amazingly relaxing exercise and almost sent me to
sleep!

I've done fifteen pages of writing since you were here.
I can't work when I'm at my ma's, nor every evening
when I'm here, and only a page or two when I do
because of being tired, so it's very slow; but I think it
feels as though its going to continue. [*It didn't – I've even
forgotten what it was.*]

Love from both to both, Diana

[*UNDATED*]

Dearest Edward –

Glad to have served as one of those valuable – oh,
what is the technical term for when an animal suddenly
starts tearing up grass or something when what it ought
by the logic of the situation to be doing is challenging
another animal to a fight? 'Displaced activity'? Not
quite – I've watched a lot of nature documentaries on
telly, but not, it seems, attentively enough. Anyway, I

know the feeling well. The letters I've written, the floors I've swept, the buttons I've sewed on when sending in my tax returns becomes Seriously Overdue. And tackling a publisher over terms would be far worse. Perhaps by now you've done it? If so, how I hope it was successful.

You are a tease, writing on the back of that review of the New and Selected, and not sending all of it. Barry said he thought the tone of it was 'a bit patronizing' – but I think it might be going to become better as it goes on? Barry, by the way, was also greatly entertained by your saying that 'my' workmen 'lose their anxiety about doing the job well and getting paid', which is, he says, exactly what happens. It was indeed quite interesting to see how quickly, after a long conversation about how it was only natural to want to change after living with the same girlfriend for seven years, the painter started forgetting to spread plastic sheeting over all of the carpet – and by the time he finished the job there was hardly an object in the flat without specks of white paint. However, all is clean and looking fine if not inspected too closely, so I'm happy to be back from Scotland (I feared he might still be here!). Barbara is pleased with her quarters too – and now her things have arrived from Washington it looks quite good – also the catamaran-sailing Dwight has made her hot-water system work properly, one must grant him that.

Much love from us both, Diana

18 JULY 1989

Dearest Edward,

I owe you two, if not three, letters. God knows why I've been in such a whirl – nothing important being done – and yet a constant state of not having a minute to spare. Barry went off to Jamaica in May, planning to be back on June 18, then finished a play and decided to put it on there to make some money, so called to say he'll be there another month – and now is only just coming up to the opening so will probably be longer ... which all seemed in anticipation like a marvellous opportunity for me to get a lot of writing done: and I've hardly done a word. If it wasn't my Ma it was the builders and decorators, and if wasn't the b. & d. it was some sort of evening out, and if it wasn't some sort of evening out it was falling into bed exhausted. I feel as tho' I can't remember a time when there was not someone hammering or painting or whatever in the house, nor can I foresee a time when they'll no longer be here. Barbara's flat is done, and she's back and very pleased; and now my flat is being done; and when that is finished extra things wanted by Barbara, such as the verandah and the front steps etc. will start. The painter working in my flat, a dear innocent soul but not a ball of fire, tackled a wall with the minute attention to detail of a miniature painter and can take three days to finish a closet. Just as well B is still away, as his room can be used for all the clobber out of whichever other room is being worked on.

Your account of your Moroccan trip inspired passionate envy – it really did sound a good experience, and even the unsuccessful bits such as getting nowhere with Paul [*Bowles*] must have been interesting. Alfred's house being so haunted is very strange. You must look up Dris. I've lost your last letter – everything is heaped in the centre of my sitting room, under dust sheets which, if disturbed, raise a dense cloud of the white plaster dust which they are keeping off (??) the buried furniture, so I hesitate to dig for it although I'm sure it had other things in it I wanted to respond to – (pause, during which I learn that Barbara's vacuum cleaner as well as mine is sick unto death with a surfeit of the above plaster dust, so there's nothing for it but a dustpan and brush) – and realizing as I write that, although I'm quite enjoying all this domestic chaos, and very much enjoying having Barbara back, I had become, because of it, unfit (temporarily, I hope) for human consumption and shouldn't even think of letter writing, having nothing else to talk about except office gossip about writers unknown to you, and a marvellous performance of *The Three Sisters* by a visiting Hungarian company which you are unlikely ever to see (the acting so splendid – that one quite forgot that one was not understanding a word they spoke).

So forgive this boring scrawl, darling Edward, the purpose of which is simply to say that you are both often thought of and much loved by

Diana

31 OCTOBER 1989

Dearest Ed –

No, you didn't write from San Diego – none of this
had I heard – and I want to know it all because clearly it
was an enormously frightful experience – one of life's
major faults (in the geological sense) – let me, at the risk
of causing you embarrassment, quote the last two lines of
this morning's dialogue between me and Barry. DIANA:
He's a very good man, is Ed. BARRY: Yes, an excellent
man.

I don't suppose you feel good. You probably feel that
in caring for Neil's mother you simply had no alternative
to doing what had to be done, and are sharply aware of
your own recoil and resentment, but handsome is as
handsome does, my love.

You know more about ladies now in two senses – one,
from your intimate care of that poor body you know
female bodies better, and two, from that same thing you
know the female fate better. There was a night last year
when I suddenly realized I despised men quite much
(tho' at a nothing-can-be-done-about-it-so-better-forget-
it level). I'd had to call a doctor to my old Ma and he and
I were alone with her in the still of the night – and as she
vomited, and also had to be supported onto a commode
and then cleaned up, he moved across the room and
gazed absently out of the window while I did the holding
and supporting and mopping up – and it occurred to me
that all over the world at that moment there were women
actually doing things to sick people, while men issued

advice and prescriptions, and from time to time gave a nice tidy injection ... Of course there are men who choose to be nurses, bless them, and of course there are women who are brutal to sick people; but on the whole it is true that women have to take on the job of caring once it involves touching sick bodies, while most men would be appalled at the idea of doing it. So you have crossed a great divide – and the greater because of the patient's sex. I am sure that (in cases unrelated to me) I would find it much less repellant to wash a man's genitals than a woman's, because after all I've handled plenty of them in my time, and as a source of pleasure at that, while I have never touched, or even looked closely at another woman's (until I had to nurse Ma). And the same is true for you, with perhaps an added resistance to the idea of them stemming from complex psychological reasons. So you truly were being amazingly good.

The idea of that snake-pit [*a care home for Neil's mother*] for which you are now having to pay is blood-chilling – with every year I get nearer to making plans for eventual suicide – but it's so much easier said than done, and anyway if one is smitten with a stroke, like Neil's mother, she will be unable to put even a very well-thought-out plan into action, probably.

On which merry note – au revoir and much love,
Diana

[*A letter must be missing during this long gap: I had obviously told him about my mother's death in June.*]

7 JULY 1990

Well!!! You can't say the old monster [*Norman Glass, of course*] lacks nerve! My first reaction is to feel that he's so far from sense by now that there's no point in answering, whether firmly or cajolingly – but I suppose you may feel that it's too cruel to snub someone you've known such a long time to that extent. If you do write, I hope it's firmly, not cajolingly, and v. briefly – because I'm sure it won't do any good, so the effort might as well be kept to the minimum. How on earth did he get himself to Tangier after being flat broke at Heathrow? I feel he must have terrified some perfect stranger into stumping up, given how he wears out friends. He's kind of awe inspiring in a way.

No, not pain about Ma, just sad, and a large gap left – but she was so stunningly lucky in the way she went that everything is blanketed by gratitude. She had a v. good spring and summer – lots of nice things happening, no vertigo attacks, much enjoyment of books, grandchildren, garden and gossip – but she was having to resort to her heart pills more often, and the thing she really dreaded – becoming too immobile to be able to bathe herself or get herself from her chair to the toilet – was perceptibly nearer: not yet quite here, but almost. So then, on a lovely day, she shuffles on her two sticks to the far end of the garden to oversee the planting of a new tree, and suddenly feels a bit odd. So her dear old henchman supports her back to the house and fetches Eileen Barrie, her beloved Home Help, and Eileen stays with her attentively all afternoon, then concludes that yes, she had better call the doctor and alert me altho' all that's happened at that stage is that Ma can't eat and is feeling v. dozy. Doc sends her at once by ambulance to our small cottage hospital in the village – a familiar place, and very kind. By the time I get there it's become horrid – she's in heart failure, struggling for each breath – that was a painful day, very. We think she'll die any minute – but no, she gets thro' the night and next morning is suddenly calm, and feeling no discomfort, and saying how odd it is that she can remember almost nothing of the day before. All that day sleep alternates with snatches of sensible and quite cheerful talk (will I please see to it that the new tree is tied to its support in two places, not just one – an outing she'd had four days ago was 'absolutely divine' – altho' her desk looks a mess she thinks I'll find it in quite good order): and at 5.30 during one of the sleeps, she simply stops breathing. I doubt whether many people are lucky enough to have such an easy death. I can still hardly believe how completely she – and I – were spared the kind of thing I've spent the last three years trying not to think about.

My sister, with whom I get on v. well, has come over from Zimbabwe, and we are coping with all the tidying up together. Fortunately the fact that keeping Ma reasonably comfortable in a modest way has exhausted her possessions comes as no surprise to anyone – but I have got a v. nice watercolour by a great grandfather, and one pretty cup, so it could be worse!

Much love, D

STARTED ON 27 SEPTEMBER 1990

Darling Edward,

Snatching a rare idle moment in the office to say that I
think you and they did a wonderful job on the stories – it
gives me such pleasure to have a copy [Head of a Sad
Angel: Stories by Alfred Chester, *edited by Edward*] –
every word of the stories proving how right we were to
be spellbound by how good he was. Rereading one's
Great Experiences can prove disconcerting, but doesn't
with Alfred. Oh God – how I wish this firm weren't still
teetering on the brink of god knows what, but it is, and at
present Tom [*Rosenthal, who bought the firm from André
Deutsch*] is only buying things which he calculates will
appear toothsome to commercially minded potential
purchasers. And are there any around? We don't know
(except that I suppose if there were we would know).
He's off to meetings quite often, and sometimes looks
rather cheerful the next day – but he's not one to say
anything until he has something final to say.

There was a large piece in the 'Review' section of the
Independent three Sundays ago, about the bad relations
between Tom Rosenthal and André Deutsch, making
Tom out to be a fool and a thug, and saying he hasn't a
hope in hell of finding a buyer. It included an obviously
reluctant and (if you know Tom) therefore pompous
interview, and a smug little piece about how André had
declined to be interviewed (implication: because he
didn't want to have to say that Tom was a fool and a
thug). End of forty years or so of friendship with André,

so far as I'm concerned – because the editor of the
Independent Review section told a journalist friend of
mine that the whole piece came from André. To make it
look as though this weren't so, they arranged for a
reporter to ask him for a formal interview so that he
could refuse it! He has gone completely gaga – his one
obsession now is that Tom threw him out of his firm –
whereas he sold the firm to Tom absolutely of his own
volition, with armies of his own lawyers at his elbow to
make sure that the terms of the sale were favourable to
him. He's now a rich man as a result – tho' he managed
to make the article imply, without a flat statement of
untruth, that he was cheated into letting it go for a song.
All he wants to do now is ruin Tom, and if he ruins the
firm he himself built up into the bargain, and all his old
friends still in it, he doesn't give a damn. So following
dialogue takes place: 'You don't think that I had anything
to do with that article, do you?' – 'Of course I do. Every
word of it sounded like your voice, and anyway I've been
told that you did.' – 'Are you calling me a liar?' – 'Yes I
am.' Whereupon he bolts out of the room and that's that.
Sad, after all those years. Barry says I must make up with
him because 'It isn't like you' not to, and anyway André
presumably can't help having gone gaga. So I expect I
shall sooner or later. What a bore! Because having got rid
of him I look back on those years of friendship and
suddenly see how much of the friendship was simply
habit, propinquity and good nature (the last on my part),
and what a mean, manipulative, tyrannical little shit he
always was.

I'm off to Italy for a couple of weeks' holiday on

October 13 – going with my cousin Barbara. Barry is not one for looking at things. He might enjoy a week in Venice if he could have his typewriter with him and work most of the time – or if we went en famille with our friends Sally and Henry and their children, whom he adores; but I think he gets much more pleasure simply from going to stay with them in Somerset. Once, when I was in Jamaica with him and had been spending most of the time watching him rehearse a play, he decided that he ought to give me at least one day of tourist's pleasure, so drove me off to the beautiful part of the coast to see the sights. And by the time we got back to Kingston in the evening he was so tense with irritation at the waste of time that we were no longer speaking to each other! I feel quite sad, sometimes, at the thought of what fun we could have had over the years if he'd enjoyed seeing places in the way I do – but there have always been other people to see them with, so as snags in relationships go, it's been a minor one. Barbara and I are going to hire a car in Milan and potter around for a week, ending at Venice where we'll get rid of the car and stay in a lovely palazzo having a restful time.

   V. much love to you both
   Diana

28 OCTOBER 1990

Darling Edward –
   Bless you for being there, hidden in the pile of income

tax assessments and bank statements and electricity bills, when I came staggering in from Italy. It really was like you being there – it gave me such delight – and such a vivid reminder of how incredibly lucky I was – and my mother too – in her end. Poor Muriel [*Neil's mother*]– it's so sad to know that she's still got to go through it. But at least there is the great relief of her not minding being in a place where they will cope ... so wonderful that it seems like a miracle, almost. And I remember an aunt telling me that oddly enough the heart attack which killed my grandmother was 'much less bad' than several of those which hadn't killed her; and Ma's actual dying, too, happened with a calm sort of inevitability. So I suspect that the traumatic bit is over for Neil and you, with the finding of the home and taking her there. What an extraordinary experience for you – thank you for letting me in on it.

Venice – oh Venice! – how we adored it. It's odd that Barbara and I, though we could hardly be more different in temperament, have always made the best of travelling companions (we did a lot together when we were young) because we share exactly the same way of wanting to 'soak up' a place. The first, driving-about, week was very enjoyable and took us to some enchanting places in blissful weather; but it was our week in Venice which was great. My poor old wrecked feet are always a curse, and B had just broken a little toe, so we were quite scared at the prospect of a place where you have no alternative to walking all the time (you can't spend all of it going up and down the main thoroughfare in a vaporetto). But I have found a magic osteopath-

naturopath-acupuncturist (such a dish, he is!) who gave
me a special before-going-to-Venice reflexology
treatment, and Barbara reluctantly but wisely bought a
pair of Sensible Shoes and a lot of painkillers, and we
were both able to walk all day and a lot of the night too
without turning a hair. There's something about
Venetian paving-stones which is extraordinary – you
only have to see how Venetians stride out to see that they
give buoyancy. I sometimes find that not drinking wine
any more is slightly embarrassing when with heavy
drinkers – they can take it as an unspoken reproof – but
our dear Venetian friends are sublimely easy-going (the
whole tone is – I don't know any less threatening
place) – and heavenly cooks too . . . they just shoved the
whisky in my direction and got on with their own
toping, and we all guzzled and giggled in the utmost
happiness. Our first dinner party, B and I left our map
at home as an act of faith. Come two in the morning our
host came some way with us to point us in the right
direction, then we insisted that we knew where we were
and said a fond farewell . . . and got totally lost – in the
rain, at that. It's not frightening, getting lost in Venice,
because it's such a small city that you know you're
bound to find yourself again eventually – but we were
beginning to feel rather ready for our lovely beds in our
luxurious flat – so finally we swallowed our pride and
asked someone, and she told us to go left under the first
archway we came to without remembering that there
was a little archway before the one she meant, which
would plunge us straight into the inky waters of a small
canal – and as we came back out of that archway in fits

of tipsy giggles at our narrow escape, she came running back (having realized what she'd done) and firmly insisted on taking us the whole way home. It was all full of such kindnesses and charm, in addition to its staggering beauty. And two of our days were of a radiant brilliance to put Canaletto to shame, and none of the other four were more than a touch rainy every now and then (always warm). And the luxurious and elegant delights of the apartment which we had so recklessly rented were quite alarmingly easy to get used to. So we rate it as one of the best hols we ever shared.

In Mantua we went to a concert of Mozart piano music by an ancient but distinguished Italian pianist given in the ravishing theatre which Mozart opened – when as a boy wonder he was being trotted around Italy by his daddy. For the first half the old man seemed to me to be possessed by the spirit of a young Mozart – it made the hair rise on the back of one's neck and if I'd parked the car in another street we'd never have known the concert was happening . . . So you see, it really was a good hol. And Barry was happily staying with Sally and Henry (where he still is until tomorrow) so that was OK (although they had a traumatic time when a cow died and they thought it might be mad cow disease – but it wasn't thank god). Much love to you both ('I love you I love you I love you' as our Venetian host Pietroferruccio Berolo would – and constantly does – say)

Diana

10 MARCH 1991

Darling Edward –

Great to hear from you, tho' I could have done without that bit about the rejection letters coming in all together. Since it's a feature of life at E. Terrace [*for Barry's recent plays*] I know so well what it's like, and groan for you. But I don't believe you've necessarily said a long farewell to Morocco. Perhaps the worst thing about that war [*the Gulf War of 1990–91*] has been its unreality – all those wretched people being killed for reasons that no sane person could take seriously – no passions involved (even automatic mid-east anti-Americanism blunted by the monstrousness of Saddam). I have a feeling that it won't be long before it's water off a duck's back, except to the Iraqis – and if they manage to get rid of their monster who knows but that they might do the Japanese thing and become American-oriented? By the strict logic of Islam they ought to, because surely it's the will of Allah which dictates the outcome of events, which must suggest that Saddam was being chastised for impiety and Bush (god help us!) is a kind of angel of the lord? I do, however, feel a bit nervous about the remote possibility of our getting a Labour government at our next general election. Suppose our new prime minister turned out to be not properly deferential to the angel of the lord, might he suddenly be cast in the role of Noriega?

Seriously – the Bush regime is not a reassuring spectacle. It frightens Barry so much that he can no longer look at or read the news.

Winter ailments seem to be over (touch wood!), and I'm beginning to get the feel of how much less tired I am now that I don't have to devote all that time and worry to my mother. After three years of neglecting the garden and of secretly feeling that I might have even gone off it, I've rediscovered the pleasure of getting earth under my fingernails and I'm digging away like mad. And last week I signed on again for the evening class in drawing from life which I abandoned four years ago because it had become Too Much. I got a good welcome and was told that it would be a great pity not to go on with it when I had such a natural gift for it – purr purr!

God alone knows what's going to happen to the firm. Tom is very obviously aware of being short of money and is chiselling everything back to such a bare minimum that we can hardly keep going. He tries to disguise worry and keep our spirits up, but he's looking a bit green-skinned and twitchy. Pray for us.

I've just had a phone call saying my friend Calvin Hernton is coming over for four months – a sabbatical I suppose. Twenty years ago – my god, it seems about five, but twenty it is – he was my lodger for a time. We published a book of his called *Sex and Racism* (a good book) and he turned up in London as a sort of protégé of Ronald Laing, staying at first in a madhouse run by Laing in the East End of London with schizophrenics who had a lovely time being persuaded that it was they who were the sane ones. Cal's not handsome – he had bad acne in his youth which ruined his face – but he's tall and he has that lovely loose black man's walk and he

always wore very black shades day and night so he
looked splendidly sinister, and then one discovered that
(altho' he sometimes went into odd panics when he was
high – he was a terrible old pot-head) – he was the
gentlest person imaginable . . . so no woman I saw him
with including myself failed to fall into bed with him
almost on sight, and – this was the really nice thing
about him – once one had made love with him one
became his fondest friend without in the least expecting
him to be one's own true love. He really had a sort of
genius at that. During the time he was living in the
room which is now Barry's he had five women of whom
he was very fond (by that time I'd pulled out – I think
B – who was still with his wife – had come back to
London from Canada), one or another of whom always
spent the night with him (sleeping alone made him
frightened). Only once did he get his lines crossed so
that two turned up at the same time – but in fact I think
they all knew about each other and didn't mind. Of
course we were in the mid sixties (it's twenty years since
he left), when no one worth their salt would confess to
Possessiveness – and anyone who had spent an evening
with Cal was pretty well bound to be so stoned that they
were past minding anything. But there really was this
feeling that what you had with him was so genuine and
so sweet that there was no reason to fret for more. As a
lodger he was almost faultless – incredibly neat and
clean – never even a teaspoon left unwashed in the sink,
because his granny had always said 'it isn't cleaning that
matters it's keeping things clean'. (He was raised by his
granny because his mother, who was called Magnolia,

was only fifteen when he was born.) And he was a
night-bird so he was never in the way. When he was in I
was out, and vice versa. The only snag was that when
he came home, which was usually three or four in the
morning, if he was very drunk as well as stoned (which
he often was) he would start playing his record player
very loud ('I Heard It On The Grapevine' and Chicken
Shack singing 'I'd rather go blind' are engraved for ever
in my aural system). For about fifteen minutes I'd lie
with my pillow clutched to my ears, saying to myself
'Surely they must soon fall into bed'; but almost always
I had to sit up and yell – which worked without fail, but
was a great nuisance. Now I ask myself 'How did I bear
it?' but it didn't seem too bad at the time. When he got
back to the States he got a job at Oberlin [*College, Ohio*]
lecturing in Afro-American studies. Then he got
tenure – and it seems he's still there – the number of
students he must have fucked defies calculation. He was
hoping, of course, that his old room would be available.
Feeling *deeply* thankful that it is not – has made me
realize how old I've become! Nowadays if I'm woken up
at three in the morning I'm not able to go to sleep
again. But it will be lovely to see the dear thing again.
He must be well on in his fifties by now, but I doubt
whether his habits will have changed. Ah me, we've
heard the chimes at midnight, yes?

Love and love, Diana

16/17 APRIL 1991

Darling Edward,

Good that you're coming (touch wood) in May. It's soon enough for your star not to have risen quite out of reach but may it continue its upward movement. A good dollop of fame would be absolutely delicious in one's riper years, when consolations can be so sparse.

I've just met a most extraordinary person who isn't famous but ought to be. She's 85, called Marie-Louise Motesiczky, was Elias Canetti's mistress for thirty-five years, kept under thickest wraps in darkest Hampstead – and is a *marvellous* painter. I met her because when my dear friend Calvin's girlfriend was looking for a flat for Calvin she went to view one in Marie-Louise's huge and shabby and lovely house and had a mysterious feeling that Marie-Louise and I should meet, so invited us to tea together. One falls for her at once – her family was Viennese Jewish of the grandest and most aristocratic kind – huge fortune, but even more intellect and style than money – and M-L is one with whom one can talk at once about anything, and of the most transparent and profound honesty. And last week I went to see some of her paintings – and my god, one was up there with Picasso and Braque and Kokoschka – *real painting* – all stuffed away in cupboards in her bedroom. She did have shows in her youth, and there are three or four of her paintings in European museums, and one in the Tate and one in the Fitzwilliam Museum in Cambridge – but apparently she never sells, and in this country is hardly

known to anyone as a painter – I think that old brute
Canetti sat on her so heavily that she couldn't promote
herself – but also it would hardly have seemed important
to her, so long as she could go on painting. But now she's
tormented about what sort of will to make, because she
does want the work to be seen and understood when
she's dead. I'm half afraid that I'm going to get involved
in this very complex problem! She hasn't much money
[*she was quite well-off, in fact*] – lets out most of her house
to lodgers – but doesn't consider selling her work
because of that. And anyway, when she fled from Vienna
after the Anschluss a cousin said 'my dear – you'd better
take this in case you need to raise money' and gave her a
Crivelli out of his collection! Not a top class Crivelli, but
still, a Crivelli. And luckily she doesn't like it very much
so now the time has come when she does need to raise
money she won't mind selling it. A Japanese is flirting
with it so she has dug it out and hung it up in her
drawing room – and I must say it gave me quite a turn to
see it there – for a moment I thought it must be a very
large and clever reproduction.

Unfortunately the flat that was being considered by
Calvin has now been taken by a horrid young man who
has announced that he must at once paint the kitchen
and bathroom because they are unhygienic. 'But don't
you think that it really is rather tactless of him? My house
is *not a slum*.' Perhaps once he's painted the rooms she'll
dislike him so much that she'll sack him – but I fear it's
only a one-room flat, tho' a huge room, so it wouldn't do
for you! Would it? No it wouldn't – because I heard her
telling the horrid young man when he came to view it

that of course he could have his girl to stay for weekends and so on, but she did not want two people in the room all the time.

Heavens, it's half-past midnight! Goodnight, dear things, and much much love.

Diana

19 SEPTEMBER 1991

Darling Edward –

Wonderful piece – and how satisfactory to see it where it ought to be. Tell that little voice inside to shut up. True – you in your heart of hearts probably think 'what a lot of nonsense' – but the more famous you are in your old age the more fun it will be for your friends.

Oh André and I did have fun in Hungary. Can't remember if my postcard to you was one of the ones onto which I condensed the story of our excursion to Siklos, George Mikes's birthplace, for the Unveiling of the Plaque (spelt Plague on the official invitation card, English version) in his honour. The joke was the tremendous difference between the fuss André had been making about it in advance, and the event itself. Having organized the presence there of George Mikes's son, his daughter, the woman who was his love during his last years (not on speaking terms with son and daughter because they think she forced him to change his will in her favour literally as he lay dying, whereas he implored her to write out the codicil for him with almost his last breath and would have died unhappy if she hadn't); plus the novelist Stephen Vizinczey (very snappy writer, difficult man, great friend of George's), a distinguished journalist called Phil Knightley (nice) and a couple of other people from London; and having tried hard to persuade our ambassador in Budapest to make the six-hour drive to Siklos (luckily he couldn't make it), André had created the impression that the whole town would come to a halt for the occasion, and probably most of literary Hungary would turn up for it.

In fact no literary person in the country cares a fig about dear old George (a rather simple humorous writer little known outside England except for one little book forty years ago, called *How to Be an Alien*), and Siklos had only thought of giving him a plaque because it's ashamed that it let George's poor old grandmother, the last of the family to live there, be carried off to die in a camp (there is only one Jew living there now). It was a dear little village occasion. For the actual Unveiling police blocked off traffic at both ends of the street, down which local passersby peered with mild curiosity before plodding on about their rural occupations, and the attendance was about fifteen people in addition to the English contingent. However, the young actor in his tuxedo read his patriotic poem with enormous verve, and the beautiful beautiful burgomeister made a long and patriotic speech, and later we all made very short speeches in a library of the school, and everyone felt it had gone very well, even tho' George's son had not brought a wreath to hang on the wall (none of us had thought of it) so a fierce last minute scramble had to be made to find one (I think from the baker's – it looked as tho' it had been designed to sit on a cake).

Except for George's love, who was very sad, we all enjoyed ourselves greatly, even tho' the drive was long – because the dinner on our arrival the night before had been so lovely. We'd had no idea what was awaiting us – were carried off some three miles into the hilly vine-clad countryside, turned out in pitch darkness – the night warm and still, but starless as well as moonless, and told that we had to walk only half a mile – which we did on a narrow little path between vineyards, following a faint and wavering torch, while all round the crickets sang. The fact that we could also hear the distant thudding of Yugoslav artillery from across the nearby border [*this was the beginning of the war in Yugoslavia*] ought, of course, to have lowered our spirits badly, but I'm ashamed to say that all it did was add to the oddness and interest of the occasion. The barn we eventually reached, lit by brilliant, hissing compressed-oil lamps, had a big cellar full of huge casks, and there we first had a Tasting, to decide which of the farmer's wines we would drink for supper. Even I tasted – and they were so delicious and so obviously pure that I did venture to drink one glass of white and one of red with the meal, and came to no harm [*alcohol had, alas, started to disagree with me*]. The white tasted of lovely unknown flowers. In the barn was a long narrow table with a white cloth and benches, where the grape harvesters are given their harvest feast, and the farmer's wife, on a cylinder-gas stove, had cooked an Enormous tin bath full of stewed pork. I was terrified that I would be unable to eat enough to satisfy oriental-style hospitality, but as it turned out she dished the stew into bowls set along the table, with plates of salad between, and everyone was expected to help himself and one could eat as much or as little as one liked; so I could happily concentrate on falling in love with the Burgomeister who – although in fact a vet – was the very image of a nineteenth-century Hungarian poet, complete with beard, aristocratic nose, large, expressive grey eyes, a noble brow and a touch – a casual touch – of the dandy in his dress. Scrumptious. How terribly sad to be old enough to be his grandmother! The stew was sublime.

All the rest of the visit was more ordinary but really enjoyable because of much hospitality, a perfectly *marvellous* hotel (one of the greatest Art Nouveau buildings of Central Europe) and the fact that battered, down-at-heel Budapest is a fascinating city. And as for the Cakes and Pastries – words (perhaps fortunately) fail . . .

Much love, Diana

28 NOVEMBER 1991

Dearest Edward,

The situation in this place is becoming boring – it goes on and on being the same: none of us seeing how we can possibly last more than another two months or so, and Tom [*Rosenthal*] behaving as though all were well (except for looking like Lazarus) and bringing down an Iron Curtain whenever anyone tries to ask him about it. We are hardly taking anything on (hence lack of desperate overwork), but on the other hand, since we started thinking 'We can't last more than a month or so' we have lasted quite a lot of months, so perhaps there is a glimmer of hope? If all turns out well I shall feel terribly guilty, because we've just lost a brilliant young novelist – Chris Wilson, he was at our garden party but I don't know if you talked with him– entirely because, without quite putting it into words, I warned him off. He's very shrewd about the publishing scene, so put me in an awkward corner by saying 'I know I shouldn't put you in this awkward corner, but is the firm going to last?' He's recklessly given up his teaching job (fool!) so it really does matter to him to get as much as he can out of his writing. He's good, and I really like him – he's become a friend, so when I had to do an instant balancing between loyalty to firm and loyalty to my writer – the scales tipped in his favour and I told him than while I knew nothing definite and was still hoping, I was unable to feel sure. 'Nuff said – Chris instructs his agent to be totally unreasonable in her demands, and I find myself having to hold Tom's hand through a lot of huffing and puffing at the monstrousness of agents until finally there's no alternative to letting Chris go. Oh dear, tangled web ... I hate lying (as I was in effect doing to poor Tom) but usually find that when I have to do it I'm very good at it.

Have you got your new flat yet? I do hope so, because surely it would brighten the prospect for 1992. [*They did move from their charming but rather subterranean*

apartment, to a larger, airy one with a tree so close that Edward could watch a bird sitting on a nest in its branches.]
For which, beloved two, I send you lots and lots of love and wishes for everything good. Diana

20 JANUARY 1992

Dearest Edward,

Given your awareness of growing old, I thought you might take a wry pleasure in the following, which turned up this morning in an obituary notice of John Sparrow, former Warden of All Souls, Oxford. It said that he produced it off the cuff towards the end of his life, when his memory was going:

> I'm accustomed to my dentures,
> To my deafness I'm resigned,
> I can cope with my bifocals –
> But oh dear! I miss my mind.

I found myself chanting it all the way to work.

Sparrow's position was the most prestigious in British Academe, and he was a very sharp man indeed who struck terror into the hearts of those who feared he might think them fools. I met him only right at the end of his life when he was no longer Warden but still lived in All Souls, which had become his home. My glamorous friend Andrew Harvey (now sitting at the feet of a Holy

Mother) was then the youngest Fellow of All Souls there
had ever been and used to invite me to dinner there on
Ladies' Nights (rare and exotic occasions then – tho'
now All Souls actually accepts lady Fellows – good
God!). After dinner we withdrew for coffee and brandy
in the Fellows' Common Room – an exquisitely
comfortable book-and-print-lined room, marinated in
centuries of intellectual privilege – where old Sparrow
would already be lurking, hungry for a taste of life as he
used to know it. On the first occasion I was flattered that
I was instantly pounced on and taken over to be
introduced to this famous and venerable figure, and
gratified by the kind welcome he gave me; but I soon
realized that I was in fact a Human Sacrifice. There the
old boy was, every evening, telling the same stories – his
memory was going fast – having become, alas, a terrible
bore – but pathetic in his longing and anyway they were
all very fond of him, so inevitably someone would have
to take him on and keep him happy until he got tipsy
enough to be steered off to bed. So if a kind-looking
guest happened to turn up – *swoop*, and he or she was
delivered up, upon which the rest of the company
quickly ebbed away to far corners of the room where
they could merrily get on with evidently fascinating
conversations – Laughter at the Other Side of the Room,
it was. Poor old Sparrow was sweet – pathetically grateful
for attention, funny and touching, and his stories were
good, so the first time it was no hardship. But the second
time I realized that it was word for word the same as the
first time ... and the third time ditto ... in fact one saw
only too well why they did it. It must have been a relief

when he finally turned up his toes. But they'd given him a happier old age than most, and he'd still been able to be funny about his own plight – which I suppose is why his little verse seems to me like a spell against decay.

You are responsible for turning my mind towards poems. I've just begun tinkering away at another. I shall now resist the temptation to mail them off to you one by one (Barry can't feel very interested in anything which doesn't address the question: How Are We To Change Human Nature? so I've no one to bounce them off easily to hand), and see whether a little group accumulates. Then you will have to say what you think.

Love, Diana

[*Andrew Harvey had turned his back on an academic career, in which his friends had expected him to shine, and after a visit to Ladakh, about which he wrote an excellent book, had embarked on the pursuit of spiritual illumination. At one time this led him to become the follower of a young Indian woman who was believed to possess extraordinary powers, which apparently led to disenchantment. He moved to the United States, after which, with regret, I lost touch with him.*]

20 JANUARY 1992

Darling Edward –

What a Feast of Poetry! It really was a lovely bundle, and kept me happy for several evenings. Barry enjoyed

The Exquisite Corpse best because in addition to you he very much likes the liveliness of the thing. Such variety in your poems – I love 'Callas' and 'The Stumps' specially. And also, with what brilliant simplicity you have given me the image of the grizzled poet's performance.

I didn't quite enjoy all the interview, because it disturbs me when you say you are a neurotic mess, and about not liking yourself, and being not good at things – like it disturbs me when you go on about being old. This is because ever since I've known you, you have been in my eyes so sane – dear heart, you're my sanest friend! – and have had so much natural authority, just as you have always been so astonishingly young – not only in your appearance but in your responses. I think it even shocks me a bit to hear you say your vulnerability out loud. *But* I did simply *love* the bit about always feeling that poetry had a duty to be true and clear. And what a sublimely valuable statement this is; 'half of writing is learning to put down what is there. You never know if it's ordinary or not until you put it down.' That's the best thing that could be said to any writer, and it comes with such force from you because you are a writer who has fought his way through to it. So thank you very much for that envelope of riches.

I just had an adventure in a hospital. Because of various twinges and uneasinesses I went to my doctor and told her that I thought I had a stone in my gall bladder, and she said it did sound like a classic case of same so I'd better go to the Middlesex Hospital Out-Patients Dept. and have an ultra-sound scan. Which I did. (In London, anyway, the dear old National Health still functions quite efficiently, whatever they say in the papers.) It is a mild and amusing procedure, and sure enough, there was a stone in my gall bladder. But the specialist said that many an autopsy reveals stones that big, or bigger, in gall bladders that have never given their owners the least discomfort, so my twinges might be caused by it, but they equally might be caused by an ulcer, so now I must have an endoscopy. Shock-horror! Because an endoscopy is when they feed a tube down your throat into your stomach and part of your guts, with a bright light at the end of it and take photographs of the inside of you ... which I've always thought sounded Nightmarish, on top of which, when it was done to an old friend of mine (admittedly about twenty years ago) they ruptured his oesophagus and damn nearly killed him. So I went very green and ran home to my doctor and said 'I think I'll say I won't have it.' She – a good doctor and nice woman – said 'It's your guts and you have a perfect right to say that ... but you should, possibly, take into account this, that and the other' – and finally, very gently, worked me round to saying 'well – I suppose it would be pretty silly not to have it done.' So after two weeks of getting more and more nervous I tottered back to the hospital, was given an enormous shot of Valium, felt convinced that the shot was having no effect on me at all, was hardly aware when the tube went down, hadn't a clue what the doctor actually did (in fact he took lots of pictures and a biopsy), thought that the whole thing lasted about three minutes when really it takes twenty, didn't feel the tube being withdrawn, and didn't even have a sore throat afterwards although they'd warned me I might. After an hour or so resting and a cup of tea Barry came to pick me up and took me home to a delicious lunch, whereupon I went to bed and slept soundly for eighteen hours. So, if ever you hear anyone being anxious at the prospect of such an examination, tell them to relax – there's nothing to it! The doc did find a small area of inflammation and has put me on ulcer pills for three weeks. He did not appear to expect the biopsy to prove anything more than a formality – well, I suppose he wouldn't, anyway – but I'm so relieved and cheered up by how easy the examination was that I'm not able to worry about hearing the result of that, which will come in about a week's time. Certainly no one threw up their hands and exclaimed 'Oh god, this woman has an inoperable cancer!!!' which is encouraging.

What news of Neil's mother?

Much love, Diana

27 FEBRUARY 1992

My darling Edward –

How marvellous to hear from you just when I was dying for company because of dreadful happenings.

Last Saturday – five days ago, it seems weeks! – I was just beginning to feel better enough after flu to get out of bed, when Barry said 'I don't know why but I've got a belly-ache' – 'Indigestion, I expect – are you feeling nausea?' – 'I'd sort of like to vomit but I can't.' And then quickly, it began to get worse. He's very bad about pain, so at first I assumed he was exaggerating something slight, but then it leapt to sweating, groaning point so I called the doctor. At weekends medical practices employ communal switchboards which supply from a pool of odds and ends. After two hours – not bad really, but oh it seemed so long! – a very small, tired shabby Indian doctor arrived, with whom B wouldn't collaborate at all, groaning only 'Give me morphine – why won't the bastard give me morphine'. B's total medical history consists of a terrifying pain in his belly thirty years go, when they told him in a hospital that he had cancer and they must operate, and he ran away from the hospital and persuaded someone who had been to Cambridge with him to supply him with morphine, which he then lived on for six weeks in perfect bliss, and the pain vanished. So I knew this morphine thing would happen and dreaded the doc getting angry. But he was very good. Firm, kind, decisive. As soon as he prodded the belly he told me 'Something nasty going on in there, we must get him to hospital', and he had an ambulance at the door in half an hour.

My cousin Barbara volunteered to drive me in the wake of the ambulance so that I'd eventually have someone to bring me home, and off we went to University College Hospital in Gower St. By the time we found a parking space they had him down in the X-ray dept. At about midnight a nurse came to find me and said I could go up to the ward with him. They had knocked him out with pethidine by then – he was just mobile, could climb off the stretcher and onto the bed, but now remembers not a thing about it. They operated next day and again the day after and for twenty-four hours I believed the garbled information given by a nurse. He was in intensive care and I thought they'd had to stop the first op in the middle because his lungs were in such a terrible condition. But at last I got the surgeon, thank god, and learned that his lungs were in a very bad way, which was why he was in care, but the first op had been completed and had consisted of removing a section of his lower bowel which had died because of lack of circulation, which was not caused by an evil growth but by a twisted gut; and the second op was to check that the blood-flow had been restored because there is a very rare condition which just occasionally causes blood-flow to fail spontaneously, and he was not one hundred percent sure that it didn't cause the trouble – but all was well, it looked much healthier now, so now it was just a matter of keeping an eye on his lungs ...

God knows how his lungs got so full of gunge – he doesn't smoke all that much, and hasn't smoked for all that long – but there he had to be until today, in an oxygen mask, with tubes and wires in every orifice, looking so dreadfully ill. He was much cheered up by the sweet, pretty, kind, competent girls caring for him so beautifully, and by the thought that the treatment he was getting for free must cost about £10,000 a day. Now, thank god, he's back in an ordinary ward and is no longer having to use the oxygen mask – still being fed via a tube up his nose, and drained by other tubes, so still terribly uncomfortable, but they do let him have plenty

of pethidine. He can read a newspaper and is taking in
the condition of his neighbours – and still adores his
nurses. Heavens, how good they are in these great old
teaching hospitals, and how sublimely lucky we are to
have a great old teaching hospital as our 'local'. Today
they took the plaster off his wound – they are very very
pleased by the way it's healing but I was stunned by the
sight of it. It runs from about eight inches above his navel
right down to vanish into his pubic hair, making a little
swerve to avoid the navel – they must have had the whole
of his innards out on the table. And it's not stitched, but
held together with stout metal staples at one-half inch
intervals. Jesus, what a sight. It's going to take his body a
long time to recover from such a trauma. But today he is
permitted to swallow very small sips of water, and he did
one fart which is, as it were, the first swallow of summer.
They will keep him in until he manages a shit – which I
can't imagine him doing and neither can he, poor love.
And then our darling Sally and Henry in Somerset say
that he can convalesce with them. Sal is being a huge
help to me, telephoning all the time, full of sense and
love. But oh oh what a harrowing and exhausting time,
and how much discomfort and horridness he's still got to
undergo, even if he continues to get better without a
hitch.

'Say your prayers, and the body will take care of itself'
indeed!!! I have to declare myself *not* a customer for your
health book. But of course it is the National Health,
however creaky and decrepit much of it is, that enables
us to believe in medicine (and the creakiness is real –
even as Barbara and I were waiting in the bright, calm,

orderly casualty dept. of UCH, observing how swiftly
even quite minor injuries were being dealt with, I read an
item in an abandoned newspaper about an old man left
in a wheel-chair in a corner of the casualty dept. in a
small south London hospital for six hours before
someone noticed he was dead).

Poems, as you can imagine, are far from my mind at
present – a great delight at your response to the one
about Ma. You really have made me happy, bless you. I
think you are right about dropping the last two lines and
calling it 'The Gift'. I was uneasy about those lines.

Now I'm going to bed very early. It was amazing, what
adrenalin did for me at the start of B's illness, but now
the post-flu 'debility' of which my doctor warned me has
got me and I feel dim and grim. Much love, Diana

P.P.S. – A little old verse called 'In a Tetchy Mood'

The poem about his wife's lipstick on the rim of the
    cup
and the poem about his lack of nerve to kill
a rabbit caught in a trap . . .

The poem about god's presence in every leaf and
    stone
and the poem about light and darkness
being one . . .

Too little or too large – too bad
I'd rather read
a well-composed and witty ad.

3 MARCH 1992

Dearest Edward,

Barry home! Goes back end of this week to have his huge row of metal staples taken out, but they say that doesn't hurt. He's still feeling very weak (naturally) but food goes in and comes out normally – amazingly quick recovery, in fact. What a relief!

Herewith the finished Ma poem complete with your suggestions, a new verse and one afterthought alteration. B likes it, too.

Love from Diana

Attached: a poem for Edward Field, whose words made me write it. Diana Athill 3-3-92

THE GIFT

It took my mother two days to die, the first of them
    cruel
as her body, ninety-five years old, crashed beyond repair.
I found her, 'an emergency' behind screens in a
    crowded ward,
jaw dropped, tongue lolling, eyes unseeing.
Unconscious? No. When about to vomit she gasped
    'Basin!'
She was aware of what she was having to endure.

I put my hand on hers. Her head shifted, her eyelids
    heaved up.

Her eyes focussed.
Out of deep in that dying woman came a great flash
of recognition and of utmost joy.

My brother was there. Later he said
'That was a very beautiful smile she gave you.'
To me it was a moment when a love I had never
    doubted
flamed into visibility
and I saw what I believed in.

Next morning: quietness, sleep,
intervals of murmured talk: which made sense.
'She is better!'
'She is feeling much better,' said the nurse,
'but she is still very very ill.'
I understood the warning and that what seemed
    miracle was morphine.

What did I feel? I'd become Siamese twins, one of
    which
wanted her never to die, while the other
was dismayed at the thought of her coming back to
    life –
of having to go on dreading pain for her; go on
    foreseeing
her increasing helplessness and feeling guilt
at not giving up my life to be with her all the time
(she never asked for that but I knew she longed for it).
What I felt was bad at being in two minds; but only for
    a while, because

perched in my skull above this conflict there was a
    referee
saying 'Neither of you can win so shut up
and get on with doing whatever comes next.'

Her collapsed body eased, she was disconcerting to be
    with
because so alive.
There she was, on the edge of ceasing to exist,
and she was unchanged, tired but perfectly ordinary,
telling me what to do with her dog and where to find
    her will.
When someone protested 'But you'll soon be back
    home' she was impatient,
saying crossly 'I could go any minute'.

Then, after a long sleep, she turned her head a little
    and said
'Did I tell you that last week Jack drove me
to the nursery garden, to buy that eucalyptus tree?'
I too loved that garden and the drive through country
we had both known all our lives.
'You told me he was going to,' I said. 'Was it fun?'

She answered dreamily – her last words before
    sleeping again,
out of which sleep she didn't wake:

'It was absolutely divine.'

15 APRIL 1992

Dearest Edward –

High time I sent you a progress report on B. His operation, huge as it was, gave him amazingly little trouble once he was unhooked from all those alarming tubes, and he was released from hospital a week after it, still with his gleaming metal staples in him from top to bottom but able to eat and digest normally. He therefore expected to be fully himself in no time, but in fact – naturally – felt pretty wobbly for a good many weeks and was not quite strong even two weeks ago – when what did he do but go down with bronchitis. Filled with anti-biotics for a week and me thinking 'Will I be able to go away on the 12th for my week in Shropshire with my sister?' (a holiday I was dying for). Which in fact I did (I'm there as I write) because he thought he could manage OK and I'm phoning every day and could always rush home if necessary. Everyone says that it takes ages to get completely over such a big op, at his age, and I fear that's so (my macabre old brother's immediate comment: 'He'll never get over that') but he's basically so healthy that I think he'll be alright again in another eight weeks or so – I mean quite alright. He can already potter down to the shops and so on – just feels more tired afterwards than he should. So that's him.

As for me – I'm less exhausted than I might be, but still very ready for this break, and I wish it were longer. My sister and her husband live in Zimbabwe, but he inherited this house from his stepmother, two years ago, and now they manage to spend a part of each year here. It's a heavenly part of the country – my favourite part of it – and the house is a charming old farmhouse, long and low and white and a bit crumbly – very old, and with an extremely relaxed and friendly atmosphere about it. My sister could hardly be less like me and is a bit of a racist, so no question of her and Barry having more than the slightest acquaintance. But I'm very fond of her all the same, and she of me – we tolerate each other's habits of mind because of the thickness of blood I suppose, and actually like each other's natures a lot otherwise. And part of me enjoys revisiting the pastimes of my youth, such as going to horse fairs and feeding chickens and such. She's gone off today to collect a couple of her younger grandchildren, whom we are entertaining over Easter, which will be fun. If change is the essence of holiday, then this is a good one. Must now buzz off to the local (and ravishing) market town to buy in a supply of ice cream, Coca-Cola, etc. for the children. Much love, Diana

9 SEPTEMBER 1992

Dearest Edward,

Today I told Tom that I'd rather leave the firm at the end of this month, than wait until the end of the year – did I tell you that I told him some time ago that I would retire then? He's been away for a couple of weeks, on holiday in Spain, and during those weeks hardly a single telephone call came in, hardly a manuscript arrived ... the place was dead, and those of us left in it sat doing crossword puzzles and reading paperbacks. He still goes through the motions of believing that a last-minute sale of the property (the two houses) could save the firm, but does so in a very low-key, zombie-like way. He didn't make the smallest attempt to persuade me to change my mind. Dreadfully depressing tho' it is for all of us, it's worse for him. He's always been so macho – how will he be able to bear the humiliation of failure?

As for me ... I've got a record of Big Bill Broonzy singing the blues, and my favourite song on it is 'Walking down the road feeling bad. / Walking down the road feeling so mis'able and baaad' and all the way from the carpark to the office, this morning it was going through my head ...

I find that it's actually frightening, to one who has been going to an office every weekday for fifty years (dear God! but it really is at least that long), to realize that in less than three weeks – no more office. And that in spite of the fact that the office has become intolerable, so that I've been longing to be rid of it. But I don't doubt, really, that I have been right in believing that retirement will be enjoyable once the first shock of it is over. One thing I shall do instantly; write for an application form to Hawthornden Castle – a Scottish mini-Yaddo (you get only six weeks there at a time), so that I can get dug into my story of the Rise and Fall of a publishing house. It will at least, now, have a Shape! People who have been to Hawthornden go weak at the knees when they remember the bliss of it. While on the home front nothing could be more timely, since Barbara has just acquired the most magical puppy – a cube of white swansdown with three shiny black currants stuck in it, which is convinced that it's the Hound of the Baskervilles – which needs someone to spend the day with while Barbara is out. Barry is benevolently inclined towards her (the puppy – called Hannah), but is not good at interpreting the signs which mean 'Quick – pounce on her and get her onto a sheet of newspaper before it happens!' So that until I can be there, I rather discourage her presence on my carpets. And on top of that, a lot needs doing at Barbara's mother's house in Norfolk, which we are slightly expanding so our builder, a beguiling gnomelike being who recognized us at once as two times the sucker than just one of us would have been, has been making the best of us. It wasn't surprising that he discovered the whole house needed re-wiring – it obviously did – but did it really have to be entirely re-plumbed? And did the foundations for the new conservatory-garden room really need to be (as he proudly declared) 'strong enough to hold a cathedral'? And did two bathrooms have to be wholly re-tiled because showers were being put in? And did . . . and did . . . Finally, of course, the whole bloody thing is having to be redecorated, including new stair and hall carpet, just because we wanted one bedroom added for me. And we are ending up with a new kitchen so stunning that we will have, like it or not, to give dinners to swarms of neighbours whenever we go there for a weekend – which isn't all that often. So the sooner I can get down there and keep an eye on colours, the better. (You would think that, after all that, I'd have a country retreat for writing my book in, and not have to go to Hawthornden Castle – but actually, once down in Norfolk (or up in Norfolk?) one never has a moment's peace.)

Much love, and do for heaven's sake, prosper. I long to hear of people I love doing well.

22 OCTOBER 1992

Darling Edward –

Writing in the country, where Barbara, her daughter Polly and I are spending two weeks instead-of-a-vacation, trying to get her mother's house free of builders, and habitable again to be our 'country place'. The end of the tunnel is in sight – but builders in despair because of the recession are very reluctant to say goodbye to a job once they've found one. We're spending alarming amounts of money – I guess we have spent, by now, a good deal more than we'd have done if we had gone on the Italian holiday we decided we couldn't afford.

As for 'Feeling so mis'able and baad' – it seems that I got all of that out of my system in the days just before I left AD – largely I think because of the appallingly gloomy atmosphere weighing down poor old 102 Great Russell St – all but empty, filthy beyond belief, it had become the House of Usher incarnate. Two days after I left, Laura Morris, one of the two people (both part-time) left in the editorial dept, and one of the six people now constituting the firm as a whole, heard laughter on the floor above her, thought I must be paying a call on her colleague up there, and went upstairs to join us. The whole floor was empty. And the colleague who, as it happened, had been downstairs on Laura's floor, had also heard the laughter . . . It was the brew of angst fermenting in that house which had made me feel so bad. The very minute I woke up on the first morning of my retirement I began to feel *marvellous* – a couple of hours later I saw in a shop window an ad for life class and by six o'clock that evening I was having a lovely time drawing a big man with a beer-belly (teacher has let me start using oils since then, and has pronounced me Very Promising – he runs a delightful class). And what with one thing and another I'm so busy being retired and am enjoying it so much that the idea of perhaps having to take on freelance work for the money's sake freezes my blood. I'm going to try to manage without. I want never to set eyes on anyone else's typescript again.

I don't think this means that, for nearly fifty years, I was fooling myself when I thought I liked being an editor – a great deal of it I did like. But I think it does mean that even congenial work, which one is lucky to be in, remains work – something which is really basically against nature unless undertaken for one's own private satisfaction. Which I didn't let myself see while I had to (or thought I had to) continue in it, but now do see. So praise god that I'm now free of it.

I shan't hear until some time in December if I've got a

place at the Scottish castle [*I didn't*]. If I have, that's
when I'll get really dug into the publishing book. If I
don't get it I'll have to start working like mad on the Self-
Discipline.

The book about Hakim [Make Believe] comes out in
Feb. My publisher has already fixed me up with a very
good interview as soon as I get back to London with
Maureen Cleave – a woman I like a lot who is doing
pieces for the *Daily Telegraph* magazine at present. She's
one of the best interviewers we have, and we are on the
same wave-length, so that's good.

I find that an old friend of mine is now more or less
editing the *London Magazine* (no one ever sees it, but on
and on it goes) so I'll try my Alfred intro on him. They
do a lot of poetry (mostly very English I suspect) and I'll
tell Jeremy [*Lewis*] he ought to go after you. Much love
my dearest dears. Diana

[*The 'book about Hakim'*, Make Believe, *described getting to
know (by publishing him) an American from the slums of Boston
who had kicked a heroin habit, inspired by Malcolm X, but in the
end turned out to think he was God: a story that ended in the
murder of the Englishwoman he was living with, and his own too.*]

18 DECEMBER 1992

Darling Edward –
This morning *your book arrived*. What a beautiful

DIANA ATHILL

book, emerging from its wrappings like the sun from
cloud – and then I opened it and began to have just a
quick look before getting up – obviously such a lovely fat
book was going to need slow reading, so just a
preliminary squint … and darling Edward, it is now 1:30
and I am still in bed, and I'm still thinking of it as a quick
preliminary squint because that's what it is. There's so
much marvellous reading in your poems I am going to
return and return to them, and they make me love you so
much. It really is a life that you are bravely putting into
our hands, and it's awe-inspiring to see that being done
(who else dares to? Nobody, with this courage and
candour and immensely hard-won simplicity). I shall
always remember this morning as extraordinary – a
sinister dark morning with a moaning wind and fierce
bursts of rain rattling on the widow, and being snug in
bed with this wonderful book coming alive in my hands –
and it's going to continue being here, hurrah hurrah.
What a marvellous thing it is that you have made this
collection, because it adds amazingly to each poem,
being seen as part of the whole.

Of course I've read and loved a number of the poems
before, but they reappear here with added strength and
point and life.

If *Counting Myself Lucky* doesn't bring fame, then fuck
fame is what I say, because it will simply be proving true
what one so often says as a sort of flippant 'touch-wood
thing' – the people who write about writing really don't
know what's what.

But blessed Black Sparrow does, or they wouldn't have
made it look so lovely, and I do, or I wouldn't love you

94

so, and I don't doubt that Barry will, when he's able to
get his hands on it. Thank you thank you *thank you* for
sending it. Diana

9 JANUARY 1993

What do you think of this for a yummy New Year's
treat? And on the same day the *Spectator* jumped the gun
(the book [Make Believe] isn't published until the 14th)
with a lead review of a page and a half – and very
attentive and good. Better than the interview, really – but
the interview is more fun because of making one look
Famous – indeed, to our dear Indian newsagent it *has*
made me be famous. So this is Happy Day – and may we
all have lots more of them. *Love*, Diana
    Enc. 'Accidental Adventures of Love and Death'
interview by Maureen Cleave, *Telegraph Magazine*. 37

27 JANUARY 1993

Dear love,
    The thing about *fame* is that it's here today and gone
tomorrow. Delicious interviews did *not* lead to good
reviews – and so far the only letters which have come in
as a result of publication are a) One from a jobbing

sculptor asking me to commission Bust of myself, and b) A three-page effusion, illustrated, about Black Penises – unfortunately so wildly incoherent that we can't make out whether the writer is in favour of same, or against them, although it's clear that he does believe them to be much much *much* bigger than white ones. The review in the *New Statesman* was all about there being two kinds of racism, the ordinary kind, and – very much worse – the oblique kind, of which I am a shocking example.

I believe I ought to have turned the story into a novel after all. As it is, reviewers seem to be so taken up by this old woman making these 'embarrassing' (that word has occurred more than once) admissions about herself, that they simply don't pay attention to the story I'm telling. Which makes me very cross. And none of them seem to recognize a beady eye when they see one. Even the one really lovely review attributed my putting up with Hakim to the capacious warmness of my heart rather than to the inability to stop watching that was really behind it.

But *how wonderful* that your garret has become large and light and lovely! What a difference it will make. Uprooting is always panic-making, so one doesn't quite foresee how much better it is to live in a better place. I'm sure it will be like a holiday. The other day friends of mine left the place in which they'd lived for thirty years, in a state of quivering misery for a large, light apartment – and within a week both looked ten years younger and still, after almost five months, they say they consciously rejoice every morning at being where they now are.

Much love, Diana

11 MAY 1993

Darling Edward,

It's a gorgeous photo and the truth is you often do look just like that, which is why I come over incredulous and irritable when you go on about how ancient you are.

Barbara v. much enjoyed her meetings with you. She's rather cross with me and B because she says that we are the reasons for Hannah becoming so demanding – we are *feeble* about saying 'No!' Of the three of us, Barry is the feeblest. Hannah has become his child, and he feels strongly that children should be allowed perfect freedom, so if Hannah wants to go out, then out she must go even if she has only just come in. This is specially so at the moment, because last Friday she was operated on – spayed – and came home that evening the most pathetic little woozy scrap of dog you can imagine, wringing all our hearts into shreds; and now she still has to be restrained from playing in the park with her rougher friends who are, of course, the ones she most enjoys, even though she is feeling exceptionally bouncy. So Barry argues that in compensation she must not be crossed in any other way ... Your dog-sitting poem is marvellous. We both treasured it on sight. Fortunately our plight is not quite so stressful as yours and Neil's with those dogs, because as far as H is concerned we are Family – she's our spoilt infant, not our heart-broken charge; and no doubt, just as she ended by house-training herself so she will end by sobering into more decorous ways. (And we will regret the passing of her puppyhood.)

I'm glad you have your lovely tree. Your delight in it brings home to me our *incredible* luck in living where we do, absolutely embowered in trees ... The park is so beautiful at this moment that one can hardly believe it even when looking at it – the green (or rather greens, because there are lots of them) at their freshest and most brilliant, the grass thick with daisies, the hawthorn trees swooning under Proustian loads of flowers ... it's delicious.

Love
Diana

[*Here is Edward's dog-sitting poem:*]

THE DOG SITTERS (For Stanley and Jane)

Old friends, we tried so hard
to take care of your dogs.
We petted them, talked to them, even slept with them
and followed all your instructions
about feeding and care –
but they were inconsolable.
The longer you were gone
the more they pined for you.
We were poor substitutes,
almost worse than nothing

Until you returned, days of worry
as each fell ill with fever, diarrhoea and despair,
moving about restlessly on the bed we shared.
We wakened at dawn to walk them,

but there was a mess already on the rug.
We called the vet, coaxed them to eat,
tried to distract them
from the terrible sadness in their eyes
every time that they lay down with their chins on their
    paws
in utter hopelessness, and the puppy
got manic, biting our hands.

Ten days in the house by the bay
trying to keep them alive, it was a nightmare,
for they were afraid to go anywhere with us, for fear
you would never come back,
and they must be there waiting when you did,
until you did ... if you did ...

Then, the minute you got home
they turned away from us to you
and barely looked at us again, even when we left –
for you had filled the terrible empty
space that only you could fill
and our desperate attempts
were dismissed without a thought.

We tried to tell each other it was a victory
keeping them alive, but the truth is
that when someone belongs so utterly to someone
    else
stay out of it – that kind of love is a steamroller
and if you get in the way, even to help,
you can only get flattened.

17 JUNE 1993

Dearest Edward,

I can't remember if you ever mentioned a very small new press called Steerforth Press – in, I believe, Vermont. They have made an offer for *Make Believe*, which my publisher here seems to think is all we are likely to get, and they sound on the phone and by letter enthusiastic and pleasant, so I've said 'Yes'. They want me to change the title. He said on the phone that one of the things about the book which specially struck him was that it was an unusually good study of someone thinking he was god, so could I think up a title suggesting that side of it. So I said 'Why not A Man Who Thought He Was God' – which I now rather like, and which I guess they'll use. So that's done. Thank you a thousand times beloved Edward, for your attempts to get people interested – but probably I'd better settle for a bird in the hand, don't you think? Their advance is $2000, which seems fine to me.

One very pleasing result of the publicity the book had here is that the paperback publishers of *Instead of a Letter* have decided not just to reprint that book but to reissue it properly, with a new jacket and announcing it in their catalogue. What really delights me is that they want to use on the jacket some part of that embroidery I've done celebrating my mother's village (it's just finished). I'm so pleased about that that I hardly mind whether it will work or not! And after my mother died I found a photo of myself age 21 which I had taken because my fiancé ('Paul' in *Instead of a Letter*) had just been posted to Egypt and asked me to send him a new photo. They are going to use that as a frontispiece, so I think the reissue will have its authenticity as a document nicely underlined.

Still haven't started the new book! Oh dear. And now my drawing classes have gone into abeyance for the summer, I am gravely tempted to start painting at home (my work made a Great Leap Forward this spring) – but probably that is the subconscious throwing up a diversionary tactic.

At the moment Barbara is in Vienna for four days, for the *Economist*, so Hannah-and-Polly-sitting [*Barbara's puppy and daughter*] is consuming all our time. Barbara must work very hard at keeping Hannah white and unsmelly – she only has to spend two days wholly with us to become grey and decidedly rancid. Whenever her friends in the park roll her over it seems to be on a bit of grass where horrors have been perpetrated.

Now I must screw up my nerve and take her down to the garden for her last pee – nerve being needed because last night we surprised rats on the compost heap. Love, Diana

29 DECEMBER 1993

Darling Edward,

I was thrilled to hear that your friend's apartment will be available – the jaunt suddenly became something that is really going to happen. I'm so tickled by the idea of being in NY again – something I was on the edge of being sure would never again happen – that I hardly mind whether conservative and gentlemanly Tom Powers finds publicity for the book or not. However – I need hardly say that if, inspired by you, he does achieve a flash of vulgar commercial efficiency, I shall instantly be convinced of its value.

Delay in writing was due, believe it or not, to that fiendish flu, which kept me confined to the flat, and mostly to my bed, for five whole weeks. Actually, the flu itself was over in not much more than one week, but the consequent bronchitis was quite hard to get rid of, the bug proving immune to the first course of antibiotics. And the second course, which worked eventually, made me feel ill and unlike letter-writing or anything else. I'm in the country now, having come to the cottage with Barbara on Dec. 23rd – no, 24th. And the day before that I was not at all sure I could manage the journey. But it turned out that the infection had been ousted, and once that had been done I quickly felt much much better, and now I'm fine.

With much love to you both, and wishes for Fame and Happiness and Health (note: ought to have put health first) in 1994. Diana

5 APRIL 1994

Darling Edward [*circled with Thank Yous*],

When I told Barry I'd had a wonderful time and never

had I felt so deliciously looked-after in all my life, there was a short pause, then he said, hopefully, 'Wasn't that a bit boring?' Kind though it would have been to answer 'Yes, it was a bit', the lie was beyond me. If it hadn't been for you and your wickedly generous kindness to me I'd have had no more than a nice time – the wonderfulness lay in your making me 'family' and in meeting Harriet and Tobias (particularly Tobias) and in being able to feel amazingly at home in New York because you and Neil were there.

An easy journey home, and swift, whisked over the ocean by a strong following wind. Wasn't upgraded – no room – but was in the three-seater part of the row, in an aisle seat, and my neighbours were a plain but rather engaging young English couple, so much in love that they went to sleep cuddled in each other's arms, thus leaving me the maximum elbow room. Cold, wet and windy here – but green and flowery. My magnolia's almost over and my crab-apple tree is in full bloom.

I found a royalty statement from my London publisher waiting for me, covering the months July–December last year. No sales, about sixty returns, and about more than half the advance still unearned, even though Steerforth's advance was taken into account! I shan't relay this less than invigorating news to Tom Powers [*owner of Steerforth*] – it would not be good for his morale.

Must now gallop to the aid of Marie-Louise Motesiczky, the ancient painter.* It seems I've got back

* See page 67 above.

just in time for a Crisis and must help her compose a very severe letter to someone who wants to write rubbish about her – though her despair (it's never anything less than despair) over this gave way, by the end of our telephone talk, to happiness about the agreement with the great Austrian gallery [*the Belvedere*], which was consummated while I was away – hurrah! That's one of the best stories I've ever sat in on: everything coming so right for someone after such a long long time, and the person still being able to enjoy it, even though so very old. And the Austrian government is giving her an Honour of some sort, and she is going to go to Vienna to have it pinned on her bosom by the Prime Minister, even though she is certain that 'it will be very very ugly'. Maybe I'll go along for the ride! The Austrians are mad keen these days, to be seen pinning honours to the bosoms of Jews – I'm quite surprised that M-L is accepting one ... but she seems to be feeling that it's a great joke, more than anything else.

Till June, my dearest dears.

Diana

[*I did go to Vienna to see Marie-Louise's paintings hung in the Belvedere: a wonderful occasion, like seeing beautiful creatures being released from cages into their natural habitat.*]

25 OCTOBER 1994

Darling Edward,

How lovely to get your letter, of which the article in the *Kenyon Review* seemed like a particularly sumptuous part. Oh to be that young again – and how I wish that when I was, I'd been it in Paris. I'd have been rather like you – a little bit puritanical and cautious while at the same time entranced. The sentence I most sympathized with is 'Whatever hang-ups this indicated, I'd preferred men who seemed perfectly ordinary' – my sentiments, precisely, about life in general which I don't like to see pushed to fanciful extremes because it's good enough as it is. And even in my excursions with nuts, what I liked about them was getting to know them well enough to experience them as ordinary – Hakim hating my dirty pot-holder in the kitchen and fussing about what toothpaste he used, and so on.

My fall is much better, though gardening can be done only in short and rather careful instalments and I've done one editing job, pushed into it by André.

Are you hearing with delightful clarity again, after getting rid of all that wax?

Pity Neil's sister is perched so high up – though a friend of ours who spent two winters just outside Taos (which is probably where they are?) loved it. I suspect it's less grim than the Andes. Hope so, anyway. I adored it in the spring – but then it was all flowering lilacs and judas trees, and that magical air was pure intoxication.

Love to Neil and to you
Diana

10 DECEMBER 1994

I've just said to Barry: 'Now I'm going to write
Edward and Neil a lovely Christmas letter.' Then I sat
down, reached for my pen – and my mind went blank.
We never do anything. The days flow gently by and our
minds – or mine, anyway – cooks slowly, slowly into a
sort of bland, very lightly seasoned gruel. My back is
quite better, yes – but that's hardly an event. We haven't
even had – this is a risky thing to say, but it's true – we
haven't even had a cold yet, and we're almost halfway
through December. It's not much good that a great
drama is happening at this very moment to a close
friend – after nearly fifty years of developing a solid habit
of Disaster she is being Swept Away by a splendid Polish
Poet (B says *that's* no guarantee that Disaster is over) –
because you don't know her.

By the end of this month I'll be 77 – ouch! – so
perhaps it's just as well that nothing happens to me. If
anything did it probably wouldn't be good.

Although, come to think of it, today something
delicious did happen. I'm sure I told you that when it
became apparent that my pension from Deutsch would
be risible, André bought me (I thought) an annuity to
bring me in another thousand pounds a year. This year I

noticed rather belatedly that it had ceased to come in, so I dug out the papers (which I'd never examined) and saw that it was a kind of insurance policy and that it expired at my death or at Jan. 1, 1993 whichever came earlier. Well, I thought, the mean old bastard. But I didn't quite understand the wording of the policy, so I sent it to my accountant, and he said he didn't quite understand either, so would write to the issuing company for elucidation. Which replied that yes, the annual payment had come to an end in Jan. 1993, and on that date, on the 'maturing' of the policy, the sum of £11,500 had become due to Miss Athill but she hadn't yet claimed it! And this very morning the glorious cheque arrived. The temptation instantly to spend it must, alas, be resisted, and it must be invested at once in an attempt to make it replace the £1000 a year which I've ceased to get. Which it won't do since nothing nowadays brings in as much as 10% – which takes the shine out of the glory, I suppose. But still – no one could call taking a cheque that big out of an envelope anything less than nice. I try not to dwell on the thought that if I died before the start of 1993 that lump sum would have gone (I suppose?) to André, who has always believed in his right hand getting back what his left hand gave ... but no, that's probably unfair, because the policy, though bought by him, was in my name. I shall never know why he chose to do his good deed in this form, because he's decaying so fast, poor old boy, that he has completely forgotten. That really shook me. He used to remind me regularly, about once every six months: 'You know that pension thing I bought for you? You know I did it out of my own money, not the firm's?' Then, about three months ago, before all the above emerged, I happened to refer to it, and he had no idea what I was talking about. No amount of prompting could make him remember – very disconcerting and sad. Talking with him has become almost impossible because of the way his memory is crumbling.

I think of you very often, and want to read your poem about food.

Much love, Diana

24 MAY 1995

Dearest Edward,

My feet make slow but definitely steady progress, and I've managed to persuade the surgeon to advance the removal of the pin from the pin toe, from June 26th to June 7th – a handsome advance! – after which I'll be able to wear a pair of trainers and drive my car. God, how I look forward to that freedom! I'm beginning to suspect that the gloomy house doctor at the hospital who said – behind the surgeon's back – 'You won't be quite over this operation for six months' was probably right as far as walking is concerned. There may well be a bit of discomfort if I try to walk too much for that long. But once I can drive, I shan't mind that. It's been ages since I could walk any distance without discomfort, anyway. [*I'd had bunions straightened when Edward and Neil were last in*

London. Complete recovery was much quicker than expected.]

Last night friends took me out to dinner at the Camden Brasserie, quite near but unknown to me and Barry because of our cheese-paring ways – which served delicious food. We must go there when you are next here – it's really special. We miss you very much. How I did enjoy your visits, you dear dear friends for whom I shall be forever grateful to Alfred.

Love, Diana

P.S. I do wish I could remember the very first poem of yours I ever read which came to me all those years ago, via Alfred. All I can remember is that – mystifyingly – I thought 'He sounds much more like an English person than an American.' What can it have been?

6 JUNE 1995

Dearest Edward –

Marvellous package! I enjoy the poems very much. The Food Chain is marvellous, St Petersburg 1918 very beautiful – something tremendously poignant about the two images, the mother on the grass and the leaping young men. I laughed aloud at Columbian Gold ... I loved them all, though not having a cock, the penis poems I felt a bit distanced from, enjoying them through the eyes of someone who does have one, rather than through my own. Colossus '94, on the other hand, might have been written for – almost by! – me. (Thinking again of that long-ago reaction – that your poem seemed English – it occurs to me that probably what I really felt was that your poems were like poems I would have written, supposing I'd been a poet!) The poems arrived just as I was getting into Barbara's car, to be carried off for a weekend in the country (lovely) so Barry hasn't had a chance to read them yet. I've just handed them over.

By now you're seventy-one. Which, in my experience, is not noticeably different from being seventy – it's the decades which rattle one, like 'sleeping policemen' built into the surface of the road. Any age over forty is improbable and amazing if one stops to ponder it, which is why I've come to think it is a mistake to do so – but I think you rather like the complicated melange of sensations you get from a sharp awareness of getting older, which must mean that you are braver than I am. May this year of your life run smoothly and include many more pleasures than pains, with much love, Diana

14 JULY 1995

Dearest Edward,

I seem to have abandoned hope of reclaiming my typewriter from Barry. His needs repairing, which entails me driving it to a remote back street hardly on the map of the city. We've been left behind by technology. The place was crawling with typewriter menders just the other day – or so it seemed to me – and now one might as well be seeking a blacksmith to shoe one's carriage horses. (Maybe I've even forgotten how to type – another good reason for not starting the book!)

Which reminds me – the firm of André Deutsch has been sold to a large organization which makes videos. One of my ex-authors saw a little item about it in the *Daily Express*, and called me with the news. She has a squeaky voice, so try as I might I failed to hear the name of the buyer – a string of initials. But the sad comment on AD's fortune is that none of the quality papers considered the event as 'News'. Someone alerted André, who was on holiday in Zurich, and he called me later, saying that apparently Tom stays on as part of the deal; that they paid half a million for it (pathetic, considering that when Tom sold just the children's list he got a million for it); and that AD is described as being over £700,000 in debt. What can the purchasers imagine they are gaining – and why?

I've been minus pin and pain for almost a month now, and yesterday found myself able to graduate from canvas shoes to a pair of pre-op sandals. Still can't walk far, but the distance within my power increases each week – and anyway, in the stupefying heatwave we've been having, with a level of humidity almost worthy of NY, walking far is the last thing I'd want to do.

Have been spending quite a lot of time in our country lair, which is heaven. But last time, when a totally exhausted Barbara had taken a whole week in order to Flop, it coincided with the abandonment of an old friend of mine and Barbara's by her new-found and thought-to-be miraculous Polish poet lover. Our poor friend, always with a tendency to depression, has had years and years of penniless loneliness, so when this splendid apparition insisted on leaving his wife and buying a house to share with her, it delighted us almost as much as it did her. But no sooner had they moved into the house than he evidently began to think 'my god, what have I done?' – they'd known and liked each other for four years before the affair began, so he didn't have much excuse. Actually Barbara had started trying to repress doubts during the move, on observing that while she was sanding floors, tiling the bathroom, painting ceilings, and even humping the refrigerator from van to kitchen, he never lifted a single finger, not even to pack and unpack his own books. Anyway, first he stopped fucking her, then he stopped talking to her, then he started telephoning his wife for an hour every night – then – whoosh – he was gone, leaving the most extraordinary 18-point letter which he must have been composing for weeks. The house is a good half hour drive from ours, and when we weren't driving madly along twisty lanes in the expectation of finding a corpse behind locked doors, we were propping her up and mopping her up, and listening and listening and *listening* to her tale of woe. After three days and the best part of three nights of this, we had got her to the point of acknowledging that if he'd been as awful as she'd insisted he'd been, then she was well rid of him, when – whoosh, and he was back! The latest bulletin is that he says he must be allowed to talk to Barbara and me,

because it's *not fair* that we should have only her version.
Which I herewith swear by all I hold sacred will be the
point at which I go on strike. Barbara says she hopes he
does because then she'll be able to Tell Him What She
Thinks of Him, but I know that that way madness lies.
The only way to retain one's sanity as an onlooker to
such a drama is to take sides, and stick to your side
regardless, not even looking at the other party.

Wimbledon was lovely — Barry and I are still feeling
bereft without it. [*The one sporting occasion I always
watched with Barry was tennis at Wimbledon.*]

Hurrah that you may well have a new book of poems
ready by the fall.

Love, Diana

Yesterday someone must have watched me taking £100
out of a cash point – and when, fifteen minutes later, I
went to pay for some fruit I'd just bought, there was my
handbag open and my wallet *gone!* The dismay and fury
over, one can't help admiring the sheer skill of it.

28 JANUARY 1996

Dearest Edward –

Forgive paper [*lined*], but at the moment it's the kind I
like writing on – a lovely new pad for my First Draft of
the book (now sixty-six pages). I'm still stubbornly
sticking to pen plus steam-typewriter despite all the siren

songs of all the computer users I know. I *enjoy* writing like this, so there!

I knew you must be enjoying the blizzard, and thought enviously of you stumping about that amazing townscape. It's reached us now, but less dramatically – at first two days of *excruciatingly* scythe-like wind, now quite gentle but persistent snow. It collects in hard snowballs all over poor Hannah's little woolly legs, which she loathes; so she sits down to try picking them off, and when she stands up again there are snowballs all over her little woolly bum. Barry and I were very sad during the wind, cut off as we are from the Wonders of Modern Science such as central heating (how I yearn for Westbeth!). The wind didn't only drill its way through every crack and cranny of our grotty old window frames but it also forced the exhaust fumes of our gas fires back down the chimneys, threatening us with death by carbon-monoxide poisoning, so we had to depend on tiny electric heaters. By about midnight my sitting room was just about becoming too warm for an overcoat. Today I awoke to a face covered with bright red patches, particularly around the nose. Is it the weather or is it a bottle of magic *new* face-wash fallen for in the Supermarket and composed of no less than sixteen unrecognizable and ugly-sounding chemicals? To be on the safe side I must struggle out and buy a pot of my usual Pond's Cold Cream, which in the Newness stakes comes only just after an infusion of nettle-leaves and oak-bark.

Thank you for sending Tom Powers' piece. He's very good, isn't he? I'm gratified to be published by such an excellent writer. As for your naughty translation – I'm getting old, old, old. I tried hard to feel a sexual frisson – I dwelt on the images presented most earnestly – but nothing could I raise! And if you can't raise a sexual frisson at a dirty poem, you find yourself thinking 'Is it worth the trouble?' Of course if someone pays you good money for them then the answer will be 'yes!' even from Methusaleh.

At the moment I'm quite pleased with my sixty-six pages [*of the book which became* Stet], but I suspect there's going to be quite a bit of rewriting in this one. I tend to skim along too quickly, then see that I'll have to expand ('Now there,' you will say, 'is exactly the situation computers are designed for' – shut up!). The worst thing is the absolutely final disappearance of poor old André's memory: not a cheep of the facts and figures I was going to depend on him for can I now get. The other day I volunteered to visit him at Gwen's, because he'd called in a miserable state to say he couldn't get up. I was rather cheered when he responded in classic André fashion by calling back five minutes later to say: 'As you are coming over, could you be an angel and take me to Harrods?' He has never missed a chance to try to squeeze something extra out of one. But when I got there, and he returned to the subject of Harrods, he stopped halfway through and said 'But why do I want to go to Harrods? I can't remember.' He was sitting in a low armchair, wearing a very dirty and ragged little old towelling bathrobe, with his skinny knees up round his ears and his poor little shrunken balls dangling – so unlike his dapper decorous self. It was no surprise to learn that Gwen's doctor, coming to visit her two days later (she's 89 and pretty groggy) caught sight of A and whisked him off to hospital. But now he sounds a bit brighter and expects to be back home in a day or two – says he's had a brain scan and the doctor says he's fine. Oh darlings, let us hope we all go down bang.

Very much love, Diana

[UNDATED]

Dearest Edward –

I felt indignant when you claimed Pond's Cold Cream as an old American remedy. I refuse to believe that it's not English – it's been going all my life and was old-fashioned when my nanny used to apply it to my little chapped hands (a frequent occurrence for an infant reared in East Anglia). Whenever my friend Nan sees it on my dressing-table she goes into a huff. She (like most women) has convinced herself that the only thing her skin can endure is some sort of designer unguent called Luminescence or Perpetual Dew in a pink container the size of a thimble for which you pay twenty-five pounds, so she takes my adherence to good old Ponds as a tacit criticism. When I made the mistake of explaining that every one of these things is made of (or at least based on) lanolin, or else petroleum jelly, or else glycerin she actually flounced out of the room and banged the door!

How clever of you to know about those boilers-

behind-gas-fires that heat radiators. But alas – because
we are up in the roof our outside walls are not made of
brick (I think of lathe and plaster, then space, then
tiles) – which means that if you stuck through them the
kind of exhaust-pipe those boilers have to have,
everything would burst into flame. I don't understand
why the existing chimney, which must be made of brick,
couldn't be used, but have been assured twice that it
can't. However, we have come across a dreamy man
called Ivor who is a gas-fitter and who absolutely agrees
with us about the monstrosity of the privatized Gas
Board. (That awful Fat Cat who was, I think, being
Exposed in the newspapers while you were here because
of his astronomical salary, has been made to retire – with
a golden handshake of several million pounds!) One of
the ways the Board makes the profit that can support
these bastards is by doing away with all local showrooms
(we now have to go to a place called Wood Green if we
want to see samples of all makes of gas heater). So what
bliss to find Ivor, who doesn't just come when he says
he's coming, but calls the day before to confirm the
appointment – and who when asked to get me leaflets
about heaters of a given size within a given price-range
does just that, on the very next day – and all these leaflets
described heaters cheaper than anything the loathesome
Gas board said existed! And who is going to put me in a
nice little new heater next week which he promises won't
blow back fumes – and I would go to the stake for a
promise of Ivor's. It's pathetic, how thrilled one is
nowadays at coming across someone efficient and helpful
who charges no more than is reasonable . . . something

which was surely taken for granted in the days when I first met Pond's Cold Cream?

I'm in the middle of two days of Toothlessness. An ancient crown in my top jaw came to its long-expected end and has to be replaced by a new tooth added to the plate I already have. So the plate has been snatched from me and I'm going about with only two teeth (considerably more macabre than none) in my top jaw. When the same thing happened to Barbara a month ago she drove off to the country and went into purdah – but then, she's been a Beauty, so I suppose feels the humiliation more sharply. I decided simply on avoiding smiling and much talk. Have just come in from walking Hannah on the first mild, sunny morning we've had for ages, and was astonished at how intense is the social life of us dog-walkers. It's accepted etiquette among us that if we are in a hurry we don't have to stop and gossip, we just wave, call 'Hi!' – and smile. And the quicker one hurries by, the broader the smile must be ... By the time I got home I had cramp in the face from attempts to perfect a broad closed-lipped grin. And this evening I'm going to attend my chair-caning class (because my chair has reached a Crucial Stage) and say to hell with it – all this self-consciousness is too fatiguing.

My book is now over 80 pages long – it feels quite solid when one picks it up. Just finished 12 pages about Jean Rhys, which could have been much longer (perhaps it will be, a bit). I'm wondering, now, whether to use a shortened version of my Alfred intro – I suppose it will depend on how long other portraits become. VS Naipaul, for instance, has had to be fairly brief owing to his being alive, and John Updike certainly will be because there's nothing much to say except that he's a nice man and the perfect author from the editor's point of view [*in the end, because of this, he didn't get a portrait*] – so an enormous Alfred might be rather out of proportion. However – I've never been able to plan ahead when I'm writing – I always have to wait and see what comes next, so now I have to reread what I've done so far and see what happens.

How *frightful* about your computer disaster – its like air versus ground travel, the former with so many dazzling advantages but so much more likely to be fatal if an accident happens. It's getting more difficult to find cartridges for this typewriter – this to my and Barry's mind lovely, new, modern electronic machine is, according to the shops which supply ribbons etc., becoming very old-fashioned, so much so that its own cartridges have been discontinued and one has to shop around for something that will be compatible . . . So no doubt we will be driven, in the end, to getting a word processor. But I'm happy messing about the way I do, so will wait until I have to.

I've got fifteen rather measly little snowdrops, and a scattering of early pink crocuses (croci?) out in the front garden and today the sun is perceptibly *hot*. I hope you, too, are enjoying such happy signs.

With much love,
Diana

18 APRIL 1996

Darling Edward –

I do so want to read your autobiography. If you are coming over soon you must not fail to bring a copy – and if you aren't coming over soon, hijack the next person you know who is coming, and give them a copy to bring. It would, of course, be best to see it first in glorious print – but nowadays 'famous' seems to mean TV or *Hello* famous, so it wouldn't be surprising if it took your agent a while to find it a publisher, and I don't want to wait a while before reading it.

Mine has now got to page 106 – I work in fits and starts, with longish gaps between – and ought I suppose to have at least another 100 pages. Sometimes when I read what I've done I think it dead boring and sometimes I think it's quite good – but that's what always happens to everyone, so one just has to hope. I've just finished describing how I stopped liking André, but decided that it would be foolish to walk out of a job that suited me so well because of that; and need to draw breath again. The trouble with life is that incidents so often merely follow each other rather than grow out of each other . . .

I do hope Neil's poor dear nose is not going to need plastic surgery – unless a scar is terribly disfiguring people soon get used to it – and the results of plastic surgery are often quite obtrusive. I once had a minuscule skin graft done on my leg after they'd dug out a small skin cancer (I was and still am sure that they did the graft because it was good practice for baby surgeons, being small and in an inconspicuous place so it wouldn't be a disaster if it was bungled). It was declared a great success – and was indeed very neat – but it is still visible after more that 20 years, and for ages would have been most unsightly had it been on my nose. And they kept me in bed for 21 days, perfectly well though I was. I supposed it was because moving about might well be quite disturbing to a leg – but then my neighbour in the ward, who had had the same thing done on the lobe of her ear and was confidently expecting to go home in about two days, was appalled to be told that she too must stay immobile for 21 days. Apparently a graft anywhere may fail to take if blood is sent coursing through the veins by exercise ... But that was long ago, and techniques have probably improved a lot. Anyway, kiss him better for me.

I have been reading a review in the *NY Review of Books* of a translation of a Polish poet – *View with a Grain of Sand* by Wislawa Szymborska – which I like the sound of a lot. It's Harcourt Brace, paperback edition $12. Could you get it for me, next time you are passing a book shop, and convey it to me as and when you convey your autobiography? (Not by mailing it – the cost of mailing makes me feel quite faint.) One of my ex-authors who lives in Chicago although he's a Parsee called Boman Desai, has now done 1574 pages of a far from finished novel about Brahms and Clara Schumann, and having already mailed me the first 800 pages has announced his intention of sending the rest in a few days time – the mind boggles at what he's spending, and a) I'm not even a publisher any more and b) the last three novels he's sent me, all I could say was 'No' (his first I loved). It's the dreadful loneliness of not knowing a soul who is interested in writing, which is all he lives for. It is possible that the present work, which is the result of a mad passion of love for his subject and an incredible accumulation of knowledge about it, may be going to come off. I am actually looking forward to reading the next 674 pages. Won't it be lovely if it does? [*It did, and was called* Trio – *but not published in the UK.*]

Much love, Diana

Let me know of any English book you want in exchange for the Szymborska.

11 MAY 1996

Dearest Edward –

I no longer feel I should apologize for handwriting after your compliments on same. I owe it to Nicolas Bentley who wrote an italic hand so exquisite that there are examples of it in the Victoria and Albert Museum. When I exclaimed about it he told me his natural hand had been an evil and illegible scrawl, so he had deliberately taught himself italic, and anyone could. So I bought the requisite pen, and worked away – my natural hand was large and loopy like loose knitting – and was soon able to write quite a pretty italic, but only very slowly – so at last I couldn't be bothered any more, but the loose knitting had been tightened up for good, except when I'm scribbling notes – and then it turns into unravelled knitting. The natural hand is gone for good – who knows what psychic damage this represents.

OK. I'll wait patiently for my first sight of the memoirs. Why don't you buck the trend and say 'What's all this nonsense about seduction by older men? It was delicious' and then tell all? Though perhaps your compatriots are more pious than Europeans are in their observation of passing fashions in thinking, so this might not be very good advice.

Have just tidied, and put everything that absolutely must be done onto this table, on a corner of which I'm writing. Typewriter and my book have vanished under the pile – and here am I, writing to you instead of starting my attack on the mountain. For 78 years, four months and three weeks I've been meaning to overcome this fatal habit of postponing the boring by quickly doing something nice instead – oh dear!

Much love. Diana

4 JUNE 1996

Dearest Edward –

I wish the review-copy idea had worked because now (late in the day, you may well think!) I have to face the fact of how troublesome and expensive I've been! Please please please think of something you want from here which will give you as much, or more, pleasure than the

Polish poems give me. I took them to the country last weekend to be my bedside reading, and left them there, thinking that I had learnt the spelling of her name by heart – but I find that it will need at least next weekend and probably longer to fix it. I like the poems very much, but whether that's because they are good poems, or because what she says makes me like *her* I can't be sure. It's always hard to judge the goodness of a poem in translation, anyhow. The friend who looks after our country garden for us has just ended a doomed relationship with another Polish Poet with whom she went to Krakow a couple of times, and she met my nice Polish lady there and says she is, indeed, a delightful person, very witty and charming and warm. Her poet, who makes his living in this country by translating, was I think her first translator into English.

Barry got back from Washington today which was very nice, because I had miscalculated and was expecting him to return on the Tuesday of next week, just after I leave for Ireland, which would have meant not seeing him until almost two weeks after that.

Love and love, Diana

18 OCTOBER 1996

Dearest Edward,

Did I tell you that just as I had said to myself rather gloomily 'When Christmas comes you will have entered

your eightieth year', crick crack and two of my few
remaining teeth broke off, whereupon my dentist sent
me to a specialist who has announced his opinion that
there's nothing for it now but complete dentures, top
and bottom. He set about measuring me with
nightmarish metal devices resembling very elaborate
medieval Scolds' Bridles, and drawing signs all over the
outside of my face – to start with I lay there thinking
'We're not talking tens, here – we are talking hundreds
here, or are we talking in thousands?' and so, I'm sure,
we shall be, when we actually start to talk. But now my
dentist, who has received the specialist's full report and
suggestions, has deserted to Arizona (I don't suppose he
even notices the price of the ticket), so I must wait
another ten days, whistling through my gaps, until we
actually decide what to do. I considered a course of
Prozac, but chose instead to plunge into a rereading of
the novels of Anthony Trollope. I once found them
boring, but for this emergency they are just the thing,
and for days I've taken my nose out of them only to walk
Hannah and to eat.

Very much love to you both, Diana

[DATE UNREADABLE]

Darling Edward –

I'm glad to hear that your money-making plans are
ticking over so pleasantly, although the fame plans seem

to be in the doldrums. May the latter suddenly take on new life.

It's hard to find a dentist here who is still working 'on the Health' – mine slid out of it ages ago, and doesn't charge much more now he's off it than he was allowed to do when on. And 'on' is now allowed to be applied to only the most basic necessities, minus so-called 'cosmetic' features. False teeth – yes. False teeth made carefully enough not to go 'clack clack' – no. So when mine said 'end of the road', it was a Specialist he passed me on to. Because André's father was a dentist, giving him a lively interest in the trade, he has been cross-examining me about exactly what's to be done. He was reassured on hearing the specialist's name – Maurice Faigenblum (to André only Jews can be any good at any kind of medicine). Last week he said 'What is he charging?' and I told him – £2000, which I had just instructed my bank to abstract from my savings account. Whereupon there came a great crash of hot red coals on my head – because he instantly wrote me a cheque for £2000!!!! How can I possibly finish a book full of bitchiness about him? I know I'd have preferred it if he'd paid me a living wage and if there'd been a decent pension involved, because what was always his argument – 'Don't fuss, I'll always look after you' – while obviously good for his self-esteem, this was bad and still is bad for mine. But the generous things he has done for me since I began having to live on £10,000 a year are mounting up, and this last splendid gesture really has put me in my place.

I've already had three sessions with Mr Faigenblum,

and can feel myself sinking rapidly into that fatuous mood towards him that one so often sees in people being treated by surgeons, gynaecologists, or any other kind of so-called experts whose hands one has to give oneself into: he can do no wrong! Supposing he was my teacher, I'd soon be leaving shy little bundles of flowers on the corner of his desk. He has staggeringly sophisticated equipment, including a way of administering a local anaesthetic which hardly pricks at all and doesn't make any part of your face numb – just kills the feeling in the tooth concerned. This may be run of the mill in New York, where dentistry is more advanced than here, but I'd never even heard of it. At our first session he said 'Your mouth does certainly present problems that are – ' little pause while he looks for the mot juste, which he then spoke almost sotto voce, as though to himself – 'daunting'. Oh gallant Mr Faigenblum, so bravely and cleverly doing his best for this troublesome person! And also, he disagrees with my dentist's opinion that everything should go, and instead is demolishing the stumps in order to build them up again, swearing that he can make them hold. So everything dental is much better than I expected it to be, hurrah hurrah!

What Barbara [*who had just spent three weeks in Iran for the* Economist] dreaded about Iran was a) not a drop of drink, ever, b) not being allowed to sit in cafés, c) not having any contacts, d) the clothes. She says the clothes were, in fact, maddening. It was very hot, so not being allowed to reveal an inch of body or a single hair was very trying. She bought a *chador* in the end, because it was less clinging than a scarf. You can't leave your

127

bedroom at all without it, not even in the 'western style' hotel. The drink she did without better than she expected, and people were very nice and helpful. Official interviews are pointless because pure propaganda; hostile-to-regime interviews impossible because too dangerous; but she talked to quite a number of intelligent middle-class people and was able to build up a picture. And for the first week Adam [*her son*] was with her, which made cafés possible, and two days of glorious sightseeing – Isfahan and Qum – so she enjoyed it in the end although she says she'll have to pad a good deal to fill the fourteen pages of the 'special report'. [*It was brilliant – and the* Economist *broke its rule and gave her a byline.*]

Very much love, Diana

20 DECEMBER 1996

(tomorrow will be the last birthday of my seventies)

Darling Edward –

Hi! From one flu victim to another. Oh isn't it *vile?* Mine has just reached stage of temperature returning to normal and nose stopping running, but now guts have started to run, damn them . . . am very unhappy, but definitely mending and shall be able to get to Norfolk for Christmas.

My poor darling sister has got back to England, bearing her husband's ashes, which are being buried today. [*Her husband had died on a flight to Australia, where they were going to visit a son.*] It's hateful not being able to be there, but she says friends and the rest of the family are rallying well. She is good at making friends, and is a very good friend to the friends she makes and they to her, and will not be left alone until she goes to stay with her daughter on Christmas Eve, so we've agreed that early in January is the time when she'll need my company most, and I'll go then. But it feels sad and uncomfortable, not being able to join in the formal ceremony of farewell for David.

The one marvellous thing about my horrid flu is that it didn't start until the very last hour of my weekend in Amsterdam and I was able to control its first symptoms sternly enough for my angelic hosts not to notice them, and to get home to my own dear bed by the time when I really had to collapse into it. Did I tell you I'd been invited there to see the documentary about Jean Rhys for which I'd been one of the four interviewees? The interview, last May, was great fun because Jan Louter, the producer, and Valeria Schnitt, the director, and the cameraman and the sound man were all so young and enthusiastic and intelligent and nice, and they said then that I must come and see the preview, but I thought they'd forgotten – then suddenly, a ticket for Amsterdam, and Valeria waiting at Schipol, and they'd found me an absurd but charming hotel called Hotel de Filosoof, and the film was really extraordinarily sensitive and good (though I don't know how it would work for people who weren't already interested in Jean Rhys and who didn't already know *Wide Sargasso Sea*) and the dinner after it was wonderful and went on until after midnight, and they all treated me with extraordinary sweetness, and I had a lovely Sunday after all that for sightseeing, and Valeria put me back on the plane on Monday morning – and the whole thing was a delight.

I'd heard several times about Lennox Honychurch, the local historian of the island of Dominica (where Jean was raised), who was always described by people researching as 'wonderfully helpful', and I had formed a picture of an elderly and earnest black schoolmaster, so that was what I was looking for when Valeria told me that he, too, would be coming over for the film, on my plane, because luckily he happened to be visiting England. And before I left a shy Caribbean voice spoke on the phone, and I told him what kind of hat I'd be wearing, and he told me he'd be wearing his green white and blue scarf. So I peered about at Heathrow, and there sure enough was an elderly and earnest black schoolmaster, but he didn't have such a scarf, and was obviously not looking for my hat. So I went back to reading my newspaper – and a Caribbean voice suddenly said 'Diana Athill?' – and there stood a most enchanting young man, white, with the most beautiful greenish hazel eyes and an elegant black moustache, looking barely thirty years old (actually he's forty-six) a truly Lovely Surprise. And he turned out to be, indeed, a perfect honey. It's his lonely fate to be the only intellectual white person living in Dominica, his family one of the very few remains of the plantocracy, and he has made his own career as historian of the Caribbean (is at present at Oxford doing some special research). When he visits Europe he is obviously greedy for talk, ideas, intellectual companionship, while at the same time he has the cheerful self-confidence of his looks and wits, and a kind sweet nature. We were booked into the same hotel and spent a lot of the Sunday together.

I'm so grateful to my flu for not ruining that truly enjoyable weekend that I can almost like it!

My bestest love to you both for 1997 Diana

P.S. My teeth – now being a bit held up – will be both upper and lower, and will take out: *clack clack* – but he says the fit will be imclackulate.

26 FEBRUARY 1997

Dear Edward,

Barry came back from Washington with the same flu I'd had, although caught so far away, and both of us have kept on having relapses until quite recently. But now energy seems to have returned, thank god – with the result that I'm spending Enormous Sums of Money on the gardens here and in Norfolk, and also on overcoming Barbara's fatalistic pessimism about the central heating system in the latter, which made our cold spell over Christmas hard to bear. Finally I summoned a plumber and put him to work – and it's a pity the worst of the cold is over, because now the house is *too hot*! Such heaven – worth every penny of the £500 it cost.

I'd hoped that by the time you appear in London my

Teeth will at last be Done – but I doubt it. First my flu, then my forgetfulness of two appointments, then the unexpected collapse of two of the pathetic remaining Fangs – one of them a vital anchorman – have combined to make a long process an apparently endless one. Indeed, it has come to seem like a condition of normal life, and when/if it ends I shall miss Mr Faigenblum's mournful presence.

I'm in a condition of obsessive stitchery, having embarked on embroidering a seat for a very ugly chair bought by my sister. I'd forgotten how madly obsessed I become when making something – it's rather fulfilling. I hope my sister doesn't think that the rather bizarre pattern which is emerging makes the chair even uglier!

André – really hardly on his feet, nowadays – has just called to say I must help them organize his 80th birthday party. His birthday is not until Nov. 15th!! Only after I'd hung up did it occur to me that I'm going to be 80 too, just three weeks after he is and did it occur to him to say would I like to share the party with him? No, of course it didn't. I think I must bring myself to speak about this, otherwise I shall work up an irksome resentment: all that tedious work being demanded of me, as though I were a temporary secretary, and then he alone getting all the acclaim for a publishing career which was, after all, our joint achievement! What an old monster he is!

Longing to see you.

Much love, Diana

20 MARCH 1997

Dearest Edward,

Pleasure at getting your letter quickly turned to
sadness that we can't expect to see you as soon as we
thought, and to great worry at the news about those leg
wobbles. Mysterious symptoms are always hateful. Still,
there's no point in adding to our and Neil's anxiety with
a lot of long-distance mopping and mowing so I'll say no
more than give him my fondest love, and a great hug
from Barry, and let me know what the tests show.
Needless to say we are both devoutly hoping that it's
something easy to sort out – darling Edward, how
intensely I hope that for both your sakes.

The maddest people, at the moment, are Barbara and
me, who have allowed ourselves to slither into giving a
buffet on Easter Saturday at our Country Cottage for
fourteen people. And Barbara – this always strikes me as
an unexpected aspect of her – is fiercely competitive
when it comes to cooking – she admits frankly that what
really matters to her is not that her food should taste
nice, but that it should *impress*. We've both been buried
in cook-books for the last ten days, and the recipes she
homes in on make my hair stand on end. One of them we
tried out last weekend, and it made every one of its six
very expensive ingredients, each delicious in itself, taste
positively nasty – which, happily, she admitted. Finally (I
think) she is going to make an amazingly rich venison
casserole and I'm going to make a frozen chocolate
mousse and a huge dish of trifle, and I've forced her to

agree that this veritable killer of a meal must be prefaced by a simple vegetable hors d'oeuvre of artichoke hearts, asparagus, avocado, black olives and watercress … and we're having people staying in the house as well. I reckon I'll be feeling every one of my almost eighty years by the end of it!

My guest is going to be the delightful Lennox Honychurch who was at Amsterdam with me. I do wish it could be Barry, but the last two times he risked exposing himself to company he behaved so dreadfully – barking and bullying and really upsetting people – that we've agreed it's no good. I fear that all our really very nice Norfolk neighbours would send him up the wall. If he disagrees he attacks – he becomes an arrogant bully, I hate him and he hates me, and then we feel sad and sorry, so it seems better simply to avoid such occasions. Alas. Thank god for you and the Smalleys and Roger King and the few others whom he loves and is his dear self with.

Oh how we do hope you'll get here for a long time in the summer.

Love and love, Diana

5 SEPTEMBER 1997

Mes Chers –

9.30 p.m. Dinner (excellent) over, night wraps the village of Ainhoa in pitch-black silence. [*I was in*

*France – the Basque region – on holiday with my friend
Nan Taylor, my dearest friend from our Oxford days.*]
The hotel (in all other ways perfectly delightful) follows
the usual French pattern of having no lounge, and if I
go to sleep now I'll wake at 5 . . . So: a letter instead of
postcard.

Getting here was frightful. Left home at 7 a.m. to meet
Nan at Victoria Station (for Gatwick) at 7.30, and we
missed each other at the station because neither realized
that Gatwick is now served (in god's name, why) by two
lines, trains running two minutes apart, one from
platform 14, one from platform 17. Having agreed 'to
meet at barrier', Nan waited at barrier 14, I at barrier
17 . . . until, both growing desperate, each decided to go
on to Gatwick where surely we'd find each other at
British Airways desk. But I, alas, chose to go to the South
Terminal. Plane left from North Terminal, to which one
has to travel on a mini-train, and by the time I got to the
desk they reported that Nan was in the act of boarding
and it was too late for them to let me through. Next
plane in three and a half hours – I could try for a standby
seat. Got it, but didn't know until ten minutes before
boarding, so had a fairly fraught morning imagining
poor old Nan, carless and very wobbly on her legs, stuck
at Bordeaux Airport for (if I didn't get in) about ten
hours.

So by the time we set off on the long drive from
Bordeaux I was not at my freshest. Most of the drive a
dead-straight line ruled through the unutterable boredom
of Les Landes, absolutely flat and every inch of it
covered in fir trees – easy-peasy. But after about 120

miles of that we hit the outskirts of Biarritz, where we got
lost, largely because we're both too blind to read
signposts without slowing up, which Biarritz's evening
traffic was rude about. Which was probably why, when
finally on the right road, I lost my grip on the problem of
driving on the right, misjudged the car's width, and gave
it a Horrid Bump against a steep concrete kerbstone
while going off a round-about – didn't realize that I was
much too near the right hand edge of the road.
Whereupon the engine gave a gulp, and stopped. And
would not, would not, would not start again.

So there we were, stranded, well out in the country by
then, no human habitation in sight, night drawing in . . .
And hungry. And even more thirsty . . . oh dear!

A lot of the people who drove by hooted at us crossly
for stopping in such an awkward place, for many just
drove by . . . oh dear oh dear! About twenty very sad
minutes passed.

But then – oh bliss! – two cars stopped without a
moment's hesitation. Two men, friends, heading for the
same destination and thinking as one. Out they hopped –
could they help? Oh darling, lovely men. But they tried
and tried, and they couldn't help but they did have
mobile phone, so they called Hertz headquarters, which
said they would get a mechanic to us in half an hour, and
went on their way. (Also they pushed the car to a safer
spot.) So back into the wretched thing we got, and
waited – and waited – and it got quite dark – and still we
waited . . . An hour passed . . .

And then *another* car stopped. And this was a woman.
We could hardly understand her thick Basque accent, but

could see at once that she was the bossy-boots to end all
bossy-boots, and we were helpless in her hands.
Nonsense, she said, we couldn't go on sitting there. She
would take me instantly to her garage two miles ahead
and there we would ring up our hotel and tell them to
fetch us, and her husband would get the car to the garage
and repair it. So she took me – 'These two ladies of
yours', she said to the hotel on the blower, 'are elderly
persons, they are tired, they are hungry, they're sitting on
the roadside in the dark, you must send for them at
once.' – 'Yes, indeed, of course we must' said the hotel.
'We'll be there in fifteen minutes.' So she ran me back to
poor Nan who was biting her nails in the car in case I'd
been kidnapped – and at that moment the Hertz
mechanic pulled up. He opened the bonnet and instantly
discovered that the shock of bumping the kerb had
slightly shifted a little red thimble perched at a vital point
with the purpose of cutting off the electricity in the event
of accident, for security purposes. He straightened the
thimble – and the car started and instead of being cross
at being called out (plus his big towing van which arrived
in his wake) for such a tiny thing, he laughed and
laughed. And wonderful bossy-boots, instead of being
disappointed that her husband wouldn't get the job, first
rearranged all our luggage, taking out *every bag* and
putting them back in a different order, then said that
certainly we must not cancel the hotel's rescue operation
because the road between where we were and Ainhoa
was twisty, and I didn't know it and was far too old to be
driving in the dark, anyway; then conducted us back to
the garage where the hotel's gallant owner had already

arrived, and he most slowly and carefully guided me the rest of the way. And when we got here they sent us straight to bed with the most delicious meals on trays in our rooms – and I can't tell you how the *entente cordiale* flourishes in my heart as a consequence of that little adventure. I'd always rather thought of the French as being disagreeable to strangers, but shall never think it again.

This is lovely country and the weather has been perfect – though I think it's breaking now. Tomorrow we must uphold the honour of England by staying in and watching Princess Diana's funeral on French telly – they've gone almost as insane about her as the Brits – but there are plenty of things to do and see and it's being a fine holiday. I half regret missing what I gather is the really amazing phenomenon of London *in mourning*, and am half thankful to be out of it. Distance doesn't prevent one's enjoying the spectacle of the ridiculous royal family blundering from humiliation to humiliation. French telly may be dreary, as people always report, but their newspapers are so well written compared to ours that it's a pleasure to follow events through their eyes.

You will hardly be surprised to learn that now it is nearly eleven, so I'm going to turn out my light and go to sleep.

Much much love, dear hearts.

Diana

P.S. Next day. We had to watch every minute of the whole thing, seated side by side on red velvet armchairs in madame's private quarters, while the hotel's management and staff popped in and out to peer reverently over our shoulders. Was glad to do so, finally. Moved to tears at moments, and fascinated at others – how we wished the cameras had been allowed to show the Queen's face when Di's brother promised – in effect – to protect the boys from the royal family and everyone in the abbey clapped: I guess that must have been the most traumatic moment in the history of the British Monarchy since Oliver Cromwell. The basic and fascinating ambiguity of the whole situation (that foolish, flighty, unhappy girl being turned into a saint just because she was pretty, and affectionate to children and sad people) was underlined by the fact that the person who made this daring gesture is a man whose marriage collapsed in an ugly way and who went to live in South Africa – and who has, I think, the face of a bad tempered pink pig.

But I suppose what remains with me most strongly was the pity of it: the fact that in that box being carried slowly, slowly through the streets of people was the hideously smashed up body of a 36-year-old mother, and the sight of her two sons. The card on Harry's wreath on the front end of the coffin just said MUMMY. Someone had placed it carefully so that the cameras could catch it – and had, I suppose, tipped off a cameraman to get a close-up of it – though that wasn't the little boy's fault. And neither the mother nor the sons with a single really warm, reliable person in their lives – god! The sight of Di's mother teetering into the Abbey like a little mad mushroom under an enormous and enormously smart black hat and the mini-est of mini-skirts above her pathetic little bony old knees! (footnote: Nan says that was Fergie's mum – what a pity.) That on one side and the Queen on the other! Poor, poor, poor little boys.

D

8 OCTOBER 1997

Darling Edward,

Barry left for three weeks in Jamaica four days ago, and Barbara's off to the US for ten days next week. Barbara's going to her daughter Laura's wedding celebration, then on to New York for her customary United Nations roundup. I've said not to fail to call you but she looked rather Hunted – I think she gets very work-entangled when in New York.

What a wonderful letter yours was! Because the Contemporary Authors' piece seemed like part of it. I'm glad I didn't meet you in your bearded Guru incarnation – our friendship would probably have been strangled at birth by all that hair. On the other hand you and your sisters were very pretty as the Trio – and your mother was a lovely young woman. I enjoyed the whole story, but specially liked you on your poetry, which is really the heart of the matter. It made it so clear why I loved you as soon as we met –

It was because even before I'd heard you utter a word about poetry it was obvious you were the sort of person who would utter those words. (I wonder – has anyone else ever said 'writing poetry, of course, is far more fun than reading it'? A statement of crystalline obviousness, and exhilaratingness because mostly people pretend it isn't true.) You were bound, I suppose, to be nudged sooner or later into unfashionableness, because someone roaming the New York Literary Scene with such an unblinking eye for the nakedness of Emperors would make a lot of people uncomfortable. Long live (as no doubt it will) Neo-pop – and even longer live you.

Went to a book-launch three days ago. Rather a grand old boy called Sir Denis Forman had told Tom Rosenthal that Deutsch could publish his third book provided I edited it (I'd done his first two). The first was a delightful account of his childhood which made it clear that at the core of this splendid Establishment Figure there lurks a very funny anarchist, the second was the story of his war (in which he lost a leg at Casino), and this third was the story of the beginning of commercial television – he was in at the very start of Granada Television, working with an amazing Jewish Monster called Sidney Bernstein, who he adored, and finally succeeded as boss. He's a pleasure to work with, so I agreed, and edited it from home. Tom left Deutsch meanwhile, but the new Deutsch went on with it (a bit baffled, to judge by their appearance at the party, by Denis and his ilk). I couldn't help being much warmed when the little speeches came at the end of a very agreeable party, and he was so hugely flattering to me that a sort of awed hush fell on the party as one and all turned to gaze on me with deep reverence. All the evidence suggests that, in England, books are no longer edited at all (and they aren't much the worse for it except for the occasional minor nonsense like someone with a cropped head on page 1 and shaggy locks on page 24). So I suspect that the younger book people there had no idea what he was talking about and were imagining all kinds of magical mysteries at my command. And what was even nicer was when a sweet young woman who used to work for us, congratulating me on my dress, said 'But then – you always did wear lovely clothes', so I left that party with a Refurbished Self-image: how pleasant!!

Much love Diana

20 NOVEMBER 1997

Darling Edward –

When I was still working nothing about a script daunted me more than fatness, but now I have all the time in the world and am constantly buying books I can't afford with which to fill my days, the prospect of a good stout manuscript has become just the thing. So lug it down to the post office at once! (Footnote: It's only fair to warn you that at least 3 years before I retired I realized that I had lost my judgment as to what would sell: the climate had changed but I hadn't. So by now . . .!!!)

Last week there was a wonderful tea-party at the Groucho Club to celebrate André's eightieth birthday – and mine too, thirty days prematurely, which I hadn't been told about so the huge sheaf of flowers, lovely amber necklace and monster card with dozens of messages came as a touching surprise. Why it was 'wonderful' was that the two dear people who had organized it, a former secretary of André's and our former children's books editor, had managed to assemble an astonishing number of people who had worked for André Deutsch Limited, and they were all so delighted to see each other again – each person arriving being greeted with shouts of delight from all those already there, that I have never been to a party which buzzed so convincingly with genuine pleasure. I'd expected it to be rather a trial, because nowadays I dislike large, noisy parties – but in fact, from the first minute to the last I truly loved it, André was immensely rejuvenated by it, but that was to be expected because he is very sentimental, and a surprise party laid on by his old employees (it was kept as a surprise to him, very cleverly, because they knew how much he likes that) – such a party was bound to make him dewy-eyed. But I was really amazed by my own delight at seeing them all again – and they couldn't possibly have been so happy to see each other again if they hadn't been happy when they were with us ... I got home from it feeling *very good indeed*, and do you know what? – It has started me up on the book again! It suddenly gave me, like Proust's madeleine, a genuine whiff of what the nice side of all those Great Russell Street years had been like, which made me want to go on remembering ...

So you keep your fingers crossed for the continuance of my second wind, while I keep mine crossed for your agent's success with the Memoirs –

Love, Diana

31 DECEMBER 1997, NORFOLK

Darling Edward,

I seem to remember another time when I was alone in the country, thinking 'what a nice peaceful time in which to write to Edward . . .' Now it's the last day of 1997, and Barbara will soon be getting back here, driven by Adam (she had to dart back to London for three days after Xmas, to get out mini-post-Xmas *Economist*) so that we could all go to our fourth party – Norfolk is in a seasonal whirl, far more festive than London. This party is given by a pair whose fabulously delicious food is always served up at least two hours late by which time everyone is too drunk to appreciate it properly. The last time we were there I came home at midnight, pleading my Advanced Age, and Barbara got back at 3.30 a.m. – but I hadn't been able to benefit from going to bed early because Hannah was so anxious at Barbara's lateness that every fifteen minutes she jumped off my bed to see if she'd come back yet, and then jumped on again, crying because she hadn't. So this time I might as well stay to the party's end.

The best part of being here was going over to stay the night with my brother two days before Xmas, because all his four sons had come home and I came to the conclusion that it's not family partiality but they really are four exceptionally interesting, entertaining good-hearted men. Charlie, the gay one, was visiting from Buenos Aires (where he's teaching English at a posh school) and was wearing Argentinian trousers that might have been painted on him, a rib-clinging striped sweater and shaved head – straight off the most decadent tango floor, he looked, which was very refreshing, and he's wonderfully interesting and funny about the Argentine. But the most extraordinary was Willie the pirate, who used to look exactly like Harpo Marx and live a most adventurous life on the shores of East Africa, salvaging sunk ships, and sailing dhows and shooting lions. Recently came the news that he was in Bombay, 'learning to be a Merchant Banker' – and a sort of Hush fell on his family, everyone being terribly careful never to mention the name of Nick Leeson – that young man who Brought Down the House of Baring Brothers. And now he comes swanning in from New York, where it seems he's actually being a Merchant Banker, looking happy and confident and astoundingly un-like Harpo Marx, roaring with laughter at the total improbability of it all, and saying 'It's so lovely being within reach of the children again.' [*His marriage had broken up.*] – 'Within reach – in New York?' – 'Yes, I can phone them every day and I've got enough money now to fly home every weekend.' The second son ought to be dull because he's a Colonel – but he's not in fact dull, having a Persian wife and sons called Darius and Cyrus, and being both kind and witty. And Phil, the eldest, is the one I see most of. When I see how well both my brother and sister have done in the way of children, I reckon I may have deprived posterity quite severely in having none myself! (I did try for one, once with Barry; but life being what it is, that was the one which spontaneously aborted itself.)

Every time drinking has been going on over this holiday (which seems to have been most of the time) I've drunk a silent health to your agent in the hope of evoking superhuman powers in addition to the existing good-will. I keep hearing such gloomy views about publishing on this side of the Atlantic that I've come to feel that here, at least, anything which is actually good is doomed. Please god, you'll prove me wrong. Much love Diana

22 JANUARY 1998

Darling Edward –

Of course e-mail is wonderful – that's the only bit of modern technology that I can recognize as desirable – but I'm miles from being able to afford a new typewriter, so ... well, there you are. But my Chicago-dwelling friend Boman Desai, writer of monumental slabs of fiction only one of which has been published (by me – I loved it) has just written describing how a wealthy friend of his in Bombay has just given him £4000 with which to set himself up with the latest and best, hereupon printing out his latest opus, which took him three eight-hour days on his old computer, now took just three hours!!!! and it corrects typos; and all his other novels and all his correspondence now fit on a single diskette which is not even a quarter full ... Yes, clearly any actively productive writer ought to be ready to sell his soul for such magic, but it would still be pointless for me, even if I could afford it. Which does, however, rather heavily underline the fact, which I've been accustomed to disregarding, that I now belong to Another World!

On the 8th of March I'm flying to Dominica in the Windward Islands, to stay for two weeks in the cottage belonging to the mother of dishy Lennox Honychurch (who I met last year on my jaunt to Amsterdam). Barbara was coming too but has now been invited to Mexico to stay with a beloved old friend. She feels she must accept because although she detests Mexico she would feel dreadful if John died (as well he might) without her seeing him again. I found a very cheap charter flight which will be long and horrid, but I feel that when I'm established on my veranda 'in a large botanical garden from which there are views of mountains and waterfalls' it will prove to have been worth it. Everyone says Dominica is the most beautiful of the Caribbean islands, and the Honychurch mother and son are very congenial.

With much love – Diana

30 AUGUST 1998, NORFOLK

About Singing Words [*words used primarily for the beauty of their sound, which Edward dislikes*]. I don't see the singingness of words entirely as an evil, although it can certainly lead writers astray. It is a part of their power, and recognition of that part is very ancient – almost as ancient as speech itself – witness magic spells and chanting. Song is surely older than poetry. Sound-patterns catch attention and engage the memory. I'm not good at remembering poems word-for-word and it's not accidental that one of the few passages of poetry that I never forget is absolutely without importance meaningwise but sounds luscious – a piece of one of Milton's masques:

> Sabrina fair,
> Listen where thou art sitting
> Under the glassy, cool, translucent wave
> In twisted braids of lilies knitting
> The loose train of thy amber-dropping hair.
> Goddess of the silver lake
> Listen for dear honour's sake.
> Listen, and save.

Never, now, would I want to read a poem written like that, but I don't think it's a sin to let touches of verbal beauty creep in when it can happen without distorting the naturalness. 'Behooves' is, as you say, a mistake; but playing with vowel sounds as Milton did in that song, can add something to a statement. You, of course, do it with rhythm rather than with sounds because of wanting to keep your sounds inconspicuous. And it works. So all the above is just a general thought, not a comment on your work.

This weekend our neighbours in the village's big house – dear scatty people, great friends of ours, lent their house for a Reading by a very well-known and popular Lady Novelist who lives nearby, as a fundraising exercise. The funds to be raised are for a theatre in Bungay, our small market town. In about the 1750s it had a theatre, built for the use of travelling companies, which almost fell down, was then propped up to become Bungay's first cinema, then almost fell down again when a purpose-built cinema was put up, then became a warehouse ... and now some earnest and energetic citizens want to return it to its original purpose plus Art Centre. So, handsome Elizabeth Jane Howard, who was Kingsley Amis's second wife, read cleverly chosen bits of her novels very well to one hundred very enthusiastic people; and after it Gill and Michael Stanley, the house owners, who would do anything for a party and have never been known to leave one until everyone but them is under the table, gave a huge and delicious supper entirely cooked by her – and with the wine which ran almost ankle deep it must have cost a pretty penny – to about thirty of us. It's funny how much more Social Life there is in the country than in London – although country friends always suppose that we Londoners live in a constant whirl. But perhaps my life here would be just as quiet as it is in London if it were not for Barbara. She's a great joiner-inner when she gets down here.

Love, and great delight at having *Frieze* at my bedside. [A Frieze for the Temple of Love *was Edward's latest book of poems.*]

Diana

23 SEPTEMBER 1998

Darling Edward –

Such an advantage today to be deaf! Builders are at work in the middle flat, adapting it for Adam and his Georgia, and although the major horrors are over (the insertion of vast iron girders under my floor-boards from which to suspend the ceiling of Barbara's living room to prevent it from falling down) they are still using drills from time to time. If I could hear fully I'd be up the wall, but as it is I know the hideousness of the din only by the extremity of poor Hannah's panic. Everything in my flat, even if shut away in cupboards, is powdered with plaster dust – yuk! I shall be glad to leave in four days time for the week in Venice which Barbara is giving Polly/Vanessa [*Barbara's daughter Polly decided to change her name to Vanessa*] for her 30th birthday present.

My dear Dominican friends have invited me for two weeks next March – insisting, this time, on no rent – and suggested I bring with me as my co-guest Carole Angier, who wrote a formidably good biography of Jean Rhys for André Deutsch Ltd, in the course of which we became very good friends, and who is now deep in a biog of Primo Levi of which I've seen the first four chapters, and they are wonderful. I think she'll overcome the competition – one book already, very bad, and another coming, not likely to be very good. We couldn't afford to finance a Dominican visit for her before the Rhys, which was sad – but she still feels enough involved to long to see it. It will be fun to go with her. Poor Primo – do you know his monstrous mother never ever embraced him, not even on his arrival back from Auschwitz. No wonder his wife, who is apparently just like la madre, is so resolute in refusing to let writers anywhere near her or hers.

Barry has become even more riveted by Clinton than he is by football – spends all day listening to American talking heads on Sky TV, and shot out to buy the miraculously instant paperback of the full report. I've become bored – there's so much repetition of what everyone knew already. The thing which shocked me most was the spectacle of Clinton's cabinet after he'd told them he'd lied to them: my god, what a sleazy-looking bunch of ninnies! Did you read the novel *Primary Colors*? I don't see how anyone who did read it could be surprised by all this. But it is still interesting to speculate on which way the country will jump about impeachment. I fear that the soap opera element of sheer entertainment that seems to operate on this side of the Atlantic must be a good deal harder to find on your side. And none of it will do any good, will it? I mean, they'll still go on picking candidates for the presidency simply because they have an effective television manner, not for any real qualities of mind or character. – The older I get, the more I think the box is essentially a *bad thing*. But that, no doubt, is just Being Eighty.

Much love, my dears
Diana

8 MARCH 1999, DOMINICA

I believe I may have sent you this very same card last
year – it was certainly pressed on me by my dear
hostess, because it was painted by a old friend of hers
who obviously landed her with a huge bundle of them.
She was brave even to think of painting Dominica,
because it's so wonderful to look at that it despises
'interpretation' by humans. I'm here with Carole Angier
(you met her once in London) who wrote 'the'
biography of Jean Rhys but wasn't able to visit Jean's
island while researching it because our advance was too
mingy. She has just said that this is the most exciting
holiday she has ever had, which is gratifying. We are
staying with my darling friends, in the little house they
have built for guests in their garden, and they are
marvellous hosts – lending a car (Carole is a good and
bold driver), escorting us on the more alarming drives
(which are, of course, also the more stunning ones),
feeding us, cosseting us, leaving us alone when we want
to be left alone – perfection!

I think I must carry a gene inherited from my remote
West Indian ancestress, because the oddest thing about
Dominica, as far as I'm concerned, is how profoundly at
home I feel the minute I set foot on it. Not only when
doing the lovely things, but even when leaning on the
counter in the police station waiting for a driving licence
to be validated: I felt that I'd heard that fan creaking
round a thousand times – and picking my way along the
broken sidewalks of Roseau, watching out for the

gutters ... just the same feeling. I had warned myself that a second visit might easily be less enjoyable than the first one was – but in fact it simply feels like a continuation and it's unimaginable that I won't come back (though I suppose only too likely, in real life). I think I must feel about it rather like you feel about Morocco – though age has eliminated sex as an element in the excitement it inspires.

Carole has just gone off for an adventurous guided trek in the rain forest – not the big trek, which is four hours up to the 'Boiling Lake' which is the centre of a volcano, continually abubble – she's training for that. It's very sad not to be able to walk, except that I think you have to watch so carefully where you tread that you can hardly take in the parrots and orchids!

There hasn't been an eruption here within historic memory, but there are ten volcanos, and the whole island is composed of their ash, and there hadn't been an eruption within historic memory on Montserrat, either ... and there have been a lot of earth tremors here recently, some since our arrival though not in our part of the island. They seem to think that it's bound to blow sooner or later, but to be determined to believe that it will be much much much later so why worry ... The truth is that no one can bear to think of it for more than two minutes at a time – certainly I can't – so *Basta!* (Although I believe they are making evacuation plans for the villages in the places in greatest danger, just in case.)

As usual I'm itching all over, though not from mosquito-bites this time, against which I came armed with magic lotions. This time it's vile invisible ticks which leap on one out of the long grass. Never mind, its worth it.

Love and love. Diana

30 MARCH 1999

Darling Edward,

I was slightly disconcerted on the flight home because when I boarded the plane, feeling very sprightly after my wholly delicious holiday, a stewardess positively snatched my very light piece of hand-luggage from me saying 'Don't worry, dear, I'll put it in the rack for you – Now, when we get to Gatwick would you like to have a little buggy?' Thinking she meant a luggage trolley on which to put my hand luggage, I said 'Why not?', although feeling it to be hardly necessary. But in fact when we arrived I was forcibly restrained from leaving the plane until everyone else had gone except for half a dozen evident cripples, and we were then, one by one, conveyed by wheeled chair down a short passage – not more than about 20 yards – and were then loaded onto a convoy of electric buggies on which we were buzzed through the whole process of arrival – passport control and all – without having to lift a finger ... the only snag being that all the other passengers had all but got home by the time we left the airport. It was certainly extremely comfortable, but I did rather wish that they hadn't decided on sight that I qualified for it!

The *Magic Words* jacket is lovely – are all the
illustrations as good? The cataract surgery is not yet –
I'm getting very slowly blinder, but it's not yet bad
enough to make it worth it, or so the doctors say. It's OK
so long as I don't have to drive an unfamiliar route and
read sign-posts – because that I simply can't do.

Much love from us both

Diana

22 APRIL 1999

Dearest Edward,

Yes – I'm going to use most of what I've written of the
general André Deutsch material as Part I, then Part II will
be Brian Moore, V.S. Naipaul, Alfred, Jean Rhys, Molly
Keane. What a pity that I did books about Waguih Ghali
and Hakim Jamal! Unfortunately my two biggest 'names',
Norman Mailer and John Updike, remain too remote.
Mailer can come in – does come in – to Part I to some
extent, as an important step in the firm's development,
but about John – although I saw quite a lot of him and
always liked him very much (more as a man than as a
writer) – I simply don't have enough to say. And the three
closest friends I made as an editor (who all became part of
my life after they'd ceased being Deutsch authors) Calvin
Hernton and Peter Smalley and Roger King, are a) not
well enough known to be interesting to the public, and b)
too dear for me to want to be beady-eyed about them.

My court case [*I'd forgotten to license my car for a whole year*] – I'd forgotten all about it! It was quite interesting because this very big Magistrates' Court in quite a tough part of London turned out to be so civilized – a pleasant modern building and tremendously 'User Friendly' – very polite and helpful people, mostly black, staffing the place and showing one where to go and what to do, and extremely clear, well-thought-out informational notices posted at every stage, carefully balanced in style between an assumption that you would know absolutely nothing about the processes of the law, and an equally firm assumption that you are not a fool. When you actually got into your court (there were six of them) the clerks and ushers and so on were still black and mostly women, brisk but motherly, and it all went very quickly but kindly. I had been pretty sure that they would not fine me the maximum – £1000 – but I hadn't expected them to be so lenient as to make it £20, which they did. Though it wasn't quite as good as that sounds, because £50 was added. One was given a week in which to pay, but could do so over a counter at once, if one wanted to, and that was that. No doubt there were people in the waiting areas who were going to have a bad time (some were meeting their lawyers – there were little rooms where they could have their consultations in private) – but I didn't see anyone looking any more stressed than they would have done shopping in Sainsbury's.

Barry will be in Washington from May 13 to May 30. The visit will be less happy than he hoped because he has just heard that Carol, his eldest brother (he's about 80, I think) is in hospital in New York (where he and his girlfriend now live) with what sounds horribly like cancer of the liver. The latest news is that the scans are conflicting, so there is a chance that it is less bad – his woman has been told that there's reason to hope, but his daughter Margaret (the ambassador's wife) has been told by another doctor that he's pretty sure that a tumour on the liver has spread to the pancreas. His daughter wants to move him to Washington, but his woman has a job in New York and doesn't want to lose it ... I don't know what they will finally do. They say he is not in pain at present, and Barry is very anxious to see him while he can. His other brother, Lloyd, and his sister Cynthia will be staying with Margaret at the same time. He will be very glad to hear from you.

Much love. Diana

13 MAY 1999

Darling Edward,

Had we heard, when I last wrote, how ill Barry's brother in New York is? Cancer of the liver, inoperable. And now he's decided that he wants to die back home in Jamaica so has already been moved down there, so when Barry left for Washington yesterday, it was with the plan of going on almost if not quite immediately to Jamaica with his niece Margaret (poor old Carol's daughter and the Ambassador's wife). He doesn't mean to stay until

Carol dies, but he wants to see him while they can still communicate. I think if I were Carol I'd kick him out – talk about the British being inhibited about expressing emotion . . . they are nothing to Jamaicans. Barry on the phone to Carol kept making jokes. He really minds a lot but he so dreads feeling pain that he just won't. Margaret is being rather the same, so I hope it's the family mode, and will seem natural to Carol – tho' he sounded on the phone, to me, to be pulling no punches about knowing that he's dying, and hating it, but wanting to accept it with as much courage as he can summon. Mind you, I oughtn't to be surprised at B's attitude – I've always known that if one's ill he's about as much use as half a wet Kleenex.

Having just spent an afternoon with poor old André, I feel that almost any kind of death would be preferable to dragging on and on in the state of physical dissolution that he's in. Apparently his doctors can't – or won't – tell him what's wrong. He's like a little skeleton – no flesh or muscle left – can shuffle two steps at a time, then a long wait, then two more steps (propped up by someone). Falls down very often. Can't remember anything. Can no longer articulate properly (that's quite recent, and very difficult for deaf old me). Longs to get out of his ancient and now quite gaga girlfriend's apartment so persuaded me to manoeuvre him down the stairs and into my car (a fearful business) and drive him to Battersea Park where we could sit in the car under beautiful trees and have a talk – and had soaked his trousers twice by the time I got him back (is obviously v. mortified by this, but tries to deal with it by pretending nothing has happened). And is still enough himself mentally to be totally and ceaselessly miserable – does almost nothing but moan and keen about his condition and say how he wishes he was dead. To me it looks like advanced Parkinson's Disease, though without the shakes, but he says his doctor says it's not. Anyway, by the time I got home I must confess that the Little Pleasures of Life had (let's hope temporarily) rather lost their efficacy.

I don't think I could do portraits of Ghali and Hakim Jamal, after those two books, but I might do a chapter on them as examples of what editors are not supposed to do – get emotionally involved with their nuttier authors to the point of spending a lot of time and energy and money on them – which, as it turned out, I am very glad I did do because of how interesting it proved to be and of how much more I know about life as a result . . . I can have a shot at it, anyway, and see if it works.

I have now reached the stage of thinking about the book on and off all the time, which is satisfactory. It means that what I've done up to now keeps on putting out little sprouts, which have to be accommodated – at which point, you will say *aha*! Didn't I tell you how useful you would find a word processor. But fortunately I still don't mind going back and doing bits of retyping – 'fortunately' because I looked at someone else's word processor the other day and not a word could I read on the screen. That green lit-up writing and my cataract are totally incompatible and however closely I peered it was just a blur. I have to peer pretty closely at ordinary typing, but at least when I do it becomes legible. (One good thing about André – he said yesterday – that when the time comes for my operation I must have it done by a specialist and he'll pay!) I've enjoyed doing the Jean Rhys portrait. I'm not sure that it's quite stopped sprouting – when it does, I'll send you a copy.

I'm so sorry that things have gone flat with you – if it's any comfort, I was quite sure that I was going to go on doing nothing for the rest of my days, but off I go again! And I'm much older than you are, dear love. So cheer up!

Ribbon ran out – so good-night my dears, & big hugs
Diana

9 AUGUST 1999

Darling Edward,

This letter is Naughtiness – because what I sat down at the table to do is my Income Tax – the day by which the filled-in forms have to be sent in is rapidly approaching. And I know that I can do it. I've done it for myself for the last two years, and a) it isn't really difficult when I get down to it, and b) it was deeply satisfying not to have to pay an accountant at least the equivalent of what he had saved one, and usually a good deal more ... Yet still I put it off, and off, and off. But I now swear that when I finish this letter, *I will start on it.* So there!

We are hugely looking forward to Sept. 2 – or the date soon after it when you're settled enough to call, and arrange our first meeting. Charlie [*my nephew*] says

you've been lent a flat this time, which is good news. He
came yesterday to Sunday brunch, with his brother Phil,
and was in very good form. He's gone back to teaching
for the firm he worked for before – not what he really
wants to do, but he says they are nice people – Unlike his
NY employers! – and he doesn't want to run out of
money. I think my family is amazingly lucky in its
younger – no longer youngest! – generation: so amusing
and charming, and yet so level-headed and un-worrying.
Nearly all the oldies I know have tales of woe about their
grandchildren – or, if the young things are not
deplorable, they are deadly dull. How rash to boast like
this – god may hear, and send a thunderbolt. *Burn this*!!
   There really isn't any news . . . But how much nicer it
is to envisage you as a recipient rather than Her
Majesty's Inspector of Taxes! Actually we are in a state of
shock, because our dear old cleaning lady, Doll, has
retired, and I've taken on in her place the youngest of
three formidable sisters from the Philippines who have
been bullying Barbara for years. They have the most
terrifyingly high standards – Barbara warned us, and we
laughed – but lo! both Barry and I have been doing,
during the past two weeks, more housework than we
have ever done before, in a vain attempt not to feel
ashamed in the light of Myrna's piercing eye. We jump to
obey her orders – this kind of toilet cleaner, not that one;
old cotton t-shirts, not shop dusters; a new mop, if you
please. And I simply can't convey to you the sense of
moral inferiority which engulfed us at her most recent
communication:
   'Hi! More Jif please. Sorry but I have used a lot

because trying to get oil off walls.' I think it's that 'trying' which is the coup de grace. One reads stories of Filipinas being imported to London and treated brutally as domestic slaves, but now I know Myrna I'll never believe a word of them.

Love and love, Diana

10 DECEMBER 1999

Darling Edward,

I'm just coming to the end of a tedious week. Barbara jaunted off to France with our Norfolk neighbours, and Barry went to stay with Sally and Henry in Somerset, so there I was faced with a week closeted with Hannah, when a) my car broke down twice in two days, and b) poor old André broke his hip. He has come through the pinning operation; and doesn't seem to be suffering any pain, but my god, he looks frightful – a tiny bag of sparrowbones, his poor little claws dark purple from where they've stuck tubes into him. When he can haul himself out of doziness, which isn't often, he's in his right mind (though his speech has gone so mumbly that it's hard to discern as much). He looks as though he couldn't possibly live another day, but the hospital says brightly that he's doing very well and will be going home next week ... His heart must be amazingly strong to withstand all his illness and now this. Luckily, some time ago, he was canny enough to attach to himself a

young man called Paulo who was a decorator working
on his house. I think Paulo asked him if he had any odd
jobs going, and André recognized a benign and willing
nature, took him on to do driving and occasional
shopping and so on, and gradually, as André has
become more helpless, Paulo has become more helpful.
I guess that André has done something major for him –
helped him buy a house, or something of that kind –
because P says 'Well, I owe him so much . . .' – but
basically I think it's that Paulo is one of the world's
natural carers. He is now administering André's life in
almost every way, as far as I can see out of genuine
loving kindness (tho' he does get a bit bossy at times).
Although Paulo can go there every day, he can't be
there at night, or at weekends . . . So I was beginning to
worry that André must be becoming too much for his
girlfriend's carers, but then Paulo told me yesterday
that he has decided he must over-ride André's
instructions and ring up an agency and order a night-
nurse for him. He says he'll be able to get the money
for it out of A once it is a fait accompli. So – thank god
for Paulo!

I never did remember to show you my *La Fontaine's
Fables*. I now send you one of them.

Love and love

THE WOLF AND THE LAMB

Might is right: if you don't know it
allow me with this tale to show it.

At a sparkling stream
a little lamb was drinking.
Out of the shadowy wood
a wolf came slinking.

'Lamb,' snarled the wolf, 'you're mucking up my
    water
and I intend to lead you to the slaughter.'

'My lord ... Your Majesty,' stammered the lamb,
'Kindly observe that as I sip I am
downstream – a long way down, I truly think
from that transparent pool where you will drink.'

'You've mucked it up.
And what is more, I know
that just a year ago
you called me an idle, cheeky, thieving pup'

'A year ago, my Lord, I wasn't born ...
Oh please, I beg of you, ask my woolly mother!'

'Well, if it wasn't you it must have been
that foul-mouthed reprobate, your elder brother.'

'I have no brother!'
'So – who cares? – it was
someone to do with you: a close relation –
your shepherd – his dog – your who-knows-what –
    and I
must now avenge my damaged reputation.'

Whereupon – snap, gobble, crunch,
he ate the lamb for lunch.

[*Pamela Royds, our children's books editor, had bought a charmingly illustrated French edition of* La Fontaine's Fables *and was wondering who to get to translate them, when it occurred to me I'd like to try my hand at it. I enjoyed it, and Pam approved of the results. Edward thought he could do better and I expect he could – but I still stuck to my versions.*]

21 DECEMBER 1999

Darling Edward,

You've given me such a lovely present in sending Alfred's letters. It shocks me that I had forgotten so much – but it delights me that I was right in the essential memory: the feeling that there was a real and warm friendliness between us. What good letters he wrote! It comes back to me now that I didn't used to bother, quite often, to type (and therefore keep copies of) letters unless they had something official in them, which is why only a few of mine are there – the same thing happened in my correspondence with Jean Rhys, and a few others, with whom the correspondence became one of friendship as well as business. It didn't occur to me, in those days, that the friendship letters would have any value beyond the time of writing.

A surprise is the extent to which I obviously was not

worried by the signs of disturbance and statements of unhappiness. With hindsight one knows how real the unhappinesses were; at the time I thought it was Alfred's way, to overstate. I am very glad to have the letters.

It looks as though we may be in London over Xmas, because Barbara has gone down with a real bad flu. Of course she persevered in her faith in Mind Over Matter long after anyone in her senses would have capitulated, and gave in only when her fever had gone up to 105 and her cough was frightful – and then wouldn't have got a doctor if left to herself. And now, after four days, when the fever 'is almost gone' – it's still 101 – and she hasn't eaten a bite for all that time – she couldn't even drink a cup of weak tea without vomiting – lo and behold, Mind Over Matter is cropping up again! This afternoon I discovered that she had just taken Hannah out 'for a very little walk' – in an ice-cold storm of mixed snow and rain, and she has just called Barry that he must not go food shopping tomorrow for her and Vanessa (who went down with it this morning) because she was now so bored that she was looking forward to going to Safeways. Oh well – it's her funeral: I hope not literally!

Had André broken his hip when I last wrote? He's still in hospital, more confused and helpless every day, but I think they turf him out tomorrow. I guess it will be the end of him. Twice in the hospital his heart has almost stopped, and they've brought him back – moved him up to a little special room near the ward's nursing station, so that they could pounce on him if and when he collapsed. If and when it happens when he's back in Gwen's flat, even with his own nurse, he'll be a goner, which I truly think he is hoping for, in so far as he is thinking at all. I do think that by now we should have evolved a way of switching our hearts off: it's such a drag, the ending of a life being so lengthily horrible.

I don't think I could face the crowds along the river on New Year's Eve, even with Charlie's [*my nephew's*] arm to lean on. Getting there and back will be impossible except by pretty sturdy walking. No doubt the telly will put on a good show.

HAPPY NEW YEAR

My dear loves. Diana

9 OR 10 FEBRUARY 2000

Darling Edward –

Brillant news about the proper trade edition of *Village* – may it bring you in lots of money. I read heaps of novels these days because Barbara scoops them up from the literary editor's desk at the *Economist* (which doesn't review much fiction) and passes them on to me after she has read them, and very few of them do I remember as clearly as I remember yours. It deserves to catch on.

I enclose a letter I wrote you after getting yours re 'The Wolf and the Lamb', and then forgot to mail! The libel niggles I mention in it have been un-niggled – but André hasn't yet read the copy submitted to him – hasn't felt up to it. Maybe he never will!

They've now discontinued making ribbons for our loyal old typewriter – though Barry, galvanized into feverish energy, has just tracked down six dusty specimens in darkest Holloway – so our farming friends in Somerset are going to give me their out of date word processor, bringing it up when they next visit London. I'm sure it won't be clever enough to do e-mail, but hope it will be primitive enough for me to learn.

Very much love. Diana

[ENCLOSED LETTER]

Darling Edward

We-e-e-ell . . . To tell you the truth I like mine better – chiefly because the varying line-length reproduces the original more closely. Barry says 'Nothing to choose between them' (but then he thinks we're playing childish games anyway). In all of mine I kept very close to the original, because that was my brief, and I did them in the office, in odd minutes during the working day, so you have more freedom than me. However, I have to admit that yours is more natural-sounding.

The libel lawyer has been niggling away at *Stet* and it seems that I'm going to have to make some more modifications to the André material. What a damnable nuisance. But – reasonably enough – they won't let it go out without André saying he'll make no trouble . . . And envisioning him reading, even in his woozy state, I saw that I'd have – damn damn damn – to make some changes. Fuck!

Our water-heater is kaput, and the man who was supposed to come today to mend it didn't turn up. Double fuck!!

And my application for a new driving licence has been returned as faulty for the second time. Treble fuck!!!

Recently they made the licence into two parts – a card with a photo, and a little piece of paper. I lost my little piece of paper, and wrote on Application form no.1, that I didn't enclose it because it was lost. The whole boiling – applic. form, card, cheque – is returned to me with a note – please enclose your little piece of paper. So I telephoned – and that takes three hours before I catch it un-busy – and I'm told 'Send it all back with a letter saying it's lost.' So I do. And now it has all come back with a note saying 'We are no longer issuing licences in two pieces, so please fill in enclosed form for just the card' – ! Are we in Kafka land, or what?

However, we've all stopped having flu (touch wood), and darling Mordecai Richler and his wife Florence are back in London so I'm having supper with them on Thursday, and that will be nice.

Lots of love
Diana

(footnote) It was – very. And so was the Whitbread Prize dinner to which I went as guest of honour of David Cairns, whose wonderful and enormous biography of Berlioz won the biography prize. I edited his first volume, 11 years ago (the thing as a whole took him 30 years!). He's a darling man and we had a lovely giggly evening.

2 MARCH 2000

Darling Edward,

I suppose everyone is right, and gossiping back and forth, which is what one longs to do, would be easier with e-mail – but the old word processor our friend Sally says she'll bring up won't do that, and if we can get a word processor for free it seems wanton to pay for something more elaborate. Certainly I can't see B and me dripping glycerine on ribbons with much success, but to advance more than one step into modern life will probably be beyond us.

How dreadful about Neil's deafness – god, it's such a bore. By now I can never hear anything B says without asking him to repeat it (he doesn't enunciate his consonants very clearly), and it must be worse for Neil because seeing people speaking helps much more than one realizes. I do hope it clears up.

The kind of book-launch you go to sounds much more fun than ours in London. I've been to two recently – so cosy and sedate! But I've agreed, all the same, that Granta can give me one. Their office is an old piano factory in Islington with a big yard, and they say they want to put up a big tent in the yard and have the party there – towards the end of August, I think. If you are in

Europe – even in remote Berlin – you must come. I've just done something which makes me feel really wicked: for the first time in my life I've ordered a dress, jacket and hat to be made for me for summer best, with the party in mind. There's an odd but nice woman who has a boutique in this neighbourhood of extreme elegance – everything very simple but made of beautiful material, and she is just getting this season's materials in from Italy and France. She has measured me and I'm to choose the stuff next week. I haven't told anybody, least of all Barry – I think because of how really shocked I am by how much I'm enjoying it, and if I'm shocked, just think what he will be!

I gave the book to André a week ago – and he's just called to say 'Disaster! I've dropped it so all the pages are out of order and they had no numbers'. Of course they do have numbers, but they are at the bottom of the page – but anyway, he's sure that putting it in order is beyond him, so I said I'd come on Sunday to do it for him, and no, that's no good, so I must call him on Monday and find out if he's feeling up to it . . . When I gave it to him he came for it, driven by his faithful Paulo. So André was tucked up in the front of the car beside Paulo, almost invisible – a wizened little face emerging from rugs and mufflers, with his mouth hanging open – and in the back seat Eva, his nurse (they'd been to see his doctor who lives near here). And it was a Bad Walking Day (sometimes he can at least get across a sidewalk and into the front door) so Paulo fetched me out to sit beside André and have a little talk, but he couldn't keep his eyes open and he couldn't speak properly – his tongue looked too big for his mouth. Paulo said, when I retired defeated, that A was playing up – was less bad in fact than he seemed to be. I hoped so. But today André said on the phone (terribly hard to hear) that he hadn't the faintest memory of having come to fetch the script, or of seeing me. It does seem very unlikely that he'll be able to get through it – though P says he does still read quite a bit. But the poor old thing could be quite a lot less bad than he seems to be, and would still be very bad.

Love Diana

4 APRIL 2000

Darling Edward –

Writing will look a bit odd, because although my operated eye is seeing with hawklike clarity in terms of long sight, it will need reading glasses – not to be prescribed until Apr. 19, when it has 'settled down' – before it is equally good at close work. And my un-operated eye is not only hopeless at both, but rather annoys my new eye by disagreeing with it. If I wear my old glasses the new eye is totally fucked up. If I wear no glasses I'm aware of the old eye being even more useless than usual. But if I go on wearing no glasses I guess in the end my new eye will find a way of living with the old one not too badly until the 19th. As soon as Moorfields tells me I can have my second op I'll go bolting back there – after which it appears that I'll have good sight without glasses, except for close work, for the first time in my life. I had not realized that the lens they put in after removing the cataract corrects short sight!

I haven't yet driven – Barbara drove me to Norfolk three days ago, the day after the op – and I'm staying here carless for the week. But in fact I could drive perfectly well, and shall as soon as I'm back in London. And as you see, my new eye is getting better at writing. The trick is – to shut the old eye and keep the paper rather far away.

Blessed Moorfields: a sacred spot, worthy of annual pilgrimage. It was a long day certainly – ten a.m. to six p.m., op at 4.30 p.m. With about twenty other operatees, all of us in hospital gowns under hospital dressing gowns, I sat in a large room resembling the lounge of a very un-smart hotel (but the leatherette armchairs were very comfortable), having drops put into my eyes about every hour by amiable nurses (who supplied cups of tea and sandwiches if asked), suffering only because I'd been told to wear my hearing aid and there was a radio at one end of the room and a telly at the other, and lots of laughing and chatter from the nurses' station (the patients were mostly rather quiet, not knowing what to expect), which sounded to my hearing aid like bedlam. But I switched it off after a while. I don't think the op took more than 20 minutes. Having it under a local anaesthetic is in fact a bit alarming (though no pain at all) because it seemed as though a violently strong light was being directed right into your head, where it whirls and eddies in brilliant colours, and your instinct is to shut your eyes (which of course you can't do – I think he sort of clamped it open after applying the anaesthetic) – and flinch away from such an assault. So one lies there rather tense and longing for it to end. But lovely when it does! And then there is nothing to recover from, except a rather tiring day and 20 not very nice minutes, so that by the time I got home (Barbara came for me in a taxi) it really seemed comic that Barry and Barbara were fussing over me as though I were an invalid. The eye stayed covered for the first night, so it was not until the next morning that I discovered how well it could see. It was marvellous to realize that I could see a good deal further down the road we were driving along, without glasses, than I had been able to do for months and months with glasses. So here ends chapter 1 of my little success story.

With much love Diana

[*Note at top of page: AND ALL FOR FREE!!!!!*]

25 APRIL 2000

Archangel (I love being called Angel!) –

This is a warning to Neil: Err on the side of scepticism vis à vis Siemans' claims re background noise. Of course they may have hit on a miracle quite recently but at the time when, for huge sums, I bought my Siemans it was because their sales pitch was 'We can cut out background noise'. And they couldn't. My brother, having lost his Siemans, felt he couldn't afford another so replaced it with a National Health aid – and reported that it was just as good if not better. So I, when I lost mine, did the same, and he was right. I suspect that it is, in fact, impossible to make a sound-amplifying device which can distinguish between one kind of noise and another, and that one just has to switch off in noisy restaurants (or avoid them). An aid remains a blessing in social intercourse, the theatre, listening to the radio, etc. . . . And it's a help, too, in *slightly* noisy restaurants. Come to think of it, David Cairns and I, both wearing aids, sitting next to each other and concentrating on each other, communicated quite successfully at the Whitbread Prize dinner, though I couldn't hear people two or three places away, against the din.

Just back from my 'passing-out examination' at Moorfields, my eyes still full of Belladonna drops, so really am writing almost blind. Operation confirmed as a total success – but I still have to wait one more week before going to an optician for my new specs. Perhaps they'll turn out to have an 'Express Service' – (some of them do), so it won't be too long before specs are then delivered, I believe they'll be able to improve the balance between new eye and old, as well as let me read normally. At present the comparative uselessness of the old eye does weigh on me rather. Seems that I now have to wait patiently like a good girl to hear from the hospital when they'll do the other eye – the surgeon I asked said no, he couldn't give me any idea when, but not to worry, I would hear eventually.

Your description of Detroit appalled me. It coincided with a talk on BBC Radio 4 about America's present prosperity – what has happened to Detroit? I thought it was essentially a car manufacturing city, and surely more cars must be being bought than ever before?

Sally has twice forgotten to bring her old word processor when visiting London – perhaps she'll never remember!

André died on April 11th, after an op on a second hip broken in a fall. Poor old boy – he never got round to reading my script. He had a marvellous press, and a huge turn-out for his funeral, at which I spoke a tribute. I'm so glad now that I modified the querulousness of the book (bless you, darlings!). I've just had a card from old Richard Ingrams, founder of *Private Eye*, to whom Granta had sent proofs, saying how much he liked it and that it's 'a splendid memorial to André, both his good and his bad aspects, so fair and so affectionate' – which, coming from that waspish old body, pleased me a lot.

We are both so happy to think how soon we'll see you.

XXX OOO Diana

[POSTCARD] 3 JULY 2000

Chers Amis –

Just to let you know that I had second cataract op. Yesterday. Was home in time for lunch, after a nice unfrightening time, and now have two hawk eyes. Will have to use a magnifying glass for reading everything but big and blackprint for the next three or four weeks, till I've been finally checked and given reading glasses, but ordinary seeing is perfect. Hurrah for National Health Service.

We miss you. We love you.

Diana

I AUGUST 2000

Darling Edward,

I've suddenly realized that I never confirmed that Barbara is expecting you to stay when you come over for the Party. She is. Though if you would prefer to stay elsewhere you mustn't feel that you have to stay here. I suppose, though, that as you seem to be planning to come for just one night, there would not be much point in being in a more central part of the city.

I'm delighted to hear about your cataract op: join the club of those who are grateful to Modern Medicine. It's so much the thing these days, to mop and mow about it, that I sometimes feel quite out-of-step when I marvel at my own new eyes and remember how wonderfully University College Hospital coped with the dreadful emergency in Barry's guts.

Until last night I wasn't quite sure that being able to drive at night had been returned to me. I'd tried when I had just one new eye, and still found it v. difficult because the as-yet-unoperated eye fucked things up. But last night, for the first time, I tried with my two new eyes – and lo and behold, it was perfect: better than it had been for years and years, and with no glasses! From now on, all I'll need is reading glasses (which I'll have in about 2 weeks' time); and dark glasses for sunny days – my eyes are more sensitive to glare than they used to be. For now I'm having to read and write with the glasses I got after the first eye was done, which work as readers for the right eye but have to have the left eye covered with brown paper and sticking plasters because that lens was designed to deal with a poor old eye that was both cataracted and myopic and therefore does frightful things to normal sight. It's not a comfortable state of affairs – I'll postpone starting a new book till I have proper readers – but it's much better than nothing.

It wasn't just because of your encouragement that I wanted to dedicate the book to you and N. Although I've always been a facile acquaintance-maker, I've never found it particularly easy to make friends – and that is something which gets harder as one gets older, anyway, so by the time I was in my seventies I really was not expecting ever to do so again. So it was truly lovely to feel, as soon as I met you and Neil, 'Now here are people with whom it's possible really to connect' . . . which seems to me to be worth celebrating.

I've now had very agreeable interviews with both *The Times* and the *Telegraph* (don't know when they'll appear, but both will be with photos, and I don't think either can be hostile after so much geniality face-to-face), and the *Guardian* has confirmed that when it runs the extract in its weekend mag. on August 5, it's making me its cover-girl!!!

The only big interview still to come is the *Independent*, but there are several small things – local radio, etc, plus BBC's *Women's Hour*. And there's already been one wonderful review in the *Literary Review* (not yet in circulation, but they sent me a copy), plus excellent trade paper reactions. So the book could hardly get off to a better start. Life without all this pre-publication fuss will seem quite flat! I feel I'm building up to knowing what it feels like to have once been famous. Let me know if you don't want to stay here – otherwise a bed will be ready for you. Much love

4 SEPTEMBER 2000

Darling Edward,

Here's the official invitation. I do hope they are going to give us food – surely they must, as they say it will probably go on till ten ... but I for one will have a substantial lunch, just in case. Barry still says he can't be bothered with it – I wish he were more sociable, but there it is. Their guest list doesn't look exciting – and mine is mostly Athills and their kin. How I wish you could expect to be dazzled – but I fear you mustn't. However, you will be there to dazzle us!

Love xxx Diana

DIANA ATHILL

29 SEPTEMBER 2000

Darling Edward –

Behold my superior new writing paper (Special Offer
to readers of the *Oldie*) which you are the first person to
see. I was so glad to hear from you, and hope the reading
went well and family affections survived it.

I've just done my first – a little one organized by my
local bookshop. They were pleased because 60 people
came – they said sometimes it's dismal with only about
15 – and lots of them bought the book. And I was
pleased because it turned out I was very good at it. I used
to be nervous if I had to speak in public, but now I think
the receding tide has exposed a streak of exhibitionism. I
knew I could make them laugh, and did, and enjoyed
doing it. Wouldn't mind doing more of it, but don't know
how one sets about getting invited.

Interviews came to a comic end last week. The tiniest
of the three local newspapers asked if they could send
someone – and I answered the door to a little girl who
looked to my eyes about 12 and spoke in a mouselike
whisper. 'How long have you been with the paper?' I
asked on the way upstairs. – 'Three weeks.' – 'Oh poor
you. Is it still nerve-wracking?' — 'It was this
morning . . .' And she told how she'd been sent to
Islington to find out why the people who bought Tony
Blair's old house are moving, and not a single person
would speak to her. And then, with considerable courage,
she confessed that she had no idea why she had been
sent to interview me! Once I'd explained to her why, she

turned out to be quite bright – her ambition is to get into the *Guardian* – and we contrived a splendid interview – pages and pages of her little notebook, far longer, I'm sure, than her paper would dream of using – and parted fondly. *Sic transit gloria mundi,* as they say.

Grove/Atlantic have not communicated with me at all – only, and minimally, with Granta. And my book is on page 24 of the 26 pages in their catalogue devoted to hardbacks. So I think it unlikely that they will want me over in March, which is when it's announced for.

I'm pottering along with a new book – Granta wanted to sign a contract for whatever it might be, offering an advance £10,000. I've said no contract till it's written, but £10,000 will be OK when the time comes. They are also going to paperback my long-long-ago novel *Don't Look at Me Like That* when they do *Instead of a Letter* next year. It's a very comfortable feeling, having them so sold on me!

Barry sends fond love to which I add Hugs and kisses.

Diana

3 NOVEMBER 2000

Darling Fieldinski –

Of course I'm not horrified at your quoting me about *The Villagers* – I love to think I might contribute a tiny push to its sales. I'm glad it looks handsome – and think there are probably more ladies who like a good fat read than ladies who want to carry a book about in their handbags.

The invalid: now either you failed to let us know about the op, or else I've had a lapse into senility – only too possible, but even so it would surprise me to forget something so important. Because I don't know what he's had done to him. I'm appalled to think of his poor scrotum with a tube coming out of it, out of the blue, so to speak – and to hear that the op was 'ghastly'. Thank god you can say that he's pretty well recovered now – but it's dreadful to think of him going through horrible things, and you too, doing the looking-after – and us unaware! I would have telephoned if I'd known. Give him my love, and tell me what it was.

You and your computers!! Surely you had a new one just the other day? All I can say is you'll have to start doing desk-top publishing to justify this immersion in technology. Because I don't know what a Scanner is I'm not as impressed as I ought to be by your treatment of the piece from *Tears in the Fence* – although I am tremendously impressed by the piece. He is a lovely man to get the point of you so thoroughly and to write about you so fully – I'm so glad you sent it to me.

My own Fame is dying down: no more readings, and an outing to Cheltenham Festival last week to talk about Jean Rhys, not me. We were a panel of four and it went very well – one lady said afterwards that she'd attended seven Festivals and ours was the best evening she'd been to. So that was nice – and the hotel, too – although all we were given to eat was sandwiches! But I did have one very splendid belated review, in the *Spectator*, by the

novelist Tim Mo – who I thought hated me! He flounced
out on André Deutsch because André fucked him about
over his second novel, and I'd assumed that he'd blamed
me, too – but no! So that was nice. And so, very, was a
reunion with the Canadian novelist Margaret Atwood,
whom I admire a lot but had thought was lost to me for
similar reasons. Her new novel, *The Blind Assassin*, is hot
favourite for this year's Booker Prize. She was in England
for a short visit a little while ago, and somehow our local
bookshop persuaded her to come to our local library and
sign copies – it was part of a 'Support Our Threatened
Libraries' campaign – and when I saw it announced I
thought I really must go – we knew each other really
rather well when AD was publishing her, and I liked her
a lot – and hoped that after all this time she'd forgiven
me. And I was shuffling up in the queue, and Peggy
looked up from her signing to run a weary eye over the
queue to see how many more, and her glance passed over
me, paused, came back to me – and her face lit up with
delight. She said of course she had never blamed me for
that ages-ago nonsense, and she was in the middle of
reading *Stet* and was loving it, and was absolutely
delighted to see me again – and now she has ordered
Bloomsbury, her publisher here, to invite me to the
Booker party which will be fun even if she doesn't win it
(she's so famous, and rich with it, by now that she
doesn't need it) ... I 'discovered' her for England, so it
will feel something of a triumph if she does win, as well
as being lovely to know her again.

I'm worried about Barry, and so is his brother Lloyd.
He hardly ever gets out of bed now, and does absolutely

nothing but watch sport, eat and sleep. He's ceasing to exist as an intelligent person ... Lloyd said the other day 'He's fading away in front of our eyes'. I've been watching this slow shrinking of his boundaries for such a long time that I hadn't really taken it in until I saw it through Lloyd's eyes. L and I agree that there's nothing we can do about it – Barry flatly refuses to go anywhere or meet anyone or take any interest in anything. And he's happy in his room with his television and his food, which he enjoys – so let him go on being happy in that way, we feel. But it is sad. It must be partly because of the diabetes, but I'm afraid it's more because he's developed a sort of tunnel-vision about his writing – if people don't want to put on the one and only play he wants to write, which is about the one set of ideas on which he's become fixated, then he's not going to do (or perhaps has become unable to do) anything else. He'd rather just fade out ... He's so sweet and ungrudging about me having a nice time – God, how I wish this wasn't happening to him.

As for me, I'm getting on with what – I think – is going to be called *Child's Play*. [*It became* Yesterday Morning.] I'm not at all sure yet, if I'm going to be able to give it any shape. I've just done 6 pages about my father hoping that it will become apparent how to fit it in – it hasn't, yet! But it won't really matter if it doesn't work, because I'm having fun doing it.

Good luck with the Pomeroy-Kuh novel – and even better luck with the group of literary portraits.

Love and love

Diana

23 NOVEMBER 2000

Darling Edward,

The Booker evening turned out a funny mixture of appalling and magic. It was not the prize-winner's table at the Guildhall I was invited to – at the dinner itself only authors, their spouses if any, and the top people in their publishers, are allowed, to which the sponsors add a lavish number of the flashier kind of VIP. So Bloomsbury, Peggy Atwood's publisher, had decided to give a separate party of their own, to which Peggy would come after the award had been announced, to be consoled if she hadn't won, and to celebrate if she had. It was that party to which she had asked them to invite me, and also Xandra Hardie, my neighbour across the road, who by a strange coincidence is a very old and dear friend of hers. So we were each duly sent an invitation to that, which was headed BOOKER DINNER PARTY. So both Xandra and I assumed – not, I think, unnaturally – that it was to be a dinner party: probably 15 or 20 people sitting round a table, eating a civilized meal, with a television set in the room so that we could follow the proceedings. Well, what in fact it meant was that it was a party, given in connection with the Booker Dinner – a very different kettle of fish, particularly as it was intended by the firm as a treat for all their lower ranks, who could bring their boy and girl friends and have a high old time whooping it up. (This, of course, Peggy didn't know when she asked them to invite us.) So the first, and mild, surprise came when Xandra, and I, who had shared a taxi, arrived at the address in Soho which had been given simply as a street number, and found it to be an Irish pub. No doubt, we thought, it had rooms, or a room, for Functions upstairs. Surprise increased as the stairs turned out to be uncarpeted, splintery and dirty; and increased further as it appeared they were leading towards a god-awful din. Surprise turned to dismay when we arrived at a fairly small room, *absolutely crammed* (literally, all the bodies touching each other) with young and rather drunk people yelling at the tops of their voices. There was a television against one wall which no one was watching – and indeed no one could hear, except those right up against it – and when those happened to hear the commentators uttering a name they recognized, they all went '*Whoooaaaargh!!!!!*' at the tops of their voices, whereupon all the rest of the room went '*Whoooaaaargh!!!!*' too.

Xandra bravely ploughed her way through to the opposite wall, where there was a chair – I think the only piece of furniture in the room – onto which she steered me. I took out my hearing aid. I truly think I might have fainted if I hadn't, so appalling was the noise in the room when magnified by it. And without it, of course, I could hear nothing but the generalized roar of voices reduced to a more or less endurable volume – and no individual voices at all. There was no food, and although there was obviously lots of drink somewhere, the crowd was so dense that we couldn't see where. And it was eight o'clock, and Peggy couldn't possibly get there till 10.30 or 11.00 – and when she did get there, there would have been no hope of communicating with her. For a deaf

person one month short of her 83rd birthday it was
simply not to be endured. So Xandra (who is much
younger) hacked me a path through the living jungle and
found me a taxi, before returning to the fray (unwillingly,
but she felt and I agreed that Peggy must find one of us
there), and home I went. I was very disappointed and
cross, having looked forward to this dinner party
(hahaha) so much!

Then, having got home, and divested myself sadly of
my best evening glad-rags, I thought that probably by
now the award ceremony must be reaching its climax, so
I went into Barry's room, got him to agree to switch off
the current football match for a few minutes, and tuned
in to BBC One ... and there on the screen was Peggy's
face, and the words she was saying as I tuned in were:
'And I want to thank Diana Athill ...' It really was a most
extraordinary moment – almost uncanny. And because
of the amazingness of that coincidence, it suddenly made
the whole ridiculous evening much better than the
civilized dinner-party would have been. And Peggy is
going to be taking a flat in London for a few weeks come
the spring, so we'll have plenty of time to get together
then.

Another nice thing to happen last week was ... I don't
know if you are familiar enough with the British press to
recognize the name Lynn Barber. She's a journalist who
specializes in interviews and became famous for being
unbelieveably beady-eyed about her interviewees. I
always used to read her with pleasure because in fact she
was less bitchy than extremely shrewd and sharp-eyed,
and didn't hesitate to say about people exactly what she

felt – though she did, I think, sometimes choose frightful people to munch up, because munching was her thing. One used to wonder what possessed them, even to allow her into the same room with themselves, to say nothing of offering themselves to her for interviewing. Anyway, there she was, last week, frightening Lynn Barber, choosing her best books for the season – and there was *Stet*, being described by her as 'a winner'. I was pleased.

About *Child's Play* the worrying thing is that I don't think it can possibly be spun out to more than 100 pages of typescript – if that – which will make a terribly short book. My feeling is that it will work at about that length, but not if I stretch it. They'll just have to (if they take it!) use a large type-face and wide margins. At this stage I really have no idea if anyone but me will find it interesting – but it's still a bit too soon to try it out on you. I shall do so sooner or later.

Much love

[*Addendum*] 7 December
Wrote this ages ago – and buried it! Disinterred it by accident just now. Recently gave your address and telephone number to my young and dear friend Andrea Ashworth. She and her partner, Mark Greenberg, are just settling in at Princeton, where he is lecturing on Philosophy. Andrea wrote an amazing book called *Once In A House On Fire*, about her absolutely horrific childhood – which she now, being very beautiful, very clever, and very sweet-natured, appears to have recovered from in an astonishing way. I think she is, in fact, still pretty frail, and perhaps always will be – still

tormented by guilt, however much money she gives her poor feckless mother, at having more than one pair of shoes, lots of books, some pretty clothes and a man who loves her. She tends to hero-worship, and is at present endowing me with so many rare and wonderful qualities that I almost collapse under the burden – but still she herself is really so remarkable, and so dear, that I love her. If she does call, on one of their escapes from Princeton, give her a big hug. I've not yet met Mark (an American who has been studying at Oxford) – but he sounds OK.

20 OR 21 JANUARY 2001

Darling Edward –

Well here it is: *Child's Play*, not yet read by anyone, not even Barry because I've been so uncertain about it that I thought he easily might not like it, and if he said anything in the least critical I'd have gone into a flap. I took it to Granta yesterday, on the understanding that alterations could of course be made – though not much can be added, without taking it into territory already touched on in *Instead Of A Letter* – which it already overlaps a little, in places. Luckily they like little books so at least its shortness won't be against it.

Barry's in Washington for a couple of weeks – probably the last time he'll be able to stay there in ambassadorial splendour, because Richard (his niece's

husband [*and Jamaican Ambassador to the US*]) thinks
he'll soon be recalled. He's had a good long stint in the
job, and can feel jealous people treading on his heels.
Lloyd is staying here in Barry's absence, which means
lots of Healthy Eating. He eats like a horse and never gets
fat – but luckily quite enjoys cooking, so I'm doing well,
and consuming many more vegetables than lazy old me
and Barry usually bother with.

I do rather wish at this point that I had fax or e-mail,
so could hear from you quickly ... but never mind. If the
thing's not going to work, the later I know it the better!
And if it's going to work, then it's nice to spin it out.

Now for making some soup, which I've undertaken to
do this evening ...

Much love

Diana

12 JULY 2001

Darling Edward—

I'm ashamed of not writing earlier, and your e-mail to
Barbara made me feel worse. Somehow, getting used to
living in the present climate seemed to consume so much
energy ... but we are getting used to it. Its nature is
determined by Barbara, who is absolutely determined on
Normality and makes it amazingly easy for the rest of us
to act on that determination, but of course the feelings
going on under the surface are still there.

[Barbara had been diagnosed with an inoperable cancer. It eventually responded miraculously to treatment, but of course no one knew this would happen. For some time my letters were full of concerned reports on her progress. Because she would find such material displeasing I have cut almost all of it, which has made this letter and many of the following ones shorter than they were.]

Barry's chapter from his book has not been accepted by Granta. Ian [*Jack, editor of* Granta *magazine until 2007*] said the material was interesting but the manner was 'too telegraphic and lacking in feeling'. Wimbledon has cheered him up (and the intensely dramatic men's final match really was exciting) – but he's persistently stuffing himself with more and more sugary food and becoming more and more lethargic. I know I ought to fight him about this, but I can't – he just won't take it.

I'm the only one who is all right. While not allowing the dear reflexologist [*who they met when in London*] to brainwash me into following her raw food diet at all seriously, I have taken her advice to eat many more vegetables, much less dairy food, and no bread (I'd pretty well gone off meat already) – with dazzling results. No more runny nose in the morning. No more diffuse aches and pains. And I've already lost 12 pounds. The weight loss, together with the arrival from Wales of my magic handmade and exorbitantly expensive and hideous shandals (I think he calls them that because they are as much like shoes as sandals) has already made a considerable difference to my walking. The shandals are bliss – I hate to take them off. They are proof of how acutely painful feet affect the knees and hips, indeed the whole body. My stride is becoming longer and freer every day, and my carriage more upright. I'm not going to become a marathon walker by any means, but I'm quite surprisingly better than I was two weeks ago.

I had fun at the Festival Hall discussion with Mary Karr [*the American poet and essayist, and author of* The Liars' Club]. She rode into town with a Retinue: two people who figured in her last book (both very friendly and entertaining), 'my student' who I took to be the current lover, 'my assistant', and of course her American/English publisher who used to be her lover (they very nearly got married). This was not – as it might have been – at all daunting, but created a cosy and welcoming kind of family atmosphere. Mary is very attractive, sparkly and intelligent. She has quite clearly not read a word I'd written, but I like her stuff and liked her and we had lots to say to each other about memoir-writing, so all was well. Afterwards her publisher gave an enormous dinner for the lot of us, and at first I was horrified to find myself seated next to Rushdie: I've never been able to read him, and although one certainly doesn't have to talk to a famous novelist about his work at a dinner party it is most uncomfortable to know one couldn't. But luckily it was a long narrow table, and he and his smashing girl (a model, and how!) were opposite Mary and her publisher and they were all very old friends so talked to each other all the time. So I was able to concentrate on my other neighbour, a writer called Elena Lappin whose stories I'd read and loved and who is a most delightful person – we had a very happy time together and I was astounded, when I got home, to find it was 2.30 a.m. and I was not tired at all. So, you see, nice things are still happening in spite of everything.

That's all for now, my dears. How I hope NY goes on being cool and pleasant, and Neil is getting over the radiation, and that you are both well. Love and love.
Diana

I AUGUST 2001

Darling Edward,

I'm afraid I've decided not to show your poem to Barbara because I don't think she'd find it helpful. I'm sure that – like me – she finds the concept of 'no error in the universe' impossible to accept ... except in the sense that the notions of error and rightness etc. are products of the human mind, and given that in terms of the universe humans are infinitesimal atoms inhabiting a grain of sand, notions which seem to them important must be totally irrelevant universally speaking ... No, I think B's courage, which is marvellous, finds support in more mundane ideas, such as: Well, so long as one is still alive let's be alive – if one has to die, do it with as much dignity as possible and don't let anticipation of it spoil things for other people, or oneself more than it absolutely has to. A Stoic approach rather than a Christian Scientist one.

I was a good deal shaken by your reference to Neil's condition, which makes it pretty clear that Barry and I have been allowing ourselves to fool ourselves. Oh my dear loves, how I do wish you were near by so that if there was anything we could do we could do it. Barry, too, is increasingly a member of the invalids' club – I hope to heaven not even more so than before. He has at last agreed to have a scan (on August 7) because Barbara added her nagging to mine – our worry being that his belly is growing bigger and bigger all the time but the rest of him is actually quite thin. I've been muttering about it for ages, to no effect – but B now has Authority on this subject, so he obeyed her without a murmur, thank god. And touch wood. What healthy old things like us need to do is to concentrate on being *robust* god help us!!!

Which in fact, to a quite extraordinary extent, I am. In spite of all the heavy reasons for anxiety and sadness, I have been experiencing amazing and inexplicable moments of well-being – perhaps some kind of hormonal quirk? Who knows! It first happened some time ago, on my first visit to Dominica. Getting out of the plane at Antigua's scruffy little airport, I suddenly felt Wow – I'm seeing things properly again like I did when I was young – and it went on for that whole holiday: a feeling of being in direct contact with everything – not thinking 'now I'm doing this' or 'now I'm seeing this', but just doing and seeing – just being, really, and it was marvellous. And recently these delicious times of being have been coming back in fits and starts. Three weeks ago, for example, I went to a concert of chamber music in a little church near our place in Norfolk (piano and cello, which are not distorted by my deafness like fiddles and voices) – and it was absolutely glorious: I haven't been in the music like that since god knows when. And sometimes I wake up in the morning and look out of the window, and am suddenly quite amazed by how lovely everything is. And a really funny thing happened two evenings ago. I went to a party and there was a woman I know slightly but like a lot called Robin Dalton – an Australian almost my age who used to be a theatrical agent, very exuberant and in the swing and knowing everyone, so she used rather to overwhelm me. But then she loved *Stet*, and sent me a memoir she had written ages ago and had published in Australia, and I loved that – she writes exactly as she talks, very honest and funny – so I began not being overwhelmed. So there was dear Robin sitting on a sofa next to me at this party, and we were nattering away like mad and got onto the subject of being old, and for some reason I was moved to tell her about my 'moments' which I've never mentioned to anyone not even Barry, and she screeched '*My dear* – you too!!!!' and it turned out that she has begun to have exactly the same experiences. 'Do you think,' she said, 'that it means that we are going to die – die quite soon? A sort of vision of how marvellous life is, granted to us at the last moment?' – And I had asked myself that exact same question that very day. And we agreed that whatever it meant we were astoundingly lucky to have it – so we sat there hand in hand, beaming at each other and gloating over our lovely moments of pure being. It was such fun! And I rather think that getting these moments gives me, even in the times when I'm not having them, an improved ability to survive sadness.

One of the other things about Robin that I enjoy is

how she took her husband's death a couple of years ago. He'd been ailing and very miserable for some time, unable to enjoy anything and getting worse. Then he had a cataract operation and she brought him home in a taxi, and halfway up the stairs to their flat he said 'God, I'm tired – I must sit down for a moment', and he sat down on the stairs . . . and died! And Robin says 'People keep telling me what a frightful shock it must have been for me – but it wasn't really, you know . . . well, I suppose it was a bit of a shock, but what I thought was "Good God, he's dead – how marvellous!"' Which, of course, it was – the kind of death one would give anything to be sure of having. But not many people would have seen that so instantly, or would make so little bones about saying so! Now, she is a robust old person, which is what we'd all better work at being!

Lots and lots of love and give Neil a big hug from me.
Diana

[*UNDATED LETTER*]

Darling Edward,

Barry had his scan, and it seems to be OK. He says no one said anything to him at the time, so he asked the nurse, and she said 'Oh, the doctor would have said something if there was anything to worry about'. I said 'Surely the person who did the scan was a technician, not a doctor' and he said vaguely 'I think she was a

doctor . . .' It doesn't seem very reassuring to me, but I
suppose it must be. Presumably the hospital will send the
result of the scan to his doctor.

I doubt whether your 'wretched creature' would really
re-emerge if Neil died on you, because I don't think there
are two people there – I think it more likely that the
wretched person turned out to be capable of being much
less wretched than he thought he was when
circumstances demanded it – gained something from
experience that he is not going to lose. (I was halfway
between saying 'Less wretched' and 'More capable'.) I
don't see how someone could suddenly lose the self I
know. It does, after all, contain a lot of the sensibility
which comes with 'dottiness', but enlarged and
strengthened by the things that you discovered in
yourself post-Neil. The voice which speaks in your
poems is a wonderfully sensible one which knows all
about pain and dottiness, and that, darling Edward, is the
person you are – I'm sure of it.

The paperback edition of *Stet* has been getting a lot of
attention, which is nice. I've missed most of it, but people
keep saying things like 'That was a very nice bit about you
on that book programme last week' or 'I like that photo of
you in the *Telegraph* the other day.' Apparently it was the
lead paperback in the *Evening Standard* – and (this one
I saw) the *Guardian*'s literary editor made it his Book of
the Week with a very nice review.

I hope your heatwave has passed. We are shuttling
madly from one extreme to another – stifling heat one
day, having to light a fire the next! But I don't think
anything we can produce is as frightful as a full-blown

New York heatwave – only one of which have I experienced, but I've never forgotten it.

Very much love

Diana

I SEPTEMBER 2001

Darling Edward –

So you have been having rat trouble too! And much more dramatic than ours: the invader actually under your bed, and having to do the horrible deed yourself! Whereas ours [*in the Norfolk cottage*] may yet turn out to be largely a false alarm, since the only rat we've actually met was discovered by Hannah not in the house but in the little conservatory opening off the living room, where it (a pregnant female) was building a nest behind a large geranium. It was brilliantly cornered with a broom by Deirdre, my gardening lady, who then put a flower-pot over it, slipped a board between pot and wall, and carried rat two fields away before releasing it. *But* we have long had merry scamperings between floor and ceiling, and recently fruit left out in the kitchen had been eaten into – like you, I have wondered 'Teeth or Beak-marks?' and found little scraps of peel at the scene of the crime. And also we have damp stains appearing on the dining room ceiling, which is under the bathroom but the bathroom floor is imperviously tiled and we know that we have never had a flood in it ... and I suddenly remembered a dreadful occasion in my parents' house when similar stains, when investigated, turned out to be caused by rats' excrement – there was a colony of them established above that ceiling and – tidy animals that they are – they choose to pee and shit always in one place. So I had to ring the South Norfolk Pest Control officer, who came at once. He said the stains might conceivably be caused by rats, but on the whole he doubts it because of their shape. So what he did was insert rat-poison into the space between floor and ceiling, using spaces where pipes go through. If it's rats, he said, it would do for them, and we would know soon enough ... by – oh horrors! – the stink! No stink, no rats. And if no stink – then there must be a leak in a pipe under that imperviously tiled floor, at which the imagination boggles. Well, that was just over a week ago, and still no stink. There is a very pretty kind of wood-mouse, a good deal larger than ordinary mice, of which we have a good many about the place, and he thinks the fruit might easily have been eaten by one of those – and they may make the scamperings, too. If they eat the poison he said the stink would be less. What we hope is that they scamper, but don't go in to the space under the bathroom, so won't find the beastly poison. And we are having the dining-room ceiling white-washed and will then touch wood that the stains don't reappear. If they do – then it will be floor-up time alas alas.

I had a lovely call from the dear publisher yesterday. He said 'I've just been looking through your proofs – and d'you know what – you've written a wonderfully good book!' He then said that of course he already knew he liked it, but it had taken him by surprise, now that it was in print, to see how much he liked it. To me it now seems that the first and last chapters, both added at his suggestion, and I don't think you have seen them, have made all the difference. I am indeed very lucky in my publisher.

Now to work – and I've got to review Naipaul's new novel for the *Oldie*. And when I groan, all Barry says is 'You're having a nice full time'.

xxx Diana

Last week we had 2 days of almost NYork-like heat and humidity, and I did feel for you! I wish I could send you over some of the pleasant freshness we're having now.

13 SEPTEMBER 2001

Darling Edward –

I've been trying and trying to phone – someone I know got through to a New York number on the 12th, so why not us – but all that day [*the day after the 9/11 attacks*] all I got was a recorded message that all the lines were busy – and same even this morning at 6 a.m. your time. Then this p.m. it changed to what seemed to be your engaged signal – then to a very odd signal I didn't recognize – then to a parrot voice repeating 'The service can not be connected'. I know I couldn't say anything to make the situation less frightful, but still the frustration of not being able to hear your voice is driving me mad. And although we tell ourselves over and over again that the chances of you being within range of the worst of it that morning are small – still, not being able to hear that you are all right – in so far as anyone in downtown Manhattan can be all right – is upsetting. By pure chance I, who hardly ever watch TV, saw it as it was happening – was by a set as the first images were appearing on the screen and no one had a clue what was really happening, and as the towers toppled – so am as near as anyone in this country can be to feel the horror of it, and imagine the result of those vast boiling clouds of frightful debris and dust settling over Manhattan. Oh my dears, how we two long to be able to speak with you.

There seems no point in speculating as to what will now happen in the world – people here are saying to each other 'At least ghastly Bush has a Democrat senate to cope with – he can't unleash total mayhem single-handed' – but how can anything but dreadfulness follow? I try not to allow myself to feel that civilization is going to end before we do – and brought to it by us in the West just as much as by those Muslim lunatics – but it will be a miracle if it doesn't.

Failing hearing your voice I've been reading your poems – particularly the last three in *Counting Myself Lucky* which are my favourites. I love you, and I love Neil – and I do so long to hug you both.

Diana

27 SEPTEMBER 2001

Darling Edward,

Life in Westbeth sounds as hard to struggle through as I feared. Why is everything going bad at once? The world's evil boiling over – Neil's head obviously unsorted-out, your back going, Barbara's cancer, Barry's diabetes – it's as though one thing is bringing down another – tipple-topple, a sort of general degringolation (I love that word – it doesn't exist in English but it ought to). It must be a good deal easier here than it is with you to hang onto small, private taking-the-mind-off things; we not having that gruesome mountain of potential stench next door.

I've just – oh lord, talk about degringolation!! At that point a man arrived to take the front door off its hinges and shave a bit off its bottom, because it's been sticking worse and worse – and what has he just pointed out but that the brickwork of the whole porch has started to crumble and the arch is likely to collapse at any moment. *Pause for rending of raiment*! He is the most dubious-looking man got through the yellow-pages, and Barry's insistence that he should come and do the job on Sunday evening because he'd only charge £400 has got to be withstood until Barbara and Adam, whose house it is and who will have to pay the bill, have had their say, so we are having a *spat*! This part of our story to be continued in our next.

So I go back to my original ball-point and to what I was about to tell you. Two weekends ago I went to the country cottage after a three-weekend gap and found there a letter in an unknown hand. And it turned out to be from the son of the man I called Paul in *Instead of a Letter* – my first love who all but wrecked my life. 'Paul' was really called Tony Irvine, and this James Irvine (now 60 years old!) was born after Tony was shot down over Greece which happened very soon after Tony and his mother got married (poor girl!). Now his mother is dead, and he has just retired, and has decided to do what he has long wanted to do: find out more about the father he never knew. He had never come across *Instead of a Letter*, and hit on my name by first finding a letter I'd written to his grandfather after Tony's death, which told him that his dad had once loved and been loved by someone called Diana (I've now seen that letter, and have to say in all immodesty that it's a remarkable one!). Then, when he was consulting *The Times* (which has superb computerized archives) with reference to one of Tony's wartime achievements, lo and behold his name also turned up in the little announcement: 'The marriage announced between etc. will not now take place' – from which he got my surname and my parents' then-address. So he found the phone number of that address – which was the home farm of my grandparents' estate, now inhabited by the manager who runs the estate for my cousin – and asked if they could help him trace me. And they, of course, knew that I am now sharing the cottage with Barbara, so gave him that address. From which he happens to live only an hour's drive away!

By the time I'd found his letter, he had (he says) discovered that I'm 'famous' because whenever he opened a paper or switched on the radio, there was someone reviewing my paperbacks, and he promptly read *Instead of a Letter*. So when I gave him lunch at the cottage last w.e. there was not much more for me to tell him. But it was a moving and interesting meeting. He resembles Tony a good deal, though he's much less uninhibited. Tony was extraordinary in the directness and wholeheartedness of his response to whatever experience came his way, while there's something defensive about James. He has four children, who look very attractive, and whom he obviously adores, and several grandchildren, and a nice-looking wife. He's intelligent, and on the side of the angels – but has since written to say he forgot to ask me did Tony share the rather old-fashioned but serious attitude of 'his grandfather, father, wife and son' towards 'religion and prayer', which took me aback a bit, and to which I could only answer 'no – not in my day anyway'. But I share his feeling of being a bit low after our meeting because it was as though 'the party had been given but the birthday boy wasn't at it.' I think we'd both allowed ourselves to imagine that our meeting would somehow 'bring Tony back' – and then, though we'd enjoyed meeting, came up against the fact that of course it couldn't do anything of the sort. Dead is dead. But we are going to meet again, and he's going to show me his account of his father's life, which he's writing for his children. [*This he did, and it is very good.*] And it has given me a week or so plunged back into the time Tony and I had together before sadness struck, reading all his letters again and remembering a great deal, which has been great. In spite of the end being sad, and taking so long to get over, it was a more interesting and enjoyable first love than most.

Another important thing in these last weeks was reading W.G. Sebald's new book *Austerlitz*. I'm not at all sure that it's readable aloud [*which Edward would do to Neil*] – it's stately pace and the lack of paragraphs might make it soporific. When reading Sebald to myself I always start by finding the continuous, paragraphless flow claustrophobic, but end hypnotized by it into complete subjection. And this book is, I truly think, a masterpiece. One has to read him slowly and attentively, whereupon it becomes like being carried along by a river past scenes that are at first only odd and interesting, then things that make you catch your breath with dismay, then stretches of extraordinary beauty, then of almost unbearable horror. The story is simple enough. The narrator meets, and over the years hears the story of, a man called Jacques Austerlitz who, at the age of 5 in 1939, was put on a *Kindertransport* by his mother, in Prague, and ended in Wales, being raised by an unspeakably bleak minister and his equally bleak wife under the name Dafyd Elias. These foster parents manage to obliterate his past, so even when he learns his real name, at school, he recovers nothing of it. But without realizing it he is almost petrified by despair and gradually shuts himself off from pain by concentrating almost entirely on his study of certain aspects of architecture. Then, gradually, he discovers that his mother was a singer, in Prague, where she stayed when his father, politically engaged, escaped to Paris, expecting that they would soon reunite. But when she realized that she was trapped, she summoned up the courage to put her little boy on that train, and soon afterwards was arrested and consigned to Theresienstadt. Neither parent was ever seen again. And as Austerlitz recovers more and more of this he half expects that the truth will break him out of his defensive shell. But it doesn't. For a time it nearly finishes him off. Then he seems to work out an odd but viable *modus vivendi*, and plods on.

Sebald, it seems to me, at any rate, has restored to this familiar material, by particularizing it with his special kind of odd intensity, its full force. I don't know when I was last so absorbed by a book or so moved by it. And much of it I have every intention of reading again, to savour the subtlety of his rhythms. The odd thing is that he writes in German, and I'm told by someone bilingual in German and English that his German is so old fashioned and formal (he's lived in England almost all his adult life) that German readers mostly can't bear him. Having lived and taught in English for years and years, he knows the language very intimately, and he always works very closely with his translator: with the result, so this person told me, that the translations of his books are much better than the originals. Certainly they don't read like translations, but like beautifully judged English prose.

Adam's just come in, and says he wouldn't dream of letting a dubious-looking visitant from the yellow pages anywhere near the porch. Barry's shrugging and muttering – 'oh well, if he wants to spend £2000 instead of £400 . . .' If any workman looks scruffy enough his heart always goes out to him on sight – rather odd in this case, since the scruffy character confessed to us that he had two hobbies, one collecting vintage automobiles and the other breeding Rottweiler dogs. Whether he has a surprisingly large income or a very fertile fancy I wouldn't like to say.

    Much love
    Di

15 OCTOBER 2001

Darling Edward,

    I'm writing this on my knee, because simultaneously the central light and the light by my table have been smitten by metal fatigue (or Bakelite fatigue) so that the bit into which the lamp is screwed has crumbled – and the one in the bathroom, too, but that's less tiresome. Probably any normal person with a screwdriver can fix a new lamp-holder to an electric flex, but not me, and not Barry. And the only electrician we know is a bit high-handed and has decided that this is not a proper emergency so he will come 'when he has a few minutes to spare' . . . so evening after evening I'm reduced to writing in my armchair. (Yes, I know I could move that reading light to my table, but then I'd have to move it back to near the chair whenever I wanted just to read.) The whole house is feeling a bit besieged by minor mishaps – Barbara's car was broken into last night – just when she decided to buy a case of much better and more expensive wine than she usually buys and had left it in the car – but hidden in the boot, so the thieves couldn't have seen it before they broke in; and Vanessa [*Barbara's daughter*] fell down stairs and hurt her foot – I think only bruised it badly, but may have cracked the bone; and Hannah has conjunctivitis. The only happy person is Vanessa, who adores medical crises and is longing to be taken to hospital for an X-ray. Hannah, on the other hand, has taken to looking at Barbara and me with dread whenever she sees us together, and creeping under pieces of furniture, because she knows that we collaborate when it comes to eye drop time.

You ask for news of Barbara: she's back at work, after managing to enjoy much of her Italian holiday, and she's looking better.

To my great pleasure Louisa – Granta's superior publicity girl who did such miracles for me over *Stet* – is back in their office now that her baby is nearly a year old, and is already getting to work on *Yesterday Morning*. She's already got me booked for the Edinburgh Festival, and is weighing up various offers for serialization, and has a major interview fixed for the *Observer*. The date they give for it in their catalogue is January. And did I tell you – no, I don't think I did – that just as I decided that evidently *Stet* had not earned its advance, a boring-looking envelope arrived from Granta, looking just like the ones which include photostats of press cuttings (which by now are likely to be six lines in the Kilkenny *Examiner*) so that I nearly didn't open it. And it

contained a royalty cheque for £3000! Yum yum!! Lots
of little treats, I'm giving myself.

This last weekend, while Barbara was being carried off
on a mock Orient Express Experience (a train journey
round East Anglia including lunch – so expensive that
she utterly refuses to tell me how much, and the lunch
was disgusting – surprise surprise) I made 18 pots of
Quince Jelly from the beautiful golden quinces born by
the quince tree I planted with my own hands. The wet
summer we had has caused huge fruit crops of every
kind. And I put up two litres of quince vodka – but that
will take months to mature. The amazing thing is that
although the quinces are golden-skinned and pale-
cream-fleshed, the jelly has come out a gorgeous deep
red. What colour the vodka will be, who knows, but
people say it tastes perfectly delicious. We will keep some
against your next visit.

Big hugs to you both xxx
Diana

10 NOVEMBER 2001

Darling Edward –

What energy, doing lunches! It's weeks since B and I
even thought of having anyone in. He hardly gets out of
bed now, and as his belly gets larger his face gets smaller.
After they scanned his belly and told him 'The doctor
will tell you if anything's wrong' he never heard another

word – so I hoped we were right in assuming nothing was
wrong. Now he will be going for another scan – prostate,
this time. When I said 'Did the doctor suggest it, or did
you ask for it' all he did was grunt and drift out of the
room. He doesn't want to communicate anymore. I know
I'm far from being a born carer, like you, so I'm sure it's
my fault – but he is very difficult now. It may be partly
that, knowing that I've got Barbara and Vanessa to worry
about, he doesn't want to add to it, but I think it's more
that his energy is at such a low ebb that he just can't be
bothered with anything. For the prostate scan, whether
he likes it or not I'm going with him. He's quite capable
of saying he won't have an operation, supposing they tell
him one is necessary, if left to himself. (I wouldn't have
known anything about it if I hadn't chanced to see the
hospital's form lying on the floor when I took him in a
tray of food.)

Granta has just sent me the first printed copy of
Yesterday Morning (they get to work well ahead of
publication, which is why their sales are so good). It
looks very pleasing – jacket is delightful and they've used
the snapshots and so on, which they squeezed out of me
very nicely. But they've done one bad thing – they've lost
the dedication, god knows how because it was certainly
there on the typescript – and the dedication is (or was) to
Barbara. I decided on that before she told me she was ill,
but of course when I knew about the illness, having her
there as dedicatee became even more important to me,
and I'm really miserable at what they have done. Of
course I will write the dedication into her copy of the
book, but it won't be the same.

How I hope that Tom Powers takes your Afghan book – but I fear that it's unlikely, simply because it was written 30 years ago. As you say, public ignorance about Afghanistan is abysmal, so most people have no notion of how little it has changed in 30 years, and would simply assume that a diary from that long ago must be out of date. I'm trying to imagine a Steerforth editorial meeting discussing the book, as though it were an André Deutsch meeting, and it seems to me that would be the argument raised against it, and that probably it would prevail. Touch wood that I'm wrong!

Have a good time with Neil's sister. How very odd that the fare goes down near Christmas! I'd expect the opposite. I love to think of your reading Robert Fisk together – though every time I read something in a newspaper which makes sense as a comment on this goddam war, I end up depressed because its never on a front page, always quite low down on page 3 or 4. The whole thing must be even more distressing to you, with your memories of the country. From the feminine point of view it's hard not to feel un-distressed at the thought that the mullahs may possibly get their come-uppance because although women have certainly always been kept most firmly in their Islamic place in Afghanistan, it does seem by all accounts as though the Taliban have been doing it a good deal more zealously. All religious zealots give me the horrors – the appalling self-righteousness with which they trample their way ahead. If only, if only our Leaders didn't see fit to behave in the same way!

If anyone could get me on-line it would be you. But Barbara apparently can't use her own computer (she has one at home) and Adam can't find the time to teach her, so I'll have to buy one and I can't afford it, so there we are.

Lots of love. Diana

25 DECEMBER 2001, NORFOLK

Darling Edward,

Starting this letter in bed (so writing may wander a bit) on Christmas evening, having retired rather early in order to get a bit of solitude. Three days of intensive family makes me realize how spoiled I am – so used to my own space and quietness that I can no longer bear unbroken company very easily. The first two days, chez my brother, were great fun but incredibly noisy – the four nephews and their spouses (only two spouses – Charlie solo, of course, and Willie divorced) being accompanied by nine great-nephews and nieces, ages ranging from six to seventeen, all bright and beautiful.

From there, yesterday, I drove the sixty miles to our country retreat, where Barbara had been with Vanessa for three days.

Adam arrived late last night, so today, although B insisted on stuffing the turkey, he and I have done most of the cookery, and he has cheered B up. And before he arrived yesterday B and I went for drinks to our neighbour with all of B's 'gang', and she was soon giggling away with them as merrily as ever, and stayed on at least two hours longer than I did. God be praised for them. They are obviously able to provide exactly the kind of light relief she needs. We'll be seeing them again tomorrow – and she insists she has to be back in London before the New Year because she has to be in her office. Up to now she's refused to take taxis – has driven her car as near as possible to the tube, and then taken that. But I think – I hope to god! – that when she gets back she'll capitulate to a taxi. [*She didn't.*]

Although my book's publication date is still in mid-January so that reviews won't start to appear until then, they've got it out into the shops already. If they'd left it until after the New Year, delivery would have clashed with the shops stock-taking, which would have been a Bad Thing. So I guess a few Xmas sales are being made, and I've had a few favourable responses – but mostly from people who would like it anyway. I looked through it again the other day, and thought it wasn't bad, but that I ought to have filled it out a bit. The trouble with writing such a personal thing is that one is so afraid of becoming boring – but better too little than too much.

31 DECEMBER – BACK IN LONDON –

Came home to find your Village Calendar – very nice to have, bless you two old legends. Many New Year hugs and kisses.

Di

DIANA ATHILL

[Poem from Edward Field, 12 January 2002]

INCOMPETENCE
for Diana Athill

Though I'm a competent, functioning man now,
managing to juggle several different careers in my
    complicated life
I keep dreaming of my old life, my years of
    incompetence,
the way concentration camp survivors can't stop
    dreaming of the horrors of the camp.

I seem to dream of nothing but missing trains,
losing the only person I've ever loved, who is helpless
    without me,
going about naked, and realizing it with shame,
and, again and again, shitting where I shouldn't – all
    over the place –
rehearsing the agonies, failures and humiliations
of my early life.

After years and years of psychotherapy
and much unraveling of these dreams,
interpretations that were mostly pure speculation,
I woke the other morning
with the absolute conviction that my dreams
had little to do with me, the present me, anymore.

After I told my friend Diana that
my dreams show that the old me

was still inside, had never gone away,
and I was afraid I'd revert to it,
she assured me I wouldn't – and now I believe her.

She thinks that this competent person she knows,
the one that I am now,
is the real me, which of course it is.
I'm pretty capable, and even splendid and admirable,
the way I handle things.

But is the concentration camp survivor
ever sure that it's truly over, that he won't wake up
and find himself back in that horror again?
For nothing was, could be realer than that,
certainly not the pleasant routine of normal life
    regained,
or even this dear one, as dear to me as life itself,
whom I can feed and take care of.

13 JANUARY 2002

Darling Edward –
    I can't resist sending you the *Observer* interview, which
I think gets the book off to a very good start. I'm
especially pleased with the photo. They so rarely reflect
one's idea of oneself – and this one does! Poor old Jane
Bown – and 'old' is the word, she's quite as old as me,
perhaps older – had such a hard time with it. She always

works by natural light, and having laboured her way to
my flat, and then up our stairs, it turned out that in my
sitting room there was no light. It was a terribly gloomy
January morning and my window is small and faces the
evening light, not the morning. So downstairs we had to
go, and then we had to heave the furniture in Barbara's
sitting room around until we got a chair right up by the
window, and then I had to sit in a position that nearly
killed my neck and shoulders (though the strain, luckily,
doesn't show) so that as much of the still-meagre light as
possible was on my face – and still she worried. But what
a good result! She's a famous portrait photographer and
has 'done' everybody who has been anybody in the last
60 years or so, but she's as anxious about each one as
ever she was, and says she's never stopped longing to
hurry away to her studio to see how it's going to come
out – such a nice woman. Actually, it's an honour to be
done by her, but she clearly doesn't think of it like that
for a moment. And charming Kate Kellaway who did the
interview, is a genuine fan of mine, and a fellow Norfolk
woman, so the whole thing was enjoyable.

There isn't quite the fuss being made about this book
as there was about *Stet* – for that I had big interviews in
all the main broadsheets, while this time only in the
Observer and in our local Norfolk paper (very good). But
there have been four interviews for radio, and it's to be
read as 'Book of the Week' on Radio 4. There have also
been some good reviews already (very good in the *Daily
Telegraph* and the *Evening Standard*). However, one big
disappointment looks very likely. At the *Mail on Sunday*
it appears that civil war is going on between Features and

News, and it looks as though Features is losing. Their
extract from the book, though ready to go, fully
illustrated and all, was not published as planned last
Sunday, and I doubt that it will be this Sunday – Features
said that they were 'still hoping' last Wednesday, but I
think in fact they'd have known for sure by then if it was
to be in. They have to pay us, anyway – but it will be
disappointing not to get that extra readership. Otherwise,
however, the omens are good.

I haven't seen Barbara for several days – she took
herself off to Norfolk for the weekend the day before
yesterday, and is going to the opera with friends next
week, so that looks good. And Barry is much less
uncomfortable than I expected after having horrid things
done to his penis. First of all they pushed something up
it, which they said ought to improve the too-frequent
peeing, then they circumcised him – doing both at one
time seemed to me brutal, but can't in fact have been all
that bad. We'd arranged it that he would call me when he
was ready for me to come and pick him up, so I was
waiting by the phone . . . and waiting . . . and waiting . . .
till I got so worried that I telephoned the hospital, and
got no answer. It rang and rang forever. So after half an
hour of that I decided to give it another half an hour,
then go to the hospital to see what was up and though I
was worried that the moment I left he'd probably ring
and then what . . . Then, in the middle of that worry,
plod-plod he came up the stairs, having come home by
bus! 'What were you fussing about?' he said. 'I told you
I'd ring if I needed you.' He was bleeding a bit, and
leaking quite much, so I sped off to buy special

incontinence pads. But he only had to use two of them before both bleeding and leaking stopped, and was cheerfully walking to the library two days later. They did the circumcision because for some time now his foreskin had been most odd – it had sort of stretched, so it dangled loose like a sad finger of a glove with nothing in it, and it was causing him a lot of itching. He'll be much better without it – and I suppose it must be the fact that it stretched like that which made its removal so easy and comparatively painless. Barry is really bad at bearing pain, so the light-hearted way he is taking this must be true, and not heroic, which is a great relief. There's not enough news at the moment to fill another page – so, much love and goodbye for now. Diana

[*note on envelope*] P.S. Your last letter came after this was sealed and stamped. Thank you for the work-in-progress, which I love. xx

22 JANUARY 2002

Darling Edward –

I'm sorry to report that we are going through a really horrid time. Having seemed to come through the doctor's tinkering with his cock very well, Barry began to feel less and less well – got antibiotics from his doctor – was uncharacteristically brave in insisting on 'giving them a chance' when they didn't work, and 10 days after the tinkering had to be rushed to the hospital in agony, having been unable to pee for 24 hours. Or rather, he could pee drops, which made him refuse to believe in a blockage, but the blockage was there, and the accumulation was backing into his kidneys, and he was finally in dreadful pain. The ambulance I called by dialling 999 came at once, and the hospital is nearby, but once in its Accident and Emergency he had to wait *three hours* before being seen by a doctor, and then almost another hour before she reappeared with a catheter, and then she couldn't get it in. So then another hour or so before a second and more experienced doctor came down from the urology ward and managed to get it in after knocking him out with pethidine and gas. It was truly a nightmare seeing him in such agony and being able to do nothing, so what it must have been like for him, being in that agony – !!! After that we had another four hours in Accident and Emergency before they found him a bed, but that was alright because he wasn't in pain anymore.

It's a bad infection, but by today (three days after he went in) it seems obvious that it's responding to an absolute bombardment of antibiotics. His fever is gone, and he's much more like himself – wanted a shower this afternoon, and didn't need all that much help having it. On Monday (two days from now) I think they are going to take out the catheter and see if he can manage without it. If he can't, he's going to have to come home with it. Then they are going to attack the prostate with drugs – and if the drugs fail to reduce it, they will do the big operation.

One good thing is that they found his blood sugar soaring, so he's been on an insulin drip for two days which has brought it down a lot. They think that when he gets home it may prove possible to control it by increasing the drug he is already on, but he may have to go on to insulin injections. 'Oh, Di'll be able to do that,' he said blithely; but I think I'll have to be brutal and insist on his learning to do it himself – otherwise I'd have to give up going to Norfolk for weekends – not to mention the holiday in Ireland which I'm planning when I go to the Galway Book Festival the end of April! He's amazingly bad at doing things – but thousands of people of whom it's true must have managed it, so let's hope! Luckily there's a bus which I catch in Adelaide Road, which stops actually at the Royal Free Hospital. It's exhausting, but less so than I would have expected. It seems to be rather good for one to have to do things.

Which reminds me of your poem – which B likes very much too: the feeling that the incompetent you of the dreams was the real you, to which you might revert. Although I know it was real, I don't think it *was* the original you. I think it was what your parents turned the original you into, and the now you is the rediscovered original. There are people with strong original selves and people with weak ones – that's why some people are undone by abuse in childhood, and some can go through exactly the same degree of abuse and not be undone. You couldn't have written what you've written and loved as you loved if you'd been one of the former. (I'm a bit tired as you can see from the writing).

Did you see the advertisement of *me* which Granta put

in the Jan. 17th *NY Review of Books*? It didn't half cheer
me up to see them putting their money where their
mouth is like that. Still can't quite believe it!

Love. D

8 FEBRUARY 2002

Darling Edward –

The letter in which the cops didn't arrest you for
peeing (thank god!) arrived today. I've been writing you
so many in my head that I've no idea at which stage in
our saga my last real letter left you. Was it just when B
came home from the first examination? Or did it report
our frightful day of emergency – ambulance, agony etc.
etc.? If it didn't, I think I'll spare you that, and the week
in hospital – from which he was supposed to come home
capable of living fairly normally, though still on the
catheter, with a pee-bag strapped to his leg. Since he's
got to exist like that until Feb. 23, when he goes back into
hospital for surgery, it was encouraging to be told that it
needn't stop him from moving about, going to the library
and so on . . . but of course it does!

Partly, I think, this is because his blood sugar remains
much too high, although they have twice increased his
medication (in the hospital it went so high they had to
put him on an insulin drip). But more because quite
often his bladder goes into spasm, which means that he
suddenly feels an urgent need to pee even though the

catheter is draining, which is not only horrid-feeling but also puts him into a panic for fear that it might be the emergency-horror starting up again. The doctor says it won't be that (unless the catheter stops draining) – but B is in a pit of pessimism about the whole thing, and is embracing invalidism wholeheartedly. He's been home nearly a week now, and he's only just started draining his pee-bag by himself – it couldn't be easier! – and doesn't even imagine the possibility of learning to work his little blood-sugar testing instrument. He has, for the last three days, got up and made himself tea and bread-and-butter for breakfast, which is a great advance – but then retires to bed, calls to have a glass of water moved a little nearer, or his light turned on or off. Because from the medical point of view he's supposed not to be helpless, the only help we are given is a visit once a week by the district nurse. I've just got to write off the rest of February, and hope most devoutly that the surgery restores him to viability. It ought to. My brother had it and is perfectly OK now, and Barbara's ex had it (after experiences very like Barry's) and is ditto. And if they finally put him on insulin, as I think they very likely will, they'll just have to teach him to inject himself, as thousands do. It's true I can't imagine him doing it – but I think I can count on myself not to accept the thralldom of being tied down by that.

I continue to get good notices – and letters come in every day, which suggests that a network of grandmothers is passing the news of the book around. They reprinted already. First printing was only 3000, I think, and the reprint is probably 1000, so it doesn't represent a fortune, but it's good news. And Granta USA is doing all my books, in minuscule editions but better than nothing. The US boss was here earlier this week, and I gave B an early supper and went to a lovely Granta dinner party – most enjoyable. I can get out in the evening, and have unbroken nights, so I'm not really too badly off. In fact, everyone at that dinner said how well I was looking.

The great thing about Andrea Ashworth's book [Once In A House On Fire] is to remember that once she escaped – which she did with her mother's encouragement in the end – she was able to soar. I had a lovely long letter from her last week, so happy with her beloved Mark. For a long time she was unable to cook – kitchens made her feel too ill because of the ghastly stepfather who used to beat the children up if they left the least smudge on a plate after doing the dishes. One of the blissful things about Mark, to start with, was that he didn't mind eating off paper plates with plastic knives and forks. But the miracle of moving right away from her background, to their very nice house in Princeton, is that she has started to enjoy her kitchen. Mark still cooks the big things, like joints and salmon, but she is adventuring further every day and has even made an almond cake!! She apologized for reporting such a trivial thing, but I don't think it's trivial at all – it's almost as good news as that she's now writing (she's on a new book) for fun, and not with paroxysms of guilt for such self-indulgence, which she's had to wrestle with a lot. They have time to decide, now, whether to stick with Princeton or move to Berkeley, which is after Mark. Apparently Princeton gives a philosopher more kudos, but Andrea was enchanted by Berkeley as a place. They've both been offered fellowships at an Australian university, but she said a visit to it nearly killed both of them with boredom. By the way, my brother thinks *Yesterday Morning* is quite good, and that I've been 'reasonably discreet'. This morning I had a letter from the little boy in a blue coat with whom my brother and I became friends in the orchard, although we were on the prowl to be enemies, and he says that although he was just five at the time he remembers that day vividly and it was just as I describe it – even remembers the blue coat, which had a black velvet collar.

Do phone Barry one of these days. He'd love it.

Much love, dear hearts, Diana

28 FEBRUARY 2002

Darling Edward –

Writing in bed, hence convenient if inelegant pad. [*Note: lined paper torn out of writing pad.*] Barry is having his op now – indeed it may be just over. He went into hospital five days ago, they took the catheter out to see if he could manage without it and of course he couldn't, and thank god, decided to keep him in, not send him home, for the waiting-for-theatre time. I say thank god, because no sooner was he in than my immune system gave a sigh of relief and said 'At last I can relax!' – and the bugs pounced, so down I went with a savage feverish cold. It wasn't quite flu – though I was deeply grateful to our dear neighbour-across-the-road for doing some necessary shopping for me, I remained able to stagger up and make cups of tea and so on – but it would have been ghastly if I'd had to minister to him. And he, during the wait, was feeling a good deal better because it had turned out that all the extreme discomfort which had made him so helpless during his month at home on the catheter had been due to the fact that they sent him home on a catheter of the wrong size. He'd complained about painful sensations whenever he moved before he left the hospital, and to the district nurse when he was at home, and I described them to his doctor over the phone – and no one had thought that perhaps he'd had too big a tube forced into him (I didn't know that they came in different sizes). They just thought he was being fussy. It was a new little duty doctor on the ward, who had the job of putting him back on a catheter last Saturday, who thought of it when he moaned to her at the prospect of the resulting pain. She said: 'They had you on a size 18 tube – I wonder if you'd feel better on a size 17 inch' – and it was like a miracle, the difference was so great. I'm in such a rage about the callous carelessness shown by everyone else, when the solution was so simple and all any of them needed to do was to take what the patient was saying seriously. God knows it doesn't inspire confidence in the surgeon's team. But it didn't seem like a good idea to throw a wobbly just before they performed an op that obviously has to be done as soon as possible, and there are people in the ward who have just

been 'done' by the team, obviously successfully. But I'm
going to write to his doctor, and to the district nurse's
office, pointing out the results of the error and how easily
they could have been avoided.

I got up yesterday, my temperature having returned to
normal, and this afternoon I shall go up to the hospital to
see how he is getting on. Our great friend Sally Bagenal
will be here over the weekend, so tomorrow I think I may
take the chance to dash off to Norfolk for couple of
days – I've been missing it a lot. Do you know about
Sally? I can't remember if I ever told you that story. It
must be about twenty years ago that Barry was
auditioning actresses for one of his plays which he was
taking to Jamaica, and Sally, this very charming farmer's
daughter from Somerset, got the part. By the time they
got back to England they were sleeping together. It was, I
suppose, about three years after he and I had stopped
having sex, so it didn't worry me, and the more I saw of
Sal the more I realized what an exceptionally nice person
she is. She was living in dreary bedsitters, but spending
most of her time here, so after a while I thought it would
make more sense if she moved in, so she did, and for
four or five years [*six, in fact*] we lived together in a most
harmonious trio, becoming fonder and fonder of each
other. But Sal was beginning to go off the life of a
struggling actress – all those grim auditions, and having
to take boring parts – so when her dad's health began to
fail she decided to take a course in farm management
and then go home to help him. It was quite a blow to
both B and me, but we thought it sensible – by that time
she was more or less like our daughter. So off she went

and on the course she met Henry, and they got married, and their two children, Jessamy and Beachy (short for Beauchamp, which was Henry's father's name) are adorable, and Barry's best beloveds. And by now they own the farm. Henry is as remarkable as Sal – both of them people of really remarkable independence of mind, and generosity, and integrity. So they are like family, and as soon as B feels well enough for the journey, will have him to stay at the farm for recuperation. So that's where we are at the moment. xxx Di

9 MARCH 2002

Darling Edward –

Barry says lugubriously that he has expected nothing but the worst from the beginning of his ordeal. I, alas, allowed myself a glimmer of cheerfulness when at last he was taken down to the cardiology department. Barry was right. It was confirmed that his heart is too groggy to allow an operation under general anaesthetic. So now he is back home and will presumably have to be on a catheter for the rest of his days.

What exactly is wrong with his heart wasn't told – nor whether there is anything that can be done for it. He is returning to the hospital to see his surgeon on Tuesday (two days from now) and we hope to learn more then. Someone did say to him 'You may have been having silent heart attacks' – whatever that may mean. It does seem likely, now, that the degree of fatigue he's been experiencing for some time, which we had attributed to the diabetes, may really have been the result of heart trouble.

He is less depressed than one would expect, for the simple reason that after suffering first a lot of discomfort, and finally great pain, from his catheter, now it's not hurting anymore. They found that it was clogged, and now it isn't. Given that he was in a large ward (though divided up into quite pleasant small rooms, each with four beds) which is entirely devoted to people on catheters, it seems extraordinary that it took them so long to think of this – as it had also taken them ages to start with, to think they had given him one of the wrong size. We have got to find out, in the next few days, who we turn to if it starts hurting again. B takes the line that so long as he's not in pain he doesn't really mind what's wrong with him, and it seems that's true.

I think most people on catheters for life have them inserted through the abdominal wall, and that it's less likely to go wrong that way. But he was told by his surgeon that it's quite a painful operation (done under a local anaesthetic – but they have to cut through a lot of muscle so it's not possible quite to abolish all the pain). And because he's so very sensitive to pain I think he'll refuse to contemplate that method.

I think he's going to need someone younger than I am to look after him! One of his nieces is coming over from Washington in the next few weeks, to give me a few days rest in Norfolk. Then his brother is coming, who will be a big help. And for the last two weeks of April, when I go off on my Irish caper, Sally will have him. I'm going to feel out the nieces – he has two in Washington, both quite well off and one who also has a house complete with housekeeper in Jamaica. They are both fond of him, and he of them. It is possible, I think, that one or both of them would accept the task. I can manage now, but am not likely to for much longer – I woke up at three a.m. last night to quite a bad attack of anxiety, and although I felt better come daylight, I don't think it was really unjustified; once one is nearly halfway though one's 80s one can fold up quite suddenly. It is really depressing to think in such terms – but probably better to do so than just go bumbling on – provided, of course, that an alternative does exist. It would have to be Jamaica, I suppose, not Washington – he couldn't possibly afford to be ill in the US.

Barbara goes off tomorrow with her merry band of Norfolk friends, to a cruise in the Far East! Two weeks – and a 'bargain' flight to Hong Kong to start with. She had thought the pain in her leg was much better – said today 'I thought it really was the result of the damage done by the treatment.' But today it has suddenly gone back to being as bad as ever. 'Such a bore!' she said. God knows how she'll get through the journey. It's impossible to imagine two people more unlike each other when it comes to bearing pain than our two Bs. Sorry to have only gloomy news – it's a relief to be able to unload it. Much love. D

18 APRIL 2002

Darling Edward,

I've been trying to call you in Paris, and get nothing but that maddening voice saying 'the number you have dialled has not been recognized'! Am not sure that I ought to communicate sudden good news in case the gods punish such hubris by slamming everything into reverse.

Last night Barry (in hospital), his brother Lloyd (staying with me) and Sally (up here for the night) were in pits of gloom not to say hysteria, because everything was going wrong and the doctor seemed pretty well certain that when he had an angioplasty today it would reveal that he'd have to have a triple by-pass, which would mean waiting months for his prostate op – if he ever had it . . . so at midnight Lloyd, Sal and I were still up, desperately discussing what to do if this, and what to do if that, and what to do if the other. Well Barry, getting more and more frantic, kept phoning from his bed and ordering us to do wild things like call hospitals in the USA and find out what operations cost. In fact, after the last dreadful catheter crisis (a week ago), his doctor had said quite calmly 'we will now keep you in here until you've had an angioplasty, and if you pass that test we will operate at once', so we ought just to have been waiting quietly and touching wood, but what with one thing and another, pessimism had got out of control (largely, I'm sorry to say, because of my two dear supporters, Sally and Lloyd, who both have an appetite for melodrama which combined with Barry's appetite for the Worst, and produced franticness).

Anyway, today, at four p.m., he had his angioplasty. And he passed the test! Oh my dears, *the relief.* The double relief, because not only does it mean that he'll have the op within days (that is what it's so dangerous to say!), but also that his heart, although wobbly, is not nearly so bad as they thought.

Weeks ago, when we saw his surgeon who told us nothing could be decided until after Easter, I said to myself 'Life being what it is, whatever the decision is it is bound to coincide with my long and eagerly awaited excursion to Ireland' and sure enough, it does! I leave on Sunday (today is Friday) – but for only a week, not the two weeks I'd originally hoped for. And Lloyd is here, fully prepared to cope. So I don't feel too bad about going. And when I got home from the hospital this evening, as I got out of the car Primrose Hill put on a sudden display of brilliant green and gold against a purple thundercloud, and an enormous and magnificent rainbow suddenly arched over it – which can only be, I think, a Good Omen. It's the first rainbow I've ever seen in London.

Can it really be that when I get back a week from this coming Monday he'll have had his op and this seemingly endless ordeal will be on its way out?

To be continued in our next.

Love

28 MAY 2002

Darling Edward –

How strange to learn that we were both being
demoralized at the same time. There were you, thrown
by the disappearance of your publisher – and indeed
what a dreadful shock that lovely Black Sparrow, which
has made such splendid books of your work, should be
gone! – and there was I, suddenly in a pit of gloom
about Barry's lack of recovery plus – in one particularly
gruesome week – Hannah being savaged by a vile dog in
the park so that on top of everything else I had to rush
her to the vet. You were beyond writing; I wrote such a
wail of a letter that no sooner was it written then I knew
I couldn't send it (getting it written was quite a help,
though). And now you are perking up, just from sheer
braveness as far as I can see, and I am doing the same
because B has actually got out of bed and cooked
himself one of his famous Jamaican chicken dishes!
Admittedly he hasn't stayed out of bed – but surely it
must be a good sign?

The really good thing is that at last I have done
something I should have done long ago: hauled him out
of bed and dragged him to see my doctor, instead of his.
He had been on the books of an old woman doctor for
years and years, long before we started living together,
and was stubbornly loyal to her. And I think she was
OK for a long time (he was hardly ever in the least bit
ill, so didn't need her anyway), but around the time of
his op on April 23 I began to have to go to her surgery

quite often to collect prescriptions, and at first I thought
in a daft way: 'What a nice civilized surgery – one never
has to wait', but fairly quickly it began to occur to me
that a doctor's surgery where there was never anyone
but me was – to say the least – a bit odd. And then,
whenever we needed to ask her something, she wasn't
there: 'Doctor won't be here until tomorrow afternoon'
and so on, every time. There was an assistant doctor,
but he was usually out, too (and when available was
very dim). And then, at a point of extreme crisis, when
Lloyd and I had on our hands an hysterical Barry
because he was having what he was sure was a bowel
blockage (Lloyd, his brother, was staying with us) – the
assistant was 'on holiday' and about the old woman all
her receptionist could say was 'I do not know when she
will be coming in – at present there is *no doctor* at this
surgery.' – 'So what can we do?' – 'All I can suggest is
you go to the hospital.' – 'We've done that, and they say
go to your doctor.' – 'Well, I'm sorry, but I can't help
you.' It turned out that the bloody woman had not even
opened a letter about Barry's diabetes sent her from the
hospital (over the phone we forced the receptionist to go
and find it in the doc's office, and open it and read it to
us) – and at that point B's loyalty collapsed. My doc has
said he'll take him on and he's already been given a
proper blood test for diabetes, and an eye-test
connected with it, and next week, with the results in
hand, my doc is going to adjust his medication (or
perhaps even put him on insulin – I don't know) – and
let's hope that he will at last start feeling more or less
normal again. Up till now, all he's been doing (apart

from eating) is lying gazing into space – not even reading or watching telly. Lloyd, who has been a great blessing, looking after him when I went to Ireland for a week, and had three glorious weekends in Norfolk, went back to Jamaica two days ago in a great gloom, saying that B was exactly like their brother Carol was just before he died a year ago.

But I'm pretty certain, now that the trouble is basically his diabetes, that if he can get the proper treatment for it he'll respond. The operation has worked OK and the wound has healed at last – it took a long time. The key appointment with my doc, when the results of the tests will be in, is on June 7, so by the time you get to London we'll know where we stand. (There was, by the way, no bowel blockage: that turned into black farce – but very exhausting for one and all.)

Am just about to listen to my tape – thank you for sending it. It will be so lovely to see you.

XXX

Di

II JULY 2002

Darling Edward,

I hope you enjoy *The Radetzky March* and its little sequel. Can't guess whether you will or not. I started off feeling only mildly interested, but Roth has gradually crept up on me until now I'm pretty well addicted.

It's so sad that you are no longer just a little way across town – I keep feeling that you must be.

Barry got back yesterday, and although he says that he still wants to flop into bed and sleep all day, he is undoubtedly a bit better than he was. Today he got up and went out to buy Barbara some flowers, without it seeming extraordinary, and this evening he asked me what I thought of Claire Bloom's account of her marriage to Philip Roth, and said 'My god, what a bastard'. That may not sound much like a feast of reason and a flow of soul – but I can assure you that it's four months since we had an exchange so nearly approaching it! And he's looking more like himself too. He has an appointment with the doctor in five days time, when I hope he'll hear the results of the latest blood test. If only he can have a bit more energy restored to him, we'll be back to normal.

In our Norfolk village a man has opened a little gallery on the walls of which are hung a few pictures at the very bottom end of what is hangable on a wall, and has announced in the Parish Magazine that he gives lessons in painting and watercolours. Whereupon I remembered that the few times I've tried to use watercolours I've ended up with a puddle of mud. This man's watercolours are not puddles of mud. The colours are clear and fresh looking. So it occurred to me that he is exactly the person I need to take lessons from; he will be able to teach me the absolute beginner's stuff – which colours you mix in order to get the colour you want, and so on – and whether you start a painting with the lights or the darks – the ABC of the method. So last Saturday

evening we had my first lesson – not doing anything, just
me asking him questions with a paintbox in front of us,
and he demonstrating things from time to time, and then
giving me a list of exactly what I must buy. So I came
back to London and bought the things, and today I did
my first exercise – copying a colour photo of a landscape,
not in order to make a picture but simply to see if I could
match the colours. And lo! I have done it, and it's not a
puddle of mud!!!! In fact, I suspect that I've got all that I
need to be taught out of him in that first session, and that
now all I need is to work at it by myself – one learns to
paint by doing it, once one has been shown what to do. I
fancy the idea of being able to do watercolours. In the
days before photography and postcards every halfway
educated person knew how. Off you went on your
holiday with your little sketchbook in your pocket as a
matter of course. My great-great-great-aunt Julie had a
sketchbook about six inches by three inches, which I've
seen. Faced with a vast panorama of Swiss mountains,
did she quail? No, indeed not. She just sat down and
ripped off a tiny watercolour of it, and very well too,
without for a moment thinking of herself as 'an artist' –
and she was one of the thousands of such people. So I do
not despair, now the ice has been broken for me, of being
like her.

    Love and love

    Diana

[*Alas, this hopeful start came to nothing. I did achieve one
watercolour that was quite good, and then the impulse fizzled
out.*]

4 AUGUST 2002

Darling Edward –

I hope your news is as good as ours is – by 'good', I mean that nothing horrible has happened, the weather is lovely, and we are able to enjoy nice things when they happen.

Barry is really a good deal better. He still spends most of his time lying in bed, watching sport when he isn't snoozing – but then, that's what he was mostly doing before the prostate crisis in February. The improvement is that since his trip to Jamaica he gets up and goes to the library or the corner shop quite often – and last week he pottered off to see a very old friend of his with whom he has had a mild fucking relationship for years, since her marriage broke up. I've always marvelled at her good humour, because she never appeared to resent the fact that he would turn up at fairly wide intervals simply for the purpose of having a quick poke, though I think there was usually a token cup of coffee, and sometimes even lunch, to make a social occasion out of it. This time, after a gap of about five months, there was not even a cup of coffee. He reports that he got an erection but that he couldn't feel anything, so he came away at once. When I asked if she had minded this total disregard of her as a person, he looked cross and said 'No'. I hope that's true.

My restored freedom has rather gone to my head, and I've reverted to coming here (Norfolk) every weekend, and have taken passionately to painting. Did I tell you that I'd found someone here to give me lessons in water-colours? He's giving me exactly what I wanted: the very simplest sort of technical tip. For instance, yesterday he positively changed my life by showing me how, if I changed the way I held my brush or pencil, it would become quite easy to draw sweeping lines and curves which went where I wanted them to go. As a result of his tuition my second finished work is quite clear and bright (instead of the disgusting little mud-puddle I made to start with) and has one or two passages which look quite technically accomplished. It's rather odd, though, to have painted something which, if someone gave it to me, would fill me with embarrassment because I couldn't possibly bring myself to hang it anywhere so would have to hurt the donor's feelings! I have to remind myself that it is only my second attempt. But what worries me is that it's not embarrassing because it's badly done – it's rather well done, considering – but because it's such a boring little picture! It looks like an illustration for a slightly down-market children's book. Help! *Is that the kind of eye I have?*

Break for returning to London, where I found your letter. I don't think I know anyone over 65 who has not got high blood pressure: join the club, my love. Speaking for my own, it was so alarmingly high when first detected that the doc sent me home with instructions to go up and down stairs as little as possible, and on no account to strain when attempting to shit – better constipation than a stroke – this extra care to be taken for at least a week until he could see whether the pill he's prescribed was working. Well, it was, and has gone on doing so. That was three years ago, I think, and regular checks have shown my b.p. to be fine ever since. So thank heaven yours has been identified. I'm sure it's a good thing to have a thorough check, because – despite your belief in the body's ability to heal itself – it is a fact that a little chemical help, sensibly applied, can make the difference between illness and health. I look pretty healthy, don't I? And I feel it. But I wouldn't if I didn't take three pills every day, one for stomach ulcer, one for b.p., one (¼ of an aspirin – it hardly counts!) for angina. Sometimes I've tested the stomach one by leaving it off, and it takes only about a week for the acid to get to work on the gut-lining and the pains to begin. I haven't tested the others, because the results of doing so might be a bit too conclusive! All of which is to say that you will probably feel much better when properly medicated.

Oh dear, one's poor old sick friends! Not so long ago I was shocked when a lively 90-year-old woman of my acquaintance said 'I'm so bored by all my friends – they've got so old' – but now I know just what she meant! And so, poor you, do you!!

But last week I made a new, much younger, friend. Not that he'll be much use to me, since he lives in Tokyo. From which he called me, two weeks ago, to invite me to lunch, because he's mad about *Stet* and has much enjoyed a letter I wrote refusing to write a contribution for a scholarly mag he edits for a Japanese university. He's most odd, this skittish and distinctly dishy son of an alcoholic Irish squire, took off for Japan fifteen years ago 'simply as an adventure', has lived there ever since, thinks in Japanese by now, and has become the editor of a publication (exquisitely elegant) devoted to Irish literature and language (Erse, or Gaelic, or whatever they call it) written for and almost entirely by scholarly Japanese nuts. Their unbelievably pedantic papers are translated into English for the mag – why? Who is supposed to read it? What does a Japanese university gain by it? The poems are mostly translated by the editor, who is himself a poet. (Some of the poems are splendid.) He wanted a piece by me about Irish writing – and having sent me a copy of the mag ensured that he wouldn't get one, because I could no more write something that would interest these mad scholars than I could fly. When I asked him what they are like he said 'Odd. Very. You would not want to have lunch with them.'

But I adored having lunch with him – largely because, when we met, he said 'But you are such a surprise – I've just read your book about that Egyptian, and he described you as an absurd looking old spinster, – and you are *beautiful*!' Is there a reverse form of that revolting term 'a fag hag'? Because if so, Peter's – 'a hag fag': he's obviously a connoisseur of old women. He's tremendously funny, full of mad enthusiasms, very open and warm. One of his most beloved hags is a vastly distinguished Irish woman (a scholar of about six medieval languages) who married a Japanese diplomat and who, on becoming widowed, was invited by the Emperor to become an official in the Imperial Household – the first woman and the first foreigner ever to hold such a post. She it was who discovered *Stet*, when on a visit to Paris, and she introduced Peter to it – and, I gather, many of the Crème de la Crème of Japanese Society! I am, it seems, quite the thing among them.

Peter has an ex-wife who lives in Edinburgh (apparently, she thought she wouldn't mind her husband being gay, but in the end it didn't work, though they are still great friends). He says she's a wonderfully creative woman who makes the most beautiful things out of whatever she lays her hands on, and that we must must must must meet when I'm there next week, so he's given me her number, and has called her ... Under the influence of his enthusiasm I got home from lunch much looking forward to meeting her, but by now I've realized that the poor woman will probably be thinking 'Oh god! Not another of Peter's impetuosities', because impetuosities are obviously what he is much given to. But I'll probably risk it, nevertheless. [*I didn't.*]

I'll write and report on Edinburgh when I get back. Oh yes – and my third watercolour, done during the weekend, is much less shaming, hurrah hurrah!

With much love, and my fingers are crossed to knotting point for the success of your high b.p. treatment.

XXOXX
Diana

15 SEPTEMBER 2002

Darling Edward –

For a terrible moment just now, I thought there was no

pen in this house! Barbara has gone back to London ahead of me – no pen in my handbag, none in the desk, none in the kitchen, none up in my bedroom ... Of course it wouldn't matter in the least if I didn't write to you – or to anyone else – today, but it gave me a moment of near panic, having nothing to write with. What a creature of words I am! I wonder if you would react in the same way if your computer packed up and you had no pen? This one – rather a nice one – was lurking in the kitchen after all.

The only nice thing that's happened is that BBC Radio 4 is doing a programme in December called 'A Letter to Myself' – or rather, three half-hour programmes – in which a memoir writer takes a moment of crisis in his/her young life and writes a letter to the young self who experienced that crisis. They are using me, and Andrea Ashworth, and (they think) Christopher Logue. I've written mine and have just heard from the producer that it's 'perfect' – I bet she says that to all of us, but still it's cheered me up! I thought at first 'what a phoney idea!' but in the end rather enjoyed doing it. But am now hard put to it to tell whether the quite touching piece I produced represents my true feelings, or a newly discovered knack for turning out touching radio pieces! I'm coming to the conclusion that real fame would be appallingly corrupting, given the qualms that can result from insy-tinsy-mini fame! My ability to make an audience beam at me because I'm so nice seems to me deeply suspect! I suppose the sensible thing is just to enjoy it while given the chance. I'm sure you make audiences beam at you, too, but have the sense not to get your knickers in a twist about it.

All the war-mongering going on is so sickening that I can hardly bring myself to read a newspaper any more. There never seems to be a photograph of anything in NY without a Stars & Stripes being brandished in it – not, of course, that it necessarily implies warlike feelings in the brandishers, but it's worrying. I've not spoken to a single person here who doesn't shudder at Blair's support for Bush, but that doesn't seem to prevent a fatalistic feeling that we'll have to go along with it, so the Brits are just as sickening as the Yanks, even if they don't brandish Union Jacks. Yuk and yuk again.

09.16.02 At that point it became time to go to bed, and this morning I got back to find your letter, with its brilliant idea about Bleecker Street Press. Oh I do hope you resurrect it! And how very gratifying to do a gig that pays a thou! I thought the £400 I am getting for my *Letter To Myself* was quite good, but now it seems very mere!

What did I notice on the way home, having just said we don't brandish Union Jacks, but a demure little house in Hendon (a northern suburb through which I drive) on the forecourt of which was planted a flagpole flying a Union Jack of a size suitable to Buckingham Palace, and lower down on the pole was a board with the proud announcement THE BRITISH HERNIA CENTRE. Now there's food for thought! What happens at a hernia centre? If an American, a French or a Javan hernia turned up would it be refused entrance? Could a hernia centre situated in a London suburb be anything but British? It joins my two other Favourite Things on my journey between London and Norfolk. One of them, painted high on a wall in a particularly seedy stretch of the route, where any reference to Shakespeare however indirect is the last thing one would expect, is the advertisement (the wall belongs to a very shabby little beautician's establishment): 'Now is the winter of our Discount Tans'. My guess about that is that the business is probably run by Indians and a British-educated son or daughter has contributed this touch of sophistication. And the second is a small shop in the Finchley Road which declares itself to be 'Jews for Jesus' in big letters, and underneath, in smaller ones, 'the Messiah Has Come'. Does 'Jews for Jesus' exist elsewhere, or is it a North London phenomenon? It's by a traffic light, so I've quite often studied it. It has the sort of shop window display made of cardboard boxes over which someone has draped a piece of shiny magenta nylon, with hand-written notices propped against it, and although there's usually a light on inside, I've never seen anyone there. I long to know if they've ever made any converts, but shall never go in to find out.

Your possible visit to London is yet another reason to pray for peace! Oh god! To think that here we are, having to force ourselves to try to believe in the reality of this totally insane situation.

Love and love. Does 'Jews for Jesus' exist elsewhere? [*It seems that it does.*]

16 OCTOBER 2002

Dearest Edward –

I'm very flattered that you and Neil are 'collecting' my letters, and yes, it would amuse me to see them eventually, because they must cover a lot of happenings. I'm delighted that they make you laugh. God knows that anything that raises a laugh is valuable at the moment, and that must be even more true for you, living in the eye of the storm so to speak, than it is for us. The only thing I can find to be thankful for is that at least you two can't be conscripted!

I'm sorry I forgot to report on Edinburgh. I had a lovely time. Flew up and spent the night before with old friends. They ferried me to my hotel the next morning, and of course attended my Event, bursting with pride. Coming, as they do, from the very earliest reaches of my life (he figures in *Yesterday Morning* as a small boy in a blue coat stumping away through an orchard with my brother and me in pursuit, and then becoming, up an apple-tree, one of our best friends) they added a pinch of something special to my success. Because the Event was a success. I was, to my surprise, billed as a solo turn, not as part of a discussion on memoir-writing which was what I had expected, and the tent – a big one – was sold out. The audience was expecting to enjoy itself, and did (this seems often to be true of audiences at British book fiestas) – which meant, of course, that the speaker enjoyed herself too. And afterwards, when we all trooped off to the enormous central selling tent (this was the

ritual end of all Events) I had to sign copies till my hand
ached – they said I sold over 100 copies! An enormous
and very beautiful Georgian square called Charlotte
Square was entirely dedicated to the book part of the
festival, and had become a city of very large tents
connected by canopied walkways. It was always teeming
with people. In the corner a most odd tent shaped like a
giant Yurt and furnished with oriental carpets and
cushions was the authors' gathering and refreshment
place – a handy sort of dropping-in place where one was
welcome at any time. My friends Carole Angier
(biographer of Jean Rhys and Primo Levi) and Hilary
Spurling (biographer of Matisse and Ivy Compton
Burnett) were there, each to do their own thing the next
day, so we dined together at my very swish hotel, which
was fun – tho' my energy rather gave out after that, so I
didn't go on with them to sample the Fringe into the
small hours – which would have been even more fun.
And the next day, before going to my friends' events, I
decided to do what I really wanted to do so instead of
attending any part of the festival. I had an Orgy of
wonderful picture-seeing. Edinburgh has great galleries –
the National Gallery, the Portrait Gallery, and the
Gallery of Modern Art. I meant to visit all three, but was
so carried away by the Gallery of Modern Art (really one
of the best in Europe, I think) that I only managed a part
of the National Gallery as well before having to return to
Charlotte Square. It's a lovely city – absolutely a city, yet
so small that sometimes, when you look down a street,
you see mountains, or the sea, at the end of it. I would
happily have stayed there much longer, but the Festival

only pays for one's hotel for one night, and a mere one night extra cost so much that I staggered under the shock! Anyway, I can't really leave B alone for more than three days or so. He's all right at present – but I have to admit that I'm pretty depressed about him. He has withdrawn so completely from life. He never actually listens to a word I say – and that extends to other people, too. The other day a friend called him and tried to persuade him to meet her somewhere, and when the conversation ended I said, 'What did she want you to do?' – 'I don't know,' he said. 'But you've just been talking to her about it!' – 'I didn't listen.' He reads quite a lot now, besides watching sport – but never anything but accounts of murders – real ones, not fiction. It's quite a big genre – boringly written (almost always) accounts of famous murders. Reading nothing but those is surely a bit creepy? And anything other people talk about as being interesting, he dismisses as worthless. Carole's book about Primo Levi, which he hasn't read (he long ago dismissed Primo Levi as 'having nothing to say') has been getting mixed reviews – some raves, two (and those two, alas, important ones) vicious. I told him the other day that poor Carole was shaken because she'd had a real stinker in the *London Review of Books*, and he perked up at once and asked to see it. I hadn't got it. A week later he asks me 'Which issue of the LRB was Carole's bad review in? I want to get it.' Only at the prospect of despising something can he feel a little cheerful! It does mean, alas, that in terms of companionship there's not much left of us.

But one of my worries about him has been eased

recently. His niece Margaret (the one-time Ambassador's wife) came to stay a week ago, and said that she wanted to have a talk with me about the future, because I wouldn't be able to go on looking after him indefinitely. This has been worrying me, too. I can't count on continuing to drive a car for many more years, and I'm already unable to walk more than three or four hundred yards, and can't carry heavy things ... It won't be all that long before I'm hard put to it to look after myself! So it was a great relief when Margaret said that she'd been thinking about this, so she was having a little extension to her house in Jamaica made habitable, where there is always a housekeeper and also a man who has been working for her for 30 years, and she herself goes there quite often – and that she intends to dedicate this to Barry. She says she has a good doctor there, and his brother Lloyd and his sister are nearby ... Her idea is that he should go out there for another visit in the new year, and stay there longer this time, so that he can get used to the idea of perhaps being there all the time in the future. He won't like the idea – he always impatiently dismisses as nonsense any mutterings of mine about getting old! But still, it is a comfort to know that if I really feel I can't cope any longer, he has somewhere to go. Sally has always said she'll take him, but I'm not quite sure that she could, really. Anyhow, one way or another he'll be cared for. And I know that I can send out an SOS if the pressure becomes intolerable. Which, of course, it is far from being while I can still go pottering off on my own from time to time.

End of paper, end of letter ... but no end of lots and lots of love
Diana

7 NOVEMBER 2002

Darling Edward,

It's wonderful to have a fellow-carer to beef to, who talks sense back. Neil's addiction to real life crime cheers me a lot.

You'll have had your physical by the time you get this – my fingers are tightly crossed. A week from today I'm having a biopsy on a tiny thing on the bridge of my nose which they say may be an incipient rodent ulcer. It's so minuscule that I don't see why they were bothering, but my doctor said that while a rodent ulcer that is dealt with at an early stage is gone for good, if allowed to develop 'it's a really horrible thing.' – 'Horrible in what way?' – 'It can eat away a whole face, even the eyes.' – Yuk! Reach for that scalpel, quick!

The other day I wrote 600 words about a biography (very dull) of Brian Moore for the *Evening Standard* – and got a cheque today for £400. I really must try to stir myself up to get more reviewing from papers that pay, rather than just waiting for the odd commission from the dear old *Oldie*, which pays £85 for something like half a page! Last week the *Sunday Times* mag devoted all of itself to what famous people are earning – page after page of White Trash earning millions – or rather making millions because few of them could be described as earning anything. It's obviously easy to earn millions if you press the right buttons, so one should be ashamed of not even earning hundreds. Yet a feeling of deep fatigue overwhelms me at even the thought of doing anything about it. What a Pity.

Now now – don't let a beautiful autumn become an omen! We've had lots of beautiful autumns since 1939. If those fuckers plunge us into war, let us at least enjoy good weather if we get it.

xxxxx
Diana

30 NOVEMBER 2002

Daring Edward,

I'm glad nothing worse turned up in your medical overhaul. I've been on medication for high blood pressure for about five years, and no side effect has ever made itself felt, in spite of all those ominous warnings they always feel bound to include in the packaging, so I think you can reasonably expect to be equally lucky. I suppose it depends on which of the various drugs you've been given – but on the whole, most of the many people who have to take them seem to get by quite well. But no red meat and no butter – of all the sobering prospects, that's one of the most!! Why not make it very nearly no,

rather than utterly no? i.e. about once every month or six
weeks get yourself a small but particularly exquisite piece
of fillet steak and eat it almost raw? That's what I do
(though the reason I eat very nearly no red meat is
because I've gone off it, not because it's verboten – but
the need sometimes seizes me, nevertheless, and then
how I enjoy that delicious little treat). I expect you'll feel
the better for your austere diet, anyway.

Alas, but I'm sure we'd get no joy from Granta about
my letters to you. I've got to write to Ian Jack about
something else next week so will ask him – but don't get
hopes up. [*I didn't approach him in the end – it was only
later when I saw the transcription that I approached
Granta.*]

Barry seems to be a good deal better, though he still
spends most of the day in bed. But when he gets up he
does quite testing things, like going into Camden Town
to buy Jamaican food from a little shop someone told
him about, and his blood sugar level isn't too bad. But I
still touch wood every time I think he's better, because
with diabetes you never know.

xxx Diana

29 DECEMBER 2002

Darling Edward –

I'd like to see a statistical study done of this subject –
but have you ever known of a serious domestic

emergency occurring on a Monday morning, with a week of working days stretching conveniently ahead? I never have.

In the night of Dec. 20, which had been a Friday, at 3.30 a.m. I – who was in the 48th hour of a bout of flu – woke up to an odd sensation. Which, it turned out, was caused by the dripping of rain water onto my prostrate body. From the ceiling of my bedroom. Next morning I was at least able to speak to Len Jones. Len is all but the property of Hilary Bach, who lives six houses along from us. For years and years he's done all the Bachs' building, plumbing and electrical things – but very occasionally as a huge privilege, the Bachs allow friends to borrow him. This time Len quite saw the urgency, and said that if the Bachs had not yet gone off to Oxford to stay with their daughter for Xmas, he could get out onto their roof and walk along the intervening roofs to ours (to which, as he knows, our house offers no access) with a tarpaulin, which would keep out the rain until the end of the Winter Break. (All London builders and scaffolders take a complete two week break at Christmas, which they observe as strictly as any Muslim observes Ramadan.) Need I tell you that the Bachs had left for Oxford the day before!

So – I moved my bed into my sitting room, put buckets in place, and concentrated hard on getting over my flu by Monday, the 23rd, when I was due to go to Norfolk to stay with my brother. Which I managed to do, give or take the odd fit of coughing – and my darling nephew Phil drove my car for me on the evening of the 23rd, and we gave Charlie a lift, and thus began a lovely

Christmas break during which I was able not to think
even once about my bedroom ceiling.

Barry reports that it's got no worse. He's been having a
very West Indian Xmas, which started with a visit to
Brixton market from which he returned laden with exotic
foods – isn't it marvellous that he's suddenly become able
to face such excursions? The last time he visited the
hospital it was because he had been summoned (to our
surprise) to the heart clinic. He was his usual clueless
self, when he got back, about what had been said to him,
but he did know that he'd been prescribed some new
pills, and he has been taking them. I think the
improvement in his energy is the result. And
simultaneously an old friend, ex-wife of one of his
school-fellows, got in touch and told him about sources
of Caribbean food.

I've moved on from my brother's to our house, where
Barbara has been over Xmas, and we have both been
asked to a couple of parties this weekend. It's deliciously
quiet in this house, after all the *va et vient* at my
brother's. This Christmas only three grandsons were
there, but they have lots of friends. Everyone was very
loving and amusing, and I had a lovely time, but a bit of
silence is not unwelcome. It was amazingly beautiful on
the coast, where he lives – a strange, shifting coastline. A
few hundred years ago the sea came right up to where
their village is, but now there's a good half-mile of
marsh-land between the village and the sea, and beyond
that a long, low stretch of dunes.

It was warm, with lovely sunny mornings – exquisite
light, the sea a deep blue for once (usually, there, the

colour of gravy) with magical mother-of-pearl effects. Two years ago my sister-in-law gave Andrew a tree-house for his 80th birthday – there's some kind of pine tree near their house, and you climb forty sturdy steps (with good hand-rails) up to the little house perched in it, and it really is magic up there. When I heard about it I thought 'what a waste of money!' – but the truth is, it was an enchantingly poetic idea on her part, astonishing in someone famous for a positively Monumental Practicality (which she has needed, raising four boys on a pittance. She has never in her life had any help of any sort in her house, doing all the decorating and so on herself – and when they were young even making the boys' clothes. A heroic woman. She still thinks nothing of having forty people in for supper after the Carol service.).

Charlie impressed me greatly this Christmas. His mother has a bad knee, which gives her a lot of pain, and her heart is in a dicey condition. She refuses to give an inch to either condition, and my selfish old brother is all too ready to ignore anything amiss unless it's forced on him. The way Charlie joked and wheedled her out of the kitchen and into an armchair, and then did a lot of work without appearing to do so, was masterly – so kind, and so clever. He is a dear person. And she, in addition to her astounding energy and practicality, is often very funny – and she has a wonderful eye for pretty things. My lucky old brother chose well.

Several fans rolled up with books for me to sign. I always feel that Barbara rather disapproves of such manifestations (she has always disliked autobiographical writing, and I suspect makes no exception for mine!).

But my brother and sister are delightfully proud of me, which I like very much.

Back to London the day after tomorrow. Oh dear, I wish our house wasn't so tall and didn't have parts of it sticking out behind – you can't get to the roof just with a ladder. Scaffolding costs fortunes. Perhaps it would be cheaper to take down the ceiling in my bedroom and get at the roof from inside: Oh well, we'll have to see.

Happy New Year (I don't see why it shouldn't be OK at a personal level) to both of you, my dears.

Love and love
Diana

I JANUARY 2003

Darling Edward –

Found Robert's [*Robert Friend's*] poems when I got home yesterday. Love them – more and more as he got older. Want to have his last one on my gravestone.

Have found five typos, for when (d.v.) it gets reprinted.

P. 56, 2nd stanza – should surely be dirtied, not dirties?

P. 61, first line – Of only should be If only.

P. 128, third stanza – who hands on you should be who hangs on you.

P. 155, second stanza. I think of rain should be oh rain, as he is addressing it?

Will give it to B today – I'm not sure that he'll read, he seemed a bit low today.

Barbara to her grief, is not writing about the Middle East nowadays because the *Economist*, under a new editor, has gone hawkish which she abominates. She says she's not walking out only because they'd like her to. For the Xmas number she wrote a long and excellent piece about dogs! (They go frivolous for Xmas Day.) Her piece was serious in a way – about how humans have manipulated dogs genetically through the ages – but was entertaining too. She's really very good, and it's a sad waste that she's always worked for a paper which allows no byline. (Though she was allowed her name on that special feature she did on Iran, as an extraordinary exception.)

Charlie will be coming round soon, bringing things I left behind by accident at his parents' house. I'll get you his e-mail address then. He's quite impossible to get on the phone, even though he has a mobile – the most elusive customer.

I'm beginning to look forward to reading my letters! Hope the reality isn't a great let down after your kind enthusiasm. xxxxx

D

21 JANUARY 2003

Darling Edward –

I'm enclosing a rambling letter which I wrote when I was in Norfolk last weekend – and by the way, yes of course you must drive there with me if you want to visit that old man. It will be fun. But this letter is really about my letters, which I found when I got back here.

Heavens! What a labour you've undertaken!! I'd no idea I'd covered so much paper to you. I must confess to enjoying them now. They recall so much, and sometimes I'm quite struck by how good they are! But I think that trying to get one's own letters published would be very unseemly. There's a good reason for publishing an autobiographical book – one is trying to get to the bottom of experiences which may be relevant to other people. But to publish one's private conversation, which is what letters are – what could that be but saying 'Hey – look at me!' and there are two other reasons against it – the first, that it would make me self-conscious in the future when I wrote to you, feeling that I wasn't just talking to you but was writing for possible publication. And the second, which is very important, is that a book of my letters would be pointless without yours – would be only half the conversation – and I haven't kept yours. I know I ought to have. How I have kicked myself for not having kept Alfred's and Jean's – I ought to have learned my lesson. But I'm not, and I've never been, a keeper – I think because I and my friends wrote so many letters to each other when we were young that it really was just like talking, so letters are fixed in my mind as being talking, and thus ephemeral. One listens, one responds, one goes on to the next bit . . . I did, when young, keep love letters, but not anything else.

I'll tell you what . . . if I die before you, which I ought to do, my letters are yours to do what you like with (I think the legal position re letters is that the letter as a physical object belongs to the person it was written to, but the contents of the letter are the writer's copyright?). You, after my death, will have copyright as well as possession of objects – I bequeath it to you herewith – so any possibility (probably, alas, very remote) of making a few pennies from the letters will be yours. But not until after I die. I think, that way, I can avoid self-consciousness, since it will mean that the letters are now just another of the many things over which, once dead, I'll have no control, so there's no point in fussing about them.

Must now speed to the post office with my Income Tax Return for the year ending last April, which I forgot about completely because of Barry's illness, and which has now reached the last possible minute before Grave Trouble ensues – somebody has advised that I should include a fat cheque with it in order to avoid Penalties – help!

OOXXOOXX

D

9 FEBRUARY 2003

Darling Edward,

We are, alas, back in the wars – not, thank god, as badly so as it first seemed, but still a worry. Four days ago Barry had a stroke. I came back from a visit to a skin clinic where I'd just been told that I'd got to have radiation on my nose of all places, and thought 'Really, he is too self-centred' when he made no response to this news – he was lying in bed, facing away from me as he usually is when not sitting in his chair with a book or watching the telly. Then he said, very slowly in a muffled voice, 'There is something wrong.' And when I asked what he meant, he couldn't answer. He could bring out, laboriously, the first word of a sentence, and then stuck, looking very distressed and pressing his hand over his left eye.

As you can imagine, I flew to the phone – and we were extremely lucky in that the doctor came at once. She was with us within 15 minutes. It soon became obvious that he knew perfectly well what he was being asked, or shown, and was struggling to make sensible answers, but just couldn't get the words to come out – and his blood pressure was so high that it almost gave the doctor a stroke. So she called an ambulance for us, and alerted the hospital, and back we trundled to Accident and Emergency in the Royal Free Hospital, where we spent so hideously much of last year.

This time, although I was there with him for four hours before he was found a bed, it was not so bad, because he was being attended to all the time, being given tests and so on. And by the time I left it already seemed to me that he was doing a little bit better with words. And by next morning, thank god thank god, he'd got them back. So it was a very small stroke indeed, such as lots of people have without suffering any after effects. They are keeping him in because they want to be sure they've got his blood pressure stabilized at a reasonable level – and also his blood sugar, which simultaneously shot up. And it seems they still have a test or two they want to do. But today he was allowed to come home to watch a particularly vital football match, though I had to return him after it. And we think he'll be properly home tomorrow or the next day.

My own problem is a minor form of skin cancer – not the most minor, but not the dreaded melanoma. Apparently once it is removed, that's that (whereas the melanoma crops up elsewhere and is very bad news). But if it's not removed it can, according to my doctor, be 'a dreadful thing', which is why, although the one on my nose is all but invisible (with make-up, quite invisible) it has to be dealt with. They thought at first that they could just knick it out and put in a stitch or two, but say now that it may have strayed too far into the neighbouring skin for that. Which doesn't mean straying very far.

The skin on one's nose (the bridge of it) is stretched very tight over the bone, so only a very tiny excision can be dealt with by drawing the two sides together with stitches. Anything a bit larger has to be dealt with by either radiation or a skin graft, and I gather that radiation is likely to leave the least unsightly results. They've made an appointment for me on Feb. 18 – a day on which I'm due to give a talk at the local library in the evening. I must find out whether the radiation will leave me looking like Rudolf the Red Nosed Reindeer – and change the day of the appointment. [*Finally they decided on a graft, which was done incredibly quickly and neatly under a local anaesthetic.*]

Love Diana

25 FEBRUARY 2003

Dearest Edward,

> Obsession with health can easily take over
> From sex as life's major problem . . .

Yes indeed! Latest news is that the stroke has left no
sign – was the kind of thing described by doctors by
three initials which I can't recall except that the first is T,
for transient. But the diabetes has got much worse. His
GP said he thinks the pancreas must have packed up and
that probably he'll have to go on to injections, and is
making an appointment for him at the hospital's diabetes
clinic. Poor Barry.

Brits and your poems: if Barbara is taken as an
indicator, leave out anything about shitting (such a pity –
I often practice the suggestions in 'From The Book of
Shyting'); and it might be a good thing to limit the
hypochondriacal ones – I think there's an automatic
flinch from Being Sorry For Yourself in most Brits. I
even have it myself, a bit: they are the ones I like least
among your poems. You don't say how large a collection
you are aiming for. If you want it to be properly
representative you'd need to keep one in – perhaps 'I've
always said that if I'd got it' – but otherwise I think I'd
skip 'Confessions of a Hypo'. I particularly like the long
poems – 'World War II' – 'Visiting Home' – for example.
But I guess going for what you are best pleased with is
probably the right line to take.

My little library talk was fun. Full house, and among all the grizzled heads one sleek black one – a rather good-looking man who beamed at me throughout with almost alarming enthusiasm, and turned out to be called Boris – Russian I think – and mad about *Stet* because he'd read it three times – 'And because of this marvellous book I pass my examination'. I couldn't hear what the examination was in, or for, or how *Stet* had helped – he had a thickish accent and there was quite a lot of background noise – but still it was very nice to know it had meant so much to him And then a lady came up and said that every month she sent a parcel to a man who is in prison in Addis Ababa, and she always includes two books, and *Stet* was one of them, and he'd let her know it was the one he loved best and it had changed his life!!

I was dying to find out what he was in prison in Addis Ababa for, but she quickly skipped away so I never did. But what a splendid far-flung fan to learn about!

I remember that you went to Detroit before – hope this one goes well.

Love, D

[*Edward was not the only person trying to convert me to computers, but only he did something about it. On one of his London visits he took me to a cave-like space in a sort of Kasbah near where he was staying, where many cheerful young men were busily selling retired computers large and small, and made me buy an astonishingly cheap laptop. We carried it off and he sat me down to my first lesson.*

I still know little more about the thing than he taught me then. It is not, I think, inability to learn that is the problem: several of my friends who are as old, or nearly as old, as I am are at home on the internet, and of course I can appreciate its usefulness. But I find that I do not want to go there, and the disinclination is active, not passive. Once someone tried to coax me into it by calling up my name, and I loathed *the fact that all this information about me was available without my consent; and when kind people send me DVDs, saying 'You can watch it on your laptop', I never do. The new world opened up by technology leaves me so cold that I shudder and shrink from it – except for that tiny corner of it which provides me with a wonderfully sophisticated typewriter, and for that I am very grateful. From here on my letters to Edward were e-mails, except when I was separated from my laptop, or when (as quite often happened with that first one) it let me down.]*

11 JULY 2003

Darlings – London seems miserably empty now you are gone. I had a lovely week in the country – greatly enjoyed both my two days as a garden-visiting Oldie and my week with my sister. At the start of the former, instantly proved my authenticity as an Oldie by a) forgetting the registration number of my car when the hotel wanted it, and b) losing the key to my room within seconds of receiving it (had automatically slipped it into my handbag without realizing). But soon recovered my wits, and the gardens were lovely. My sister's daughter from Zimbabwe was with us, looking thirty years older than her age and with an unfamiliar set of nervous habits – for example, compelled to wash everything in sight. We patiently took no notice when she removed everything from my sister's kitchen cupboards and washed it all – it wasn't very clean, anyway. But her sister, in a brand new house, was furious – until we persuaded her to cool it. But she soon began to relax, and it was wonderful to see her easing up and beginning to enjoy things. My nephew from Australia was there too, with his family, and when at the end of the week the niece with a new house gave a splendid party there were 90 guests, many of them family and old friends who hadn't seen each other for years. My sister and her family lived in the Argentine for a while and it has become a tradition with them to celebrate things with an Argentine-style barbecue, which means digging a big pit, filling it with huge logs, and cooking whole animals over it – in this case two sheep. I've never tasted meat so delicious. And after it, bowls as big as wash-basins heaped with strawberries, monstrous piles of meringues and pints and pints of cream – it really was a most gorgeous feast, but the best part was all the reunions. So all of that was lovely, but coming home ... Well, it's no good going on about it, but how I wish you lived here! xxx Diana xxxxx

22 JULY 2003

A nice full diary sounds fine to me! Maybe I did meet Mrs Sullivan, but if so I've forgotten her. As for Barry and eating – it's the kind of attitude a child has: if Mum says it's good for him ... *yuck!* Anything he's told he *ought* to do, he has an instant reaction against. He's always been like that – it isn't anything to do with illness.

I went to the theatre last Friday – the first time for ages. Was given some comps for the Jean Rhys play [After Mrs Rochester], which has been moved into the West End. Interesting direction and brilliant performances, but was spoilt simply as a play by a weak second half, and as a life of Jean Rhys, which is what it rashly declares itself to be – very inadequate. What was nice was that the theatre provided excellent head-sets for the deaf, so that I heard everything, and that afterwards the friend I'd invited to go with me drove me round to see what the new pedestrianized Trafalgar Square is like, and it's lovely. The post-theatre West End, which had been getting more and more squalid, seemed suddenly to have become spacious and calm and pleasant.

I'm going to have an interesting lunch tomorrow with the mistress dumped by Vidia Naipaul when he married his Indian wife – after 25 years together she learnt about his marriage from a newspaper. She's been trying to meet me for ages, since reading *Stet*, but her rare visits from her native Argentina have never so far fitted in. To be continued in our next. XXXXX Diana

24 JULY 2003

I know what you mean about dining out – I like the idea of it much more than doing it, these days. In fact I sometimes don't go to things I've said 'yes' to when it actually comes to the point. I say I'm ill, or something. But still, it is nice to have people wanting to see you.

Vidia's lady is still very much the Argentinian beauty – of course, she's looking older, but expensive raw silk dress in vivid lemon yellow, very close fitting and low-necked and exactly matching her elegant sandals and handbag. She was not only cheerful, but triumphant: he's been getting in touch with her quite often recently, trying to persuade her to meet him, and she has been greatly enjoying saying No. She gave several amusing examples of his monstrousness . . . but all the same, I would not be surprised to hear that she ended by capitulating. Their affaire was obviously passionate enough to embrace a lot of monstrosity and was equally obviously the centre of her life for 25 years, so I guess life without it is pretty boring. The reason why she is determined to dodge his biographer [*Patrick French*] is because, she says, her letters to him are not only embarrassingly 'soppy' but also appallingly illiterate – I don't think she'd mind being written about but shrivels at the idea of being quoted. By an odd coincidence, the biographer called me on the very day I met her – I saw him yesterday. I like him – he wrote an excellent biog of a famous British soldier-explorer called Younghusband about which I once wrote him a congratulatory letter which he remembers with pride and joy. We had a v. interesting talk about Vidia – I said nothing about my meeting with Margaret, referring to her only in relation to what he knew I knew of her. Don't want to get mixed up with his dealings with her. He will write a good book, I think. He's got the right sort of intense interest in how people work. And Vidia may have made a mistake (from his own point of view) in giving him permission to 'do' him. Patrick will certainly not try to hurt anyone for hurting's sake, but he has got an astonishingly clear eye! But whether I'll ever see it, who knows. He thinks it'll take him about four years to finish. [*He was right.* The World Is What It Is *was published in 2008.*] This has got too long for an e-mail – sorry! xxxxxxx Diana

13 AUGUST 2003

Dearest Edward,

I've been in a rather peculiar relationship with my e-mail recently. When I open the window it always tells me no messages are waiting – then I diddle about and it divulges that one message is there – then quite suddenly it says four messages are there so I've just (hurrah hurrah) printed out your lovely four last messages, with the two attachments. At the stage when it was divulging only one message I wrote you a rather frantic heatwave-influenced reply, but it didn't seem willing to send it. So now I'm falling back on good old letter-writing ... Have learnt how to get my window back into its proper place, which I did by borrowing a 'for Dummies' book from a neighbour in the country, to which I had fled for five nights. Allow me to tell you how I did it. Click on any part of window. Hold down Alt key and press spacebar. A menu appears. Select the word move. A four-headed arrow appears. Press arrow keys until windows border moves to an acceptable position. Press enter. And there you are. What a relief.

To put you in the picture which my lost e-mails would have done: Barry came home a week earlier than he'd said because he was too bored to stand another minute of it. It's hard to see why, since by his own account he was living in exactly the same way there as he does here – except that he 'couldn't be bothered' to give himself injections and reverted to the pills all the time he was there. He seemed neither better nor worse than when he left, and has resumed his old regime. On the whole he is surviving this god-awful heatwave better than I am because he's got a very good electric fan and doesn't have to do any shopping or domestic tasks.

But last Thursday (today is Wednesday August 13), when Barbara had just left for a five day jaunt to Kenya on behalf of the *Economist* and I had taken over Hannah, it was impossible to sleep a single wink all night, so at 3.30 a.m. I thought what the fuck, why don't I just get up and spend the rest of the night driving gently to Norfolk, and since I'd just filled the fridge, and Barry said yes of course he could manage, off Hannah and I went in the comparative cool of the night outside. And there I stayed until yesterday

(Barbara came home this evening and would have been appalled had her little dog not been back to greet her). Even there it was too hot to do anything much during the day, but it did cool down pleasantly each evening so that one could sleep at night.

Barry had sounded cheerful on the phone and had said he was going out to buy food, but on my return I found that all he had bought was a chocolate cake and chocolate ice cream 'which' – reproachfully – 'sent my blood sugar up a lot'.

On top of which, I had forgotten that I was due to pay for renewal of my parking permit, so this morning I discovered a fifty-pound ticket on my windscreen. The renewal office isn't far away, so I thought 'I'll just nip round there when my shopping's done', which I did – only to be sent home to get the car's registration document, my full driving licence (as opposed to the little card one carries around all the time) and a minimum of two documents from a Camden source proving that I am me. So back I go ... and find that I have lost my purse. One, as they say, of those days. Oh yes, and in addition to all that – a couple of weeks ago I was put on a course of antibiotics because for the first time in my life I've got cystitis, and it has now become apparent that the antibiotics haven't worked. To tell the truth, *fuck* is an understatement of my feelings about today. The only nice thing was when all your e-mails turned up, adding up to a lovely long letter. I'm entering all your Tips in my Tip List, and wish indeed that I could be sipping some of your yummy Dutch liquor with you. Love and love

28 AUGUST 2003

Disasters do not come singly! Instead of waking up refreshed today, I have the most frightful sciatica which prevented me from getting any sleep at all. It started two days earlier, first with only a shadowy twinge, then worse so that it did in fact keep me awake for half of Tuesday night, and last night it came in full-blast, and is still at it today, so this morning I hobbled off to the doc, who confirmed after a good deal of tapping and tweaking, that the source of the pain is not the hip, which is what it feels like and which had made me fear bad arthritis, but is the lower back, where the sciatic nerve is being pinched. Doctors can do nothing about sciatica except give one strong painkillers and say that it will go away sooner or later, with luck. Ouch!!! Because a pain which gets *worse* when you lie down in bed is really nasty. I called my osteopath, only to learn via an answering machine that he has emigrated to New Zealand. His friend who had taken over the practice said on the machine that she would call me back if I wanted an appointment, but hasn't yet done so. The painkillers are making the pain less at the moment although they don't abolish it, and I'm praying that they'll enable me to go to sleep tonight.

The financial disaster I mentioned in my last (if you got same – Outlook Express came up with a sinister message and I'm not at all sure that I interpreted it properly) – is distinctly odd. When I got my last bank statement I nearly had a heart attack: there was only

ninety pounds left in my account and I had written a
cheque for a hundred and something since the account
was made up. I knew I'd become a bit light-hearted
about money since book money had been coming in –
but surely not so light-hearted as that? And surely even I
would remember if I had written a cheque for £3100 on
July 22, as the account says I did. So I called the bank (it
took a good 25 minutes to get through to the appropriate
part of it) and the bank said 'But you did write that
cheque.' 'Who to?' I screamed, and she said she didn't
know (being miles away from where the account is kept)
and would instruct them to send me a photo of the
cheque. Which would take about a week. And which has
not yet come. I phoned again today and had the exact
same conversation. If it doesn't come in the next few
days I shall have to go to my branch and throw hysterics
until something is done. Meanwhile Barry, bless his
heart, is keeping us. Pray God it's a silly mistake of the
bank's and not some evil crook at work. On the stub of
the cheque I'm supposed to have written it is recorded
that I wrote a cheque for thirty pounds to our London
gardener, and I don't think he would be up to the really
quite difficult task of altering in both words and
numerals 'thirty' to 'three thousand one hundred'.

There was, by the way, a long piece about Outlook
Express in the *Independent* the other day saying it was
teetering on the brink of collapse. Any other bad news?
Can't think of any at the moment but am sure I could
find some if I really looked. Another 'by the way' – the
reason why there was enough money in my account to
cover a cheque of three thousand plus was that when my

last Granta cheque came in I reckoned that it would make such a minuscule interest in a savings account and would probably vanish in the form of shares, so I might just as well keep it there until it was spent on groceries and so on – at least it would be safe! xxxx D

16 SEPTEMBER 2003

Darling Edward –

Three lovely e-mails from you when I got back from Norfolk today (Sept. 15). I've just printed out that invaluable instructive one, for which thanks thanks thanks!!

The cheque saga – it's been a bit exhausting, the bank being fatuous beyond belief, its right hand never knowing for a moment what its left hand is doing and a long session at Hampstead police station where I had to go to report the matter was very hard on the sciatica (if that's what it is – it's still rampant although I'm sort of getting used to it and with the help of constant painkillers I'm a bit less immobilized than I was). The cop there was v. thick – had to move his lips when reading – and v. bored, and it took him nearly an hour to produce what turned out to be an extremely simple form for me to sign. But the next day I had a phone call from the Fraud Squad which cheered me up a lot. He said they really hadn't a hope in hell of catching the villain, because it looks like a job of a kind which they are getting all the time now, organized by a gang which corrupts people working in the post office sorting offices to procure them a harvest of likely-looking mail, and such cheques as they then get out of it are then 'processed', and are cashed in China (or Hong Kong, which is the same thing), over which the UK has no jurisdiction. They think most of the firms which get things paid-for with these cheques have no idea that they are forged, so tracing them is no help. But – and here comes the good news – he said that as soon as Barclays had let them actually examine the cheque (the forms I had to fill in were authorizations for this), and (I guess) they have conclusively cleared my gardener, as they expect will happen and so do I, which will not take long, I'll get my money refunded. I always thought I probably would, but fully expected to have to fight with the bank for it, but he seemed to think there would be no question about it, and I don't think he would have called to tell me that if it were not so. Which is, of course, a huge relief – though I shan't rejoice a hundred per cent until I've actually got the money! The moral of the story is only too obviously *don't send cheques through the mail*, which is a bore when one has to pay people like my gardener who don't deal with cards – it will mean always being here when his two lads turn up and thrusting cash into their sticky hands, which I don't think he's in favour of because I guess he gets his labour where he can find it – they change quite often. If only you were here when the money comes home, we'd open a bottle of champagne!

What I'm hoping is that the next e-mail I get from you you will tell me what Chris Carduff has to say about the

Collection [*of Edward's poems*], and that it is Yes! Love &
Love. D

18 SEPTEMBER 2003

Darling Edward –
   In spite of being still hideously sciatic and beginning to
fear that I *always* will be, I'm feeling pretty good today.
With the utmost dubiousness I sent to Ian Jack at *Granta*
a piece based on something I wrote forty years ago based
on the experience of very nearly dying when I miscarried
a baby which I badly wanted to have, and discovering as
I came round from the operation which saved me that it
was so *marvellous* still to be alive that it mattered much
more than losing the child! I put it into the third person
and trimmed it a bit, but I still feared it was too personal
to be presentable . . . and this morning a postcard came
from Ian saying it was very good – as good as anything
I've ever done, so he will be using it in the mag. I want to
send a copy of it to you, and know I have to click the
paperclip ikon, but I don't know how to tell the pc what
it is to attach to the e-mail. The piece is there inside my
computer somewhere. How do I bring it together with
the paperclip? I know it's as easy as pie to do, but not
what it is.
   Oh dear what dimness. However I have just, with
infinite laboriousness, managed to send an order for
groceries to Waitrose to be delivered on Saturday

morning . . . a great step forward in computer sophistication. This tiresome machine went into its freeze mode quite madly two days ago. Among other things it froze every time I tried to get it to clean itself. So in despair I called a lovely computer tutor known to my neighbour across the street. He's been working in computers for years, and finally had the bright idea of specializing in sorting out the problems of elderly writers who had at last decided to get a computer – and he put just one tiny ad in the *Spectator* (arguing that its readers were mostly over fifty and literate) – and has never looked back. He says he could work day and night if he wanted to. Anyway, he put my box through a brief medical examination and diagnosed the trouble as hardware beginning to wear out, which would cost over a hundred pounds to mend – whereupon he recommended living with the problem after he had persuaded it to do the clean-out, which he promptly did, which would make it a good deal better for a while anyway. And when it gets too bad to bear, which may not happen soon considering how little I use it, then if I decide to get a new one he'll give me an estimate for procuring and setting up the cheapest one we can find. Today, chastened by his attentions, it has been behaving very well. Thank goodness. There certainly won't be any new computer, however stroppy this one gets, till Barclays has refunded my money. Love and love D

8 OCTOBER 2003

Darling Edward,

Here I am yet again reverting to Olde Worlde ways.
The reason is one I hardly dare to confess, because I
know you will disapprove and I fear you are right. The
IBM, even after a most thorough house-cleaning, just
went on getting naughtier and naughtier, so that every
operation was interrupted by a freeze-up about every 20
minutes, and the amount of time the freeze-ups lasted
was steadily increasing. It really was becoming too
tedious to bear. So when I got my money back I decided
I must be a devil and get a new one.

So yesterday Francis Hughes brought me a Toshiba
(because it was the least expensive new one he
considered acceptable), and transferred everything from
the IBM onto it, and introduced me to it. It's a neat little
silver job, much quicker than my dear but naughty IBM
(the printer leaps into action at its command!), which
works on a battery if you want it to and which has a little
glass plate built in instead of a mouse – you direct the
pointer by moving a finger tip about on the plate, which I
think I'm going to prefer to the mouse. But I'm not yet
used to its touch, and this evening, when I began to use it
for the first time, got into silly muddles and was too tired
to persist until I got over them. The introductory lesson
F. Hughes provided as part of the service still has an
hour to run, so I'm to save up problems until next week,
when he'll come to sort them out for me. There won't be
many, I can tell. I really have learnt all the basics with

you and the IBM, I found, so I'm now quite confident that I'll soon feel at home with this one. The chief problem is learning not to touch the glass plate by accident as one types, because it responds to very light touches you hardly know you've made. It astonishes me to realize how much I learnt from you – between you, you and the IBM took me onto a level of confidence I couldn't imagine before we started. I find myself looking at the Toshiba in a completely different way from how I looked at the IBM to start with: that appeared as a Total Mystery demanding a sort of blind faith that only you could have inspired; this one is just another word processor! Hurrah!!

Why I'm so tired tonight is that this morning I suddenly realized (shock horror – but thank heavens!) that I was supposed to be in Norwich Magistrates' Court, to which I have been Summoned, because one of those fiendish police cameras caught me driving at 51 mph through a village with a speed limit of 30 mph. What with the cheque drama and the beastly sciatica, and Nan's holiday, I'd utterly forgotten receiving this summons – it was pure chance that I turned it up this morning while looking for something else. It's Terribly Fierce about how one must appear, so I called the Court in fear and trembling ... whereupon a dear, kind little girl told me that all I need do was write apologizing, and explaining and pleading guilty, enclosing the necessary documents. So that's all right and I shan't end in jail – but one of the Necessary Documents was a vastly complicated form to fill in about my finances – they explain that without it they might fine me more than I can afford, so it's important to be accurate. My dear – it was worse than an Income Tax declaration! I went nearly mad digging about for the information they asked for – why oh why do I always throw away receipts and so on? It aged me about 10 years. Finally I let my writing go more and more quavery, and my sentences sound dafter and dafter, in the hope that they'll think, Poor Old Thing – and now I'm worrying that they may start questioning my ability to drive!

Your poet friend bravely returning to his shack in the woods before the snows set in gave me a very complicated dream last night in which I was staying with a rather cross sandy-bearded man in such a shack. The snow was so deep that I couldn't go out to pee – there was, of course, no loo – so I had to use a soup bowl and tip it out of the window.

A lot of people say that they really hate revising something they've written, but I've always enjoyed it, so can well understand the fun you're having with the memoirs. I don't have a pic of me and Alfred, alas. Wish I did. I look forward so much to reading the mems.

Love. Diana

9 DECEMBER 2004

Darling –

I wrote you such a long and rambling one, I can't possibly recap it. What I must do is write you a whole new one, but now it's too late to do that, so I'll do it tomorrow. I wonder how come you didn't get it ... my fault I'm sure, as you always so encouragingly point out!!! For now – just *love* Diana

10 DECEMBER 2004

Darling Edward – 2nd attempt at this recap. 1st interrupted by a phone call and when I came back to it the thing had turned itself off, and when turned on again I couldn't find my beginning! So: what it said was good that you were glad to be home, worrying about Neil – but Barbara's thing on her temple which definitely was a cancer, and which caused concern when it didn't heal after removal, now at last HAS healed, so no doubt his will too. After that the lost message – the first lost message, not the start of this one – was all about Barbara's Conservatory, a saga which has finally reached a happy ending, which we were celebrating when we were in Norfolk last weekend.

Our dear Lesbian neighbour in the country had a most splendiferous conservatory added to her house by one of the world's most expensive conservatory firms, and eventually persuaded B that she should do the same. B has always been more annoyed than I am by the fact that our tiny little dining room in that house was more like a passage leading to the kitchen than a real room, and has longed to expand it outwards. Which could have been done quite easily and cheaply by a local builder, but B has a *horror* of having to take thought about practical matters, and was seduced by the argument that the conservatory people just brought the thing along and hey presto there it was. And their alarmingly smooth representative said yes indeed, that was exactly what would happen, it would be a matter of two weeks' work at most – and that long only because of having to knock down a wall between it and our little dining room. I was present, and pointed out that the ground on which the thing was to stand fell away quite steeply: foundations would have to be built. Well, yes, he said: perhaps because of that it would be safer to say three weeks rather than two.

So Barbara signed on the dotted line. *That was in April* – and it was not until last weekend that the job was finished! Most of the time no one was doing anything. The conservatory people insisted that we should use the builder of their choice (they themselves did nothing but deliver the conservatory and put it together). They chose one who lived a two-hour drive away, and who never answered the phone, and when we screamed at them they said it was nothing to do with them, it was between us and the builder ... who had been paid in advance through them, so we had no leverage. I will spare you a blow by blow of the rage and frustration which ensued, but it reduced Barbara to a jibbering wreck who cursed the day she ever thought of the bloody conservatory, so that it seemed more than likely that when/if it was finally completed, she would loathe it.

However ... now that at last it is done, underfloor

heating and all, it is really rather delicious, and I'm glad to say she is allowing herself to like it, to the point of rather running amok about its furnishing. Because it's to be used as a room, rather than as a glass-house for plants, she decided she didn't want the sort of cane furniture people usually put in conservatories and on patios, and rushed off to buy a sumptuous sofa and a rocking-chair (American, circa 1880). So I volunteered to buy the little occasional tables for people to put their drinks on, and last weekend managed to discover what is quite likely the only genuine antique shop (as opposed to junk and bric-à-brac shop of which there are thousands) in Norfolk. It is full of heavenly things and is run by a charming gay couple (the senior of whom wears a toupé – I didn't think anyone did that any more), and I spent a very happy afternoon with them and came away with two ravishing little tables (price? *Don't ask*). Luckily some shares left me by my mother just happened to Mature at that very moment, landing £5000 in my bank account. Of course it has got to be re-invested pronto, but the interest one gets these days is so minuscule that it seemed quite sensible to spend a little chunk of it on having fun. Most kinds of shopping leave me cold, but antiques and paintings! If I had the money my life would be one long orgy of shopping for those.

Since then it's not been a good week: a visit to Nan led to the result I always dread: ringing and ringing and getting no answer. [*My friend Nan Taylor, having broken a hip, had become an invalid.*] Thank god her upstairs neighbour, who has a key, was in, so we got in and found her lying on the floor in the hall, having fallen on the way to answer the door. She wasn't hurt apart from a bit of a bang on the head, but before I left she got up onto her zimmer again to go to the bathroom, and down she went again – a fit of dizziness, not a stumble. But she still gets frantic if I try to edge her towards living-in care, or going into a home. I suppose it will just have to go on until one day I or someone else find her dead.

I do hope this reaches you. The one which didn't came up as a 'sent item' when I asked, which is agitating. Love and love Diana

19 DECEMBER 2004

Darling Edward,

Our fingers are crossed for the biopsy. [*Neil had a possibly evil lump – but it turned out harmless.*] If it's bad news I don't think you ought to suggest no treatment. The thing on Barbara's temple was dealt with by radiation – a very small amount of it, which caused her no inconvenience while it was going on, apart from getting to the hospital to have it done, and although it took a worryingly long time to heal it has left no unsightly scar. The thing I had removed from the bridge of my nose, which was also a cancerous ulcer, was dealt with by excision plus a mini skin-graft, and it has left a scar so slight that it is all but unnoticeable. My instinct is much in favour of having these small things dealt with promptly.

I'm so furious with myself. For the last three weeks our street has been pretty well impassable because they have been renewing the side-walks – no one could park there, and even walking to and fro was sometimes quite an obstacle-race. Two days ago I drove some heavy shopping up to as near our door as I could get, and then began to reverse out down the very narrow bit of roadway left uncluttered: one side-walk had been finished so had cars parked along it, the other side still had the workmen's barriers up. Just as I started to back out, one of their huge trucks turned in and blocked the way. When he saw I wanted to leave he kindly reversed back to the bottom of the terrace, and I resumed my reversing, concentrating hard on watching the parked cars in my wing-mirror to make sure that I didn't nick one of them. So hard that having briefly established than he had stopped, I failed to estimate exactly *where* he had stopped, so suddenly: scrunch! and a corner of the back of his truck came through my rear window! What's more, it had made a dent in the car's roof, which although it was very small had to be put right before a new window could be put in – which of course made it more expensive. So off I had to go to Mike, our local body-work repair shop, which exists in an interesting cave under some railway arches in Camden Town, and although he's very nice and pops out small dents with a sort of vacuum sucker for nothing, for this he had to buy in a window as well as undent the roof, which was not poppable, so it cost me £400! On the other hand he did stay late, so as to get it done that evening, and then drove it home to me so that I didn't have to walk to the bus and so on, and as the possibility of being deprived of my car for the whole weekend, which had threatened, was to me the worst of it (I had to get to Nan, whose bedroom ceiling had fallen down owing to a leaking pipe of her upstairs neighbour) that rather cheered me up. It's worrying, being so dependent on the car. My mind boggles at how I'll manage when I can no longer drive – and things like the lack of alertness which caused this damage do tend to bring that prospect to mind. Love – And thank you thank you for the wonderful lid-opener, which has just dealt splendidly with a stubborn jar of raspberry jam. Think how often your presence will zoom into my kitchen as a result of it! Diana

27 DECEMBER 2004

Darling Edward,

Your news about the biopsy is by far the best thing to happen this Christmas. Earthquakes and tidal waves apart (about which I'm terribly under-informed because we've had no newspapers delivered for three days, I've got no radio and Barry never tells me what he's seen on the telly).

Things here have been dreary because I went down with a cold on Dec. 21. Managed to control and disguise it well enough to carry out the essential task of cooking and delivering Nan's Christmas lunch, eating it with her, helping her open her presents and so on, then came home to collapse into bed where I've remained until this morning. Much better now, but this is the first time I've set foot in my sitting room for what feels like longer than three days, which explains why I've only just read your message. Tomorrow (if snow is not bedevilling the roads which is not impossible because they've had it in some places tho' not yet here) I shall drive to my brother for a two-day visit, then on to the cottage where our neighbours there are giving a New Year's Eve party. It will be a very familiar one because they give it every year, and it is always boring, but it has become something like a family ritual so that one would feel guilty if one didn't go. Barry will go to Sally's (if, I gather, football permits – she doesn't have Sky television so her football coverage is not up to scratch). He cooked a lovely Jamaican Chicken for us, for Christmas, with rice-and-bean accompaniment, so I didn't have to do any cooking apart from Nan's, which was a relief. Not that I wanted much to eat. I have discovered a very useful thing now stocked by Safeways (since it sold itself to the Scottish retailer and became Morrison's). It's imported from France – a bag of brioches, some with chocolate filling, some with strawberry jam, each brioche being separately wrapped in foil so they don't go dry. They are v. light and rather delicious, and most useful to nibble at when one doesn't feel up to eating much.

How maddening about your book's jacket! They probably won't make too much fuss about the blurb, because that can be altered without costing much, but I fear you may have a problem over the front of it. I was unable to get anywhere with Granta when I disliked one of theirs, and they are famously obliging compared to most publishers ... and I have to confess that when I was a publisher we never (as far as I can remember) altered a jacket design once we'd decided on it.

I'm glad you are encouraging about me and my car – because in fact I've no intention of giving it up yet. I'm still (I think) within the area of just having to remember to take more care. Did I tell you – no, I can't have – that at last the *Guardian* got round to printing their profile of me? I'd given up looking for it, having concluded that it must have been submerged by more newsworthy stuff so I failed to notice my name at the bottom of the cover of the G2 part of the paper – the part which has columns and so on in it. I also flicked through that part rather casually so must have turned over two pages as though they were one. I was reading in bed, as I ate my breakfast. Luckily it slithered off the bed and the pages came apart, so when I reached down to scoop it up ... There I was! A large photo, not exactly flattering but rather nice all the same, and a very pleasant, friendly text. I'm mailing it to you. It was more fun coming on it by surprise like that than it would have been if I'd known it would be there. It was on the 22nd.

Now I'm going to have a bath and get dressed – resume normal life, in fact. Give Neil my fondest love ... oh god! I'm so relieved about that biopsy. I've been trying hard not to dwell on it, but still I couldn't help having a fairly good idea of what you must have been feeling. Huge love. Diana

9 JANUARY 2005

Darling Edward,

Horrors! Such a long time since I sat at this machine. First there was Xmas, very exhausting because I had to battle with a cold in order to cook Nan her Xmas lunch, after which I collapsed into bed for two days. Then drove to my brother's in Norfolk only to find him on the point of collapsing with a far worse cold, but still my two days there were quite fun because three of my nephews were there and they are such good value.

Then to our own house until the 2nd of Jan., and as soon as I got back here I began to collapse again. I'd been congratulating myself that my Xmas bug would have inoculated me against further ills, but of course Bug A is effective only against Bug A, and now I've encountered Bug B (a chesty one) and have been feeling really quite ill. Barry at the best of times has never been exactly Male Nurse Material, and is now quite hopeless.

It was when, yesterday, he summoned me from my fevered bed to say 'What time is it?' when he had a perfectly good clock ticking away on his bedside table that I snapped, and posted him off to Sally's. He left this morning, and maybe it's just coincidence but I do believe that I'm now on the mend at last! Must be, in fact, since I felt quite hungry this evening and now have the energy to write this.

Goodnight now ... I do really think that I'm on the mend – for instance it now seems quite possible to put clean sheets on my bed before getting back into it, whereas only yesterday such an undertaking was beyond me. xxxx Diana

24 MAY 2005

Darling Edward –

Marvellous about the standing ovations. I trust you are keeping a copy of your speech for me to read when I come to Paris, which I'm longing to do. What do you say to Friday June 17 to Monday June 20, which will overlap with your family? Ted's flat sounds perfectly manageable. I shan't be able to go tearing about Paris as I shall yearn to do, but I'm used to gentle pottering by now, and the main object of the exercise, after all, is to see you both.

It doesn't surprise me that Neil has had relapses, because that seems to be characteristic of the vile bug (tho' I suspect the stomach thing was something else, probably taking advantage of his weakened state). It is very reluctant to let go. Even though I've been up and about for more than a week now I'm still getting attacks of coughing and stuffed up nose and throat . . . but they are diminishing, and are far from being seriously incommoding. No one seems able to give any explanation of the bug, even though it's so widespread. Can it be some evil thing released into the atmosphere by the tsunami? [*The huge Indian Ocean tsunami had erupted on Boxing Day 2004.*]

I have done a wild thing – I've bought a new car!!!!!

My dear little old one, to which I feel very disloyal, had
started to enter that state of mechanical decay when If
It's Not One Thing It's Another. The drive to Norfolk
was becoming hard on the nerves, as a result, but there
didn't seem to be anything I could do about it. But then I
had a letter from the bank saying 'Your Fixed Savings
Bond will be Maturing at the end of May. If we don't
hear from you we will simply renew it . . .' Whereupon I
remembered that this happened every two years, and
they never had heard from me because doing nothing
was what I like best, which was why I had completely
forgotten that I had such a thing as a Fixed Saving Bond.
So this time I looked more closely to see what it added
up to, and by god, it was eleven thousand pounds!!!!!!!!!
So I quickly instructed them to put half of that into my
ordinary savings account, which is one from which I can
take money instantly if I want to, and my beloved
neighbour-across-the-road Xandra Bingley, who had
practically moved in to look after me when the bug was
doing its worst, hunted up a Peugeot dealer not too far
away for me, and even drove me there to choose a used
car. And it turned out that they are having a very hard
time selling cars this season, so everything was madly
reduced and they all but spread a red carpet for us, and
instead of a car just a little less old than my old one
(which was what I was looking for) I ended up with a
ravishing little car only one year old, which has only ten
thousand miles on its clock and is absolutely bursting
with Modern Conveniences hitherto unknown to me
(tho' still with manual gear change because that's what
I'm used to). I wish I was brave enough to bring it to

Paris, but I'm not. Even when I was young enough to go for a driving holiday in France, I didn't have the nerve to tackle Paris. But I have just got back from my first Norfolk visit in it, and driving it was bliss.

I'm writing June 17–20 in my diary, but of course if it doesn't suit you you must say at once.

Love and love Diana

10 JUNE 2005

Have just booked ticket Friday 17th morning, train leaving Waterloo at 10.10. Like a fool, I forgot to ask when it gets to the Gare du Nord, but I gather it takes two hours and thirty-five minutes, so I suppose it will be 12.45. They said no point in giving number of car because meeting on platform not allowed – we have to meet at the exit from same.

I'm feeling such an idiot. Can you believe it, but I thought booking a ticket meant going to a travel agent, as it used to mean in antediluvian times, so I spent most of the day running from travel agent to travel agent only to find half of them closed down, the other half dealing only in flights to Australia or Bangladesh, not in train tickets. This was even more daft than it sounds, because it was impossible to park a car near any of them so I had to foot it far more than I easily can and reduced myself almost to collapse. As I staggered through the front door almost in tears I bumped into Georgia,

Adam's girlfriend, who often goes to Paris. 'Oh Georgia, where do *you* book your Eurostar tickets?' – 'On the internet, usually, but you can do it by phone, of course.' Imagine my total mortification at my own idiocy! I suppose it's minimally less idiotic not to have thought of the internet, given my computer illiteracy, but not to have thought of the phone!

I shall bring with me a signed copy of Peter Smalley's book [HMS Expedient] – which is *very good*. Was fully expecting that I'd have to be polite, since I'm not much of a one for sea-going yarns, but I thoroughly enjoyed it. He writes so well that he makes all the life aboard an 18th-century frigate stuff riveting (to me, anyway) and the Count-of-Monte-Cristo-like adventure bit is great fun. What is more, although it hasn't had a single review it has already sold almost 5000 copies. We are so happy for him, and he himself sounded gleeful on the phone this morning. xxxxx D

[*Peter Smalley's publishing career is unusual. In 1972 André Deutsch Ltd published his fiercely witty novel about the Americans in Vietnam,* A Warm Gun, *and after that, for years, nothing he did quite came off: always there would be sparks of fierce wittiness, but as a whole the book would go astray. Now he had tried something quite different, a seafaring novel set in the eighteenth century, with a frigate's captain and first mate who could perhaps reappear in subsequent adventures, and it was a triumph – so much so that it became the first in a series of six books following the fortunes of the two men, and I believe his publishers would like it to go on for ever. His sudden emergence as a master of this specialized craft has been as pleasing as it was unexpected.*]

13 JUNE 2005

Darling E,

Time of arrival 13.53, walking ability three blocks or so, and certainly the length of a platform, will be loaded with taxi money (just earned another £500 from *Guardian*) but what I'm really looking forward to is sitting in cafés engaging in idle gossip. Love. D

16 JUNE 2005

Darling Edward, keep trying to call and getting 'number not recognized'. So I must trust to your checking e-mails regularly to get this sad sad sad news: my bloody bug has come back. I began to fear as much three days ago, but feeling ill came and went in waves so I prayed that I was fighting it off, but this morning it is clear that I'm not, and altho' I've just been to the doc and got the antibiotics that drove it off last time, I can't trust to them working like magic overnight and daren't embark on the visit. If I continued feeling like I'm feeling now it would be no fun for me and a great worry for you and it's just *not on. Damn damn and a thousand more damns.* Can I come later when I've shaken it off? Don't suppose Eurostar will transfer the ticket to another date, but that's secondary. I can at least hope that it will be nipped in the bud quickly this time and not drag on and on like it did before – but still it's fucked up the good timing with your sister and brother-in-law. Oh darling, I'm so miserable about it I can't tell you. Love xxxxxxx Diana

29 JUNE 2005

Darling Edward –

Whenever I try to check my incoming e-mails the computer disconnects in a maddening way, so I don't know whether you've communicated since getting home. I think wistfully of you in the delicious cool of your air conditioning, because our heatwave goes on, in spite of a fierce thunderstorm yesterday evening – an extraordinarily metallic-sounding thunder, as though enraged gods were kicking gigantic old-fashioned metal garbage bins about. Can't remember whether I told you that your speech to Publishing Triangle got a one-woman standing ovation from me? Which it did – I loved it, and could so clearly envisage you standing there in front of your charmed audience. Though still mourning Paris, I've now stopped aching about it. I don't think I shall use the ticket, although I could, because there'd be no point in going just to stay in a hotel unless I could get about to see exhibitions and things, which I couldn't. I haven't any other friends there, just to enjoy-being-in-Paris with, as would have been the case with you two.

Guess I'll have to call in Francis Hughes about the

computer's problem. Hope I can get this out. Love and love Diana

15 AUGUST 2005

Hi! Just back from Norfolk to find Lloyd [*Barry's brother, who was making a long visit to London from Jamaica*] crashing on my sitting room floor again because Jess and Tony, to whom he had moved just down the road, have Tony's dad descending on them for a couple of days. He does sort of cook – but more often likes a discussion about what we will have and how done, and then (not unnaturally) likes to eat the meal properly sitting round a table, whereas I have succumbed to total sloppiness and browsing in the kitchen, on my feet, once I've taken Barry's meal in to him. Utterly deplorable, I know, but so time-saving – I'm always longing to get back to a book or whatever – and I do rather *like* eating like that. But against that, I'm sure it is really *good for me*, to pull myself together and take meals more seriously, like a grown-up person . . . Have just eaten dinner with L (Barry not wanting any) and it was good, so am rapping myself over the knuckles for being querulous.

The ward in which Andrew [*my brother*] is contains five other poor old moribunds, who all looked so alarmingly as though they had died about two days earlier, that he looked positively well. Which he is not. But they do seem to have controlled the confusion, and

Mary said that his still very swollen legs were a good deal less so than they had been. So now the consultant wants to keep him there another four or five days as he thinks they may be able to take improvement further before he goes home. So it looks as though they are in for a long haul, poor dears. He was lucid, but extremely depressed, loathing his helplessness, and the hospital (which is state-of-the-art modern and very impressive), and having been confused which he said was terrifying and mortifying beyond words. Some of it sounded quite enjoyable, like flights of wild duck going through the ward, and a helicopter landing in it, but not knowing where he was or what had happened to him except that he had been abandoned somewhere for some unknown reason among probably hostile strangers was very dreadful, and he's obviously a bit afraid that it might happen again. It might well be beyond even Mary's managing if that came over him at home, so I suppose the consultant is right in wanting to be sure it's controlled before they let him go. What I now foresee is that he will get home, to his great joy to begin with, and then he'll start getting tetchy because of the many things he'll be unable to do, and that it may be quite a long time before his heart finally gives right out, which is going to be pretty good hell for one and all. But Mary, who will bear the brunt, would certainly rather have him alive than dead at any price, and I think that he, now that his back is against the wall, wants to stay here, so one may be wrong in wishing for him to be over it as soon as possible. One can't really tell, having never been in that situation (which please god we never will be!). You ought to be able to do a marvellous piece about Tobias – poor poor Tobias! [*The anthropologist Tobias Schneebaum, who lived on the floor above Edward's.*] But thank god family has turned up so that friends, of whom you must surely be the chief, are being spared a nightmare. Love and love D

18 AUGUST 2005

Well – my gloomy predictions about a long haul proved mistaken. My poor old bro. died yesterday – snuffed quietly out in mid-sentence while his wife was with him. Charlie and Phil, both tearful, came round yesterday evening to tell me, on their way to Norfolk, where the other two sons already were. They, like me and like their mother too, for that matter, knew perfectly well that he was beyond recovery and was dreadfully depressed at the prospect of dragging on, and they were still, like her, badly shaken when it happened. He was a very good and much loved father. And anyway, death – I too felt surprisingly sad, considering how fully aware I was, and am, that his going now is a good thing.

I'm going to Norfolk tomorrow. Wasn't sure that Mary would want anyone but the boys around, but she asked me to come. I hope the funeral can be next Thursday, but the undertaker is not sure that it can be fitted in. It will be a huge affair, because almost the whole of Norfolk knew him and liked him. Phil wants to turn it into a very large and splendid party, in celebration of what was on the whole a remarkably happy life, and since he's good at such things I expect he'll manage it. He also wants me to speak at the funeral, which I shall be glad to do. It's odd how having been each other's most intimate friends in early childhood, laid down a sort of sub-structure of affection and understanding that survived a huge amount of difference in our ways of thinking and living as grown-ups.

I'm sending herewith the last-but-one draft of the piece for *The Times*, which surfaced on this chaotic table just now.

Love and love D

22 NOVEMBER 2006

Darling,

Thank god about the test results, which sound about as good as one can hope for at our age and thoroughly dealable with. Also how marvellous that your doctor (doctors?) is/are lovely. Yes, of course ailments and their medication are fascinating – really important stuff, after all, and easy as it is to slip into being snide about doctors and hospitals, they are actually much more often good than bad. I, for one, hearty old woman as I seem to be, would make a very different impression if it wasn't for the three pills I take daily, and have taken for the past five or six years, two for blood pressure and heart, one for something in my guts that is, I think, very like the thing you've got, perhaps identical. Because of all the stories one hears of doctors over-medicating oldies until they become zombies, from time to time I experiment with cutting my medications out, and it's never worked. I've always slid into feeling lousy in one way or another, and have returned to normal health on going back to them. I think your 'the body heals itself' is true enough in youth and middle age, but that it's asking a bit too much of it to expect it to do so when it's old. I'm so happy to think that you are now in Germany at last . . . have a *gorgeous* time there. You certainly deserve it after what you've been enduring.

Barry's party went well. There were twelve of us, so Barbara (who alas had to be in Norfolk on the day) let us have her dining room, and all I had to do was lay the table and supply the dishes. Sally's husband, Henry, is a wonderful cook, simply by nature it seems, he loves doing it and is quite unruffled by large numbers. He cooked, and then transported from Somerset a most delicious tiger prawn, ginger and coconut concoction, so that only the rice and the veg. had to be done on the spot. His daughter Jessamy made Barry's favourite curry in her kitchen, and brought it over, together with a cake she had made. Sally made and brought from Somerset a sublime trifle, Xandra from across the road supplied another cake . . . I only had to supply the wine, the salad, the bread and the cheese (the last of which everyone was much too full by then to touch). It was Barry, me, Lloyd, Sally, Henry, Jessamy, Beachy (short for Beauchamp, their son), Glen (a charming lost boy from the US who seems to have been more or less adopted by that family), Xandra and Clytie and Peter. Barry behaved disgracefully, grabbed Xandra's cake before the meal had started and began sawing at it although it was still wrapped up in cellophane, rejected Jessamy's curry ('I told you I wanted lamb not chicken'), didn't say thank you to anyone for the presents he was given, and stumped off back to bed half way through the first course. He confirmed, in fact, my belief that senility has set in and that it's not just 'Barry being Barry'.

So we went ahead and enjoyed ourselves, everyone knowing him too well to take offence, and sweet Sally and Jess took turns to pop upstairs from time to time and pet him a bit, so I suppose he quite liked it. But I must chase him to at least say thank you to Georgia, Adam's wife. Adam was in New York and Georgia couldn't come because she had a relation visiting to admire the baby, but she had taken the trouble to find six blocks of different kinds of diabetic's chocolate, wrap them up prettily and attach a charming card saying 'With much love from Sandy' (Sandy is Alexander, the baby, and Barry does love him). And all Barry did when I showed it him was grunt. I suppose the occasion would have been a good deal happier if he had been able to take some pleasure in it, but to tell the truth I'm so accustomed by now to what he's turned into that I did quite genuinely enjoy the cheerful kindness of everyone there. Not to mention the trifle! It would have been even more fun if you'd been there. Keep well, darlings. Diana

7 DECEMBER 2006

Darling Edward,

At last I've been able to read your two e-mails about arriving. I don't know why the computer has been misbehaving and has now suddenly pulled itself together. For the last three days when I've tried to see what e-mails have come in, it has said that it is about to access seven new ones, and that little arrow which starts pouring into a box has got to work, but nothing has appeared, and when it reaches four of seven it has just gone on and on and on saying that it is doing that one, for as much as twenty minutes, and still nothing appears! Although I do see that I have three in my inbox – but I can't make them come up on the screen. However, this evening your two have at last and belatedly come up, and I'm so glad to know you have arrived safely and that the apartment seems to be OK. We are OK too, though I've had a stinking cold for a week now – but only a cold, no temperature, quite a good appetite, so nothing to worry about. Tomorrow Barbara goes to Stockholm for the weekend, because Adam, Georgia and Alexander are there and Adam and Georgia are going to some enormously grand Nobel banquet, so Barbara has to be there to baby-sit [*Adam is employed by the Nobel Foundation*]. Therefore I shall be Hannah-sitting, which has become a worry because she now has a v. bad heart and is not supposed to go up stairs but is heavy to carry – so I think I shall take her to Norfolk where the stairs are much fewer and she can manage them. Barbara

nurses her with impassioned care, but when Barbara is ill
as she was last week with a terrible cough, Hannah most
unfairly is horrid to her – she hates her coughing so
much that she refuses to stay in the same room with her!
Luckily Hannah's vet has given her a new heart pill
which has made her feel quite sparkly, so I don't think I'll
have too difficult a time.

My book is making progress, though I don't think it
can possibly become more that 40,000 words long. But
what's wrong with very short books? I'm all for them.
My beloved Ian Jack, editor of *Granta* magazine and boss
of Granta Books, has sadly given his notice. But he won't
be actually leaving till next June, so I'm hoping he'll be
there to accept my book in – with luck – late February,
and get it started. It won't be the same once he's gone –
I'm very sad about it.

Tell me how one gets unread messages out of the
inbox! I thought you just clicked on it, but that isn't
working. Oh how awful if you really have had all your
material wiped out as it went through that machine! Love
and love Diana

12 JANUARY 2007

Darling Edward –

I delivered my book three days ago and am now
summoning up patience and touching wood. Who knows
if Ian will like the second half of it as much as he liked

the first. As soon as I know whether I am to rejoice or to rend my raiment I'll let you know. I had a bad but short cold before my lovely ten-day Xmas holiday, and then a much longer one afterwards which turned into infected sinuses and is only just clearing up under antibiotics. Have not been really ill, but feeling lousy, in spite of which I was able to write last pages of book. Barry has been having a rough time. First, a violent attack of food poisoning (we suppose, tho' what by we don't know) – which was even rougher on me, because of the enormous amount of shit I had to clean off acres of carpet at 3.30 a.m. when feeling far from at my best. For an hour or two I felt that the end had come, I just couldn't go on, but as you know, one can in fact go on. Then he had a horrid fall on the stairs, the first fall he has had. Nothing broken, thank god, but bruised and very shaken. But that has led to a good development, because our darling pocket doctor, Jess, daughter of Sally and Henry who is well on in her medical studies and lives just down the road from us, agreed to go with him to his doctor instead of me. He alone at the doc's might just as well be staying at home in bed because he never says anything about what's wrong and never listens to what is said, and I at the doc's with him am not much better because I'm not really sure what to ask and am inhibited when trying to report on his condition by his scowls and denials. But Jess, this morning, got him referred for a) a cardiac examination and b) a general neurological examination, both of which he urgently needs, and also got his medication changed because one of the things he's been taking is notoriously depressing. We now have to wait for the appointments, of course, but at least something may come of it.

Lloyd, his brother, has to go back to Jamaica next week because his tenant is moving out of his house there and will probably take most of his furniture unless Lloyd is there to keep an eye. He is v. depressed by Barry who is, I think, pleased to have him around, but who has spoken no more to him since he arrived in November than he has to me. I shall miss Lloyd, although it will be rather a relief not to have to spend so much time thinking up interesting dinners – he's a keen foodie. But on the whole it's his keen attitude that makes him a pleasure to have around. He's well on in his seventies, but is full of energy and does so enormously enjoy his theatre-going and so on – a pleasant change from poor B! He says he'll come back in March if he manages to let his house again by then. Love and love, dear loves, and touch wood for *Somewhere Near the End* (too downbeat a title? I like it). Diana

14 JANUARY 2007

Darling E,

I like *After the Fall: Poems Old and New* – and I'm good at titles: do call it that. And I'm glad it's not too long before you'll be back home, because this time of year, through to the end of Feb., is the pits. Any kind of ailment just goes on and on, making one feel low and vulnerable even if not really ill, and the cosiness of being at home is preferable to anything else in such circumstances. My heavy catarrh drags on – not noticeable when my mind's engaged, but lurking for empty moments: a bore. And yours sounds a bit worse.

I read that Stasi book and nothing would make me visit the place! I hope you follow your instinct and don't. Yes, one should know about such miserable horrors, but what the fuck good does it do to *dwell* on them? Particularly when one is old. At one's active peak one probably ought to because just possibly dwelling on evil strengthens one's ability to do something about it, but what more do we need to know beyond the plenty we know already? Did I tell you – I don't think I did – about Alice Herz-Sommer, 103 years old and interviewed in the *Guardian*, survivor of Theresienstadt from which her young husband went to his death, and of the deaths of all his and most of her own family, and not long ago of her beloved son whom she had raised single-handed in Israel, to which she went (from Czechoslovakia) after the war, and who brought her to London twenty years ago where she still lives in a one-room flat not far from here. And who practices the piano (she studied under a pupil of Liszt's) for three hours every day to this day, and says cheerfully that life is extremely beautiful – and indeed looks in her photo as though that is what she truly feels. She attributes this to her great luck in being born with an optimistic disposition, so that 'although I know about the bad I look only for the good'. Which I have decided is a good idea! xxxxxxx Diana

15 FEBRUARY 2007

Darling,

What is this airy reference to a colostomy? This must have been the medical news waiting for you on your return home – what a horrid shock [*not so horrid; Edward had mistyped* colonoscopy – *the investigation, not the operation – and all was well*]. It is of course true that lots of people have them and manage very well having done so, so you are quite right not to mop and mow and rend your raiment over it, but all the same –

What a bloody nuisance! Barbara's mother had one when she was sixty-three, and being one of the world's most squeamish women, made the heaviest weather imaginable of it. I believe that nowadays they often manage to restore the guts to normal working order, but in those days there was no question of that, it was just a new hole for the shit to come out of into a colostomy bag and that was that, and she drove everyone to distraction with her horror at this fate – but in the end managed to live very successfully with it for over thirty more years! But the most recent one I know of, a few months ago, was restored to normal remarkably soon, so I devoutly hope that will be so in your case. But obviously it's going to complicate your busy spring programme.

I can't print things at the moment – thought at first I must have done something silly to my printer, but peering into its innards I now think I can see something broken. Granta printed out the book for me (and will have to do so again because I have just greatly improved the last chapter).

Extraordinary to read about your snowfall while we are in the middle of a freakish early spring! It's true that last week we had three coldish days and a bit of snow (in London about two inches, which melted away overnight) but now it's sun with intermittent gentle showers of rain, and the magnolia in our garden is nearly out, and birds are singing. Somewhere near here a robin is reported to have built a nest in a Christmas wreath hanging on someone's door, and hatched four eggs! But I suppose your blizzard could still cross the Atlantic – the usual pattern seems to be that we get your bad weather about a week later.

Barry heard this morning that he must have a cataract operation in about a month's time – he seemed to be unaware that his sight was deteriorating, though I had noticed it. Having been assured by me that it won't hurt (which of course it won't) he is unworried. I hope the Royal Free, which is where he will have it, is as good as Moorfield's, the very old-fashioned but marvellous eye hospital which did mine. I haven't suggested he transfers, because the Royal Free is round the corner while Moorfield's entails a good many visits to quite a distant clinic where you have to endure long waits, and he's not up to that.

I'm a bit overwhelmed, having foolishly accepted an invitation to be one of the judges for the Samuel Johnson non-fiction prize (a big prize – £30,000 – organized by the BBC). Naturally this involves a hideous amount of reading. At this stage it's not too bad because we are still weeding-out to reduce the number of books to the 'long list' of twenty, which means that quite a lot of the books are obvious non-contenders so don't have to be read right through. But it's going to become a headache, because there's a lot of very good stuff there, and there are really hard decisions ahead – a big problem being that there are many kinds of non-fiction, and how do you decide between a very good biography and a very good piece of popular science? It will be like those ridiculous things at the end of big dog shows when they make the Best of Show award, choosing between a Pomeranian on the one hand and a Pit Bull on the other. But I believe – I'm not sure – that we get paid £2000, which will be nice! Goodbye for now (high time, you'll be thinking!). xxxxxxxxx D

16 FEBRUARY 2007

Darling –

Thank goodness for that! Just had a call from Ian Jack confirming acceptance of book (of which I have revised the last little chapter to v. good effect, I think). 'So now will you send me a contract?' – 'Yes of course, – I've been thinking about money. What about – ' and this is what I think I heard him say, but given my deafness I may well be wrong '– eight thousand pounds'!!! Actually I don't think it could have been that, but what other figure sounds roughly like 'eight'? Certainly not 'two' (what I was hoping for) or even 'three' or 'four' well, we'll see when the contract comes, and shan't be at all surprised if it turns out I misheard ridiculously (I often do, particularly on the phone). The more I think about it the more sure I become that I must have done [*but I hadn't*]. xxxxxxxxx D

21 FEBRUARY 2007

Darling,

Love hearing that you enjoyed *Somewhere Towards the End*. I took the disc over to Granta today, so now they've got the final thing, and Ian confirmed that it is £8000. I'm sure I only got £2000 last time, tho' of course more came in when they paperbacked my other books. It seems that nowadays eight is nothing special – he was very tickled when I asked him to confirm it because I couldn't believe it was so much, he thought I was raising the subject because I was going to ask for more. Perhaps I should have done!!!

I thought my printer was just choking on a piece of paper, but now I've peered into it while the ink cartridges are sliding back towards their parking place (into which they won't fully go, which is the trouble) and I see there is a sort of comb-shaped white thing against which they are supposed to come to rest, and two of its teeth are sort of sticking up – in a broken-looking way, so that's probably the trouble. Francis will be back from Italy in

about two weeks and I'll have to get him to come and
look at it. Will see about e-mailing revised end soon, but
must now cope with poor sick Hannah who I'm dog
sitting today. xxxxxx D—

8 MARCH 2007

Darling,

V. sad here, because Hannah died yesterday. At last
Barbara called in the vet to give her a lethal injection,
which she should have done days earlier – the poor little
dog has been dying slowly, slowly for so long, but B
stubbornly clung on to refusing to admit it. I, though
thankful that it's over, feel v. sad, but B is so distressed
it's unbearable to see it. I'm sure she loved Hannah more
than any human except Adam. A kind neighbour put us
on to a lovely gardening lady who came to dig a grave in
our garden – a very hard task because in London you
only have to go down about ten inches before you strike
a most evil, solid, slimy yellow clay. Adam had made a
little coffin and the funeral is tomorrow – but I shall be
taking Barry to an appointment with his doctor, I'm glad
to say, so will miss it.

I did tell you, didn't I, that I have rashly let myself in
for being one of the judges for the BBC's Samuel
Johnson non-fiction prize? Can hardly get into my sitting
room for the piles of books and my eyes are beginning to
give out. Up to now, of the five contenders I've sieved

out, the two most likely are a very elegant life of a savage old Welsh poet, and a *gigantic* history of the 1950s (tremendously impressive tho' utterly exhausting to someone like me who is far from being at home in the field of economics). How the hell anyone could decide which of two such unlike-each-other books is 'the better' god alone knows. It makes for rather infrequent reading of e-mail, I'm afraid, and short answers. Better soon, I hope. xxxxxxxxxx Diana

12 MARCH 2007

Darling –

How adventurous you are! The idea of making a film by means of a computer seems to me to belong in the realm of science fiction. You will, I know, fight your way through to familiarity with your new machine, and I'm so envious and admiring of your courage and cleverness that I can hardly bear it. How can I be so dim that I don't even know how to delete all my old e-mails from this old thing? It is a sort of idiocy, into which I seem to be sunk – and look at you, soaring into the computer empyrean like an eagle!

Your earnings are impressive, but with no National Health Service you don't half need them! One of the books under which I am buried is a history of the 1950s – a very serious one, all about the politics and economics of the time, and I think tremendously good (tho' being illiterate as regards economics I have found a lot of it hard going). It makes it hideously clear that when they embarked upon the Welfare State none of our politicians and thinkers had got round to understanding that we were no longer an immensely rich World Power, so they bit off far more than the country could chew . . . they were doing something we simply couldn't afford, the consequences of which are still mounting up. It's very frightening, actually, but still how glad I am that they did it, considering that the NHS is at least staggering on for long enough to see me out (God Willing!).

This Prize's workload is not really too appallingly heavy. Only about three hundred books were submitted, and at our first meeting (a long and exhausting one), we most ruthlessly weeded out most of them (actually it was easier to do than I expected – so many of them were just obviously not going to make it). We left ourselves with a mere fifty, which we have all been reading with the aim of reducing them to a long-list of twenty, out of which we will have to choose a short-list of six, and that will be when the agony begins, when a decision will have to be made between books all good and all of completely different kinds! Out of my fifty I already know that there are five obvious contenders. It's going to be interesting to learn at our next meeting, in two weeks time, what the other three judges have been deciding.

It is strange what an emptiness poor little Hannah has left – Barry and I keep thinking we hear her barking, or scratching at our door demanding to be let in, and of course it is worse for Barbara. But to my great surprise, at the weekend she switched on the telly in order to watch Crufts, the huge and internationally famous dog show that happens once a year (it used to be a London event, but has been moved to Birmingham now). At one point the camera concentrated on some little dogs called Papillons (because they have big ears rather like butterfly wings) and she was so charmed by them that I realized she may well invest in another puppy before long. I think she's too old to take on a new dog, because she's almost as bad at walking as I am, but probably she's envisaging moving permanently to the country in the not so far future (she has already made this house over to Adam) and there we have enough garden for a small dog to run about in without needing to be taken for walks. I now think that when she does make that move, she'll probably get a new dog.

The news that spring fever has begun to turn your thoughts in the direction of London is very welcome. Love and love. Diana

16 MARCH 2007

Darling –

A lovely long one about how France was broke too, and how medical bills are mounting but you are still aiming to come in May, *did* get through, which I suppose to be the one they said didn't.

We were so broke because we had huge debts (I haven't managed to understand to whom or why) and had spent a lot more on the war than France because we went on being in it after they were out of it, and because without the Empire (which we were busily and to my mind rightly getting rid of) we are *very small*, which our half-witted politicians couldn't get their heads round. The worst thing I have always thought was utterly losing our splendiferous steel industry which we could have saved if we hadn't been haughty and refused to join a proposed European organization (the book's weakness is a very inadequate index, so when I want to check up on things in it, such as name of said organization, I *can't!*). 'We don't want foreigners buggering about with our steel' said Anthony Eden or words to that effect, whereas if we'd become part of it together with France and Germany we'd still be in business. A very fascinating part of the book is that so many hitherto secret documents have now been opened. One never, of course, had much time for politicians, but the extent of their idiocy when fully revealed is gobsmacking. But one of the qualities we judges are supposed to take into account is 'reader friendliness' so I don't know what the consensus will be about the very considerable amount of heavy going in this book – which we will after all be having to compare with other v. good books.

Today a sweet photographer turned up to take a picture of my 'work space' – the *Guardian* has been running a little feature of photographs of writers' dens, most of which have been wonderfully professional-looking, in cosy rooms with pleasant rural outlooks before which are placed huge desks covered with every kind of Modern Convenience and learned apparatus. I've been saying to myself 'Lucky I'm not famous enough for them – I bet no one else has to eat off their knee because their only table has become their work space, and has to clear everything off it on to their bed if they want to serve a meal to guests.' But they got round to me in the end, and declared themselves delighted to have found a writer in my circumstances. I'll send you what they publish when it comes out. The photographer was a dear man and threw in a pic. of me for free to go on the back of the jacket of the new book. He said he liked my work space best, but I bet he says that to all the girls and boys.

Today I'm feeling a bit better. I've been having fiendish aches and pains all over for the last month or so, starting with a frozen shoulder, then spreading. At first it seemed that my osteopath was helping, but such improvement as he achieved never lasted more than a day or two, so I've just made an appointment with my doctor, who won't be back from her holiday till next Thursday, and perhaps by that time it will be all better!

Francis Hughes, my computer nanny, who has most tiresomely moved to France and also to Italy from time to time, luckily still answers his mobile and called me this morning to report that he has tracked down for me a 2nd hand printer exactly the same as my broken one, so someone is delivering it to me on Tuesday and I'll be able just to plug it in and go ahead – no new soft-whatsit to install and I can use my old ink cartridges. The broken one is out of date, of course, so it's great luck that he's found a match for it. Which is timely, because I've got two thousand pounds worth of article to send to the *Guardian Weekend* next week. They are doing a series of articles about the last decades of the last century and asked me to do the 50s – a lucky coincidence with that book! xxxxxxxxx Diana

5 APRIL 2007

Darling –

Alas, but Barry is really ill. They are talking in terms of an operation – a new valve for his heart, or perhaps a by-pass – but say they couldn't operate yet because he's not well enough. At first they seemed to think that they could get him stabilized by next Tuesday (today is Thursday) but this afternoon he struck both me and Jess as most peculiarly dopey, and thank god she was there, because being by now an almost-qualified doctor gives her the nerve to make her presence felt, and her great charm makes her able to do so without alienating the doctors and nurses in the hospital, so off she bustled and cornered the head cardiologist who came at once and examined B and can you believe it, he's been in that hospital only one night and already he's got an infection! So that'll have to be coped with. It's really desperate about hospitals – someone as ill as he is just has to be in one, yet the dangers of being there are so real. Jess says she's seen enough of them by now to understand that an old person in hospital can easily be just left there to die unless they have someone young and knowledgeable in attendance to make sure that they get properly looked after. It's the most enormous luck for us that she is here and is taking on that role wholeheartedly (Barry's been like a most favourite uncle of hers all her life). Barbara has just called from Norfolk to say that it's absolutely ravishing there at the moment and can't I come down for the weekend given that Jess is taking over at the hospital, and I am sort of dithering. It's true that today he hardly noticed my presence, and that she is the one who is of great practical use, but I feel dreadfully uneasy at the thought of not being around. I think I'll wait to see how things go tomorrow, and then discuss it with Jess. Actually it would be easier for her without me, because she has to take me up by car and there are nightmarish parking problems, whereas by herself she can nip up there on her bicycle in five minutes and no parking problems – probably, unless he's much worse tomorrow I will go ...

My own problems seem v. small compared. Went to my doc this morning and it turned out that the technician who had taken my blood for the test, who was a trainee (very sweet but rather nervous) had not taken enough blood. The lab had been able to do all the tests the doc had asked for except one – and that one was the very one we most need! It's nice to know that all the other things (thyroid, liver, cholesterol and god knows what else) are in perfect shape, and the doc very kindly took blood herself then and there instead of sending me back to the hospital for it, but now of course we have to wait for the lab to report on it, and she happens to be going off for a week's holiday, so I won't be able to hear the result for another two weeks. Perhaps it will clear up on its own by then, touch wood. I'm *so happy* that you've been released ...

Jess has just called to say that she'd pedalled up to the hosp. for another look at him and he'd perked up a lot – was sitting up and eating some supper, and that of course I should go to Norfolk for the w.e. and we can call each other all the time so stop fussing. So *I shall go*! And my computer, properly chastened by the faunlike but very expensive Sean, is being as good as gold. Are you happy with your new one – and have you embarked on the film of Tobias's apt.? xxxxxxx Diana

24 APRIL 2007

Darling Edward –

I managed, with the help of his doctor, to get Barry back into hospital this morning, having failed at breakfast time to persuade him to take even one sip of drink or one bite of food ... and collapsed into bed, suddenly feeling to the full how exhausting the last ten days have been (angelic Jess went with him in the ambulance and saw him into bed). Then, just as was beginning to recover enough to plan four blissful days in Norfolk (supposing that he would be safely tucked up in hosp. for at least a week) I hear from Jess that the hospital said they would keep him for two days. I can't see how he can possibly be put right in two days! Of course they may change their minds, but bang goes my plan of slinking off to the country tomorrow – I shall have to wait here till Thursday, when it looks as though we well may be back in square one. I can't tell you how bleak I feel that prospect to be. But at least, dear Edward, I've got tomorrow. Is it possible for me to park my car in your little yard, like I did once before, and can I visit you, if so? [*Edward and Neil were in London, staying in a block of flats with a convenient forecourt.*] Call me.

Diana

[*A long silence ensued, caused by complicated events during which communication was infrequent and by telephone. Barry became much iller and needed a heart operation too complex for the Royal Free Hospital, so they referred him to the Heart Hospital. There we were told that they wouldn't operate because the probability of his dying on the table was too great. The surgeon told us to expect his death within a year. Barry didn't seem unduly distressed ('I don't feel as though I'll be dead in a year, but I don't suppose I'll mind much if I am') but I was pretty desperate: my 90th birthday was approaching and how I was going to cope I could not imagine. It is impossible to express my thankfulness when, without warning, his niece Margaret Bernal arrived in London saying she had come to take him back to Jamaica where she had arranged a little flat for him in a house she owned across the road from her own house, where a couple lived who would look after him. Sally rushed up to London and between them the two women got him packed up and onto a plane (first class) within a week. It was a long time since Margaret had told me she was thinking of taking him in if necessary, and I had assumed she had forgotten about it, so it hadn't entered my head to call on her.*

It was a shock, and of course it was sad that our long]

relationship had come to this; but simultaneously it was a most profound relief – a relief registered in my body before it fully reached my mind. The acute pain I had been experiencing in my neck and arms vanished almost at once. In Jamaica Barry continues – still continues – to live exactly as he did here, lying in bed all day, watching a little television, hardly ever talking – except for saying to Margaret not long ago that he intended to live another twenty-five years. Sally visits him, and often telephones him, but I no longer do, because although I have explained the situation to him over and over again, in letters and by phone, all he ever says is 'When am I coming home?']

9 OCTOBER 2007

Darling –

Such a long silence! I'm getting quite worried, but tell myself to stop fussing, it's more likely owing to your having been away, and busy, than to ill health. And I too, after all, have been silent – largely due to longish periods during which my laptop was playing up. Going on to broadband, meant to be such an ease-making delight, seems to have disgreed with it. And as for bloody Skype – all it ever tells me is that people aren't there to receive it!

Somewhere Towards sold to Norton – did I tell you? So it's almost earned its advance before publication which is a cheering thought.

This week, such a lovely thing. Thirty-five years ago

my sister's youngest daughter had a baby. She fell in love at age thirteen with her riding master, and being a stubborn child hung on to him in spite of much parental discouragement through thick and thin – I remember my sister saying in despair 'We can't actually lock her up or we'll lose her forever.' They knew what a miserable little shit he was, but infatuated Jane refused to see it – until, when she was seventeen, she got pregnant and he said 'Alas, I'm not good enough for you. We must part.' (Since when, it seems, he's gone on from teenager to teenager.) She refused an abortion, or to settle for having it and letting her parents help her look after it, but she strongly felt that she did not want to condemn herself at that age to the life of a single mother, so she decided to come to England (they lived in Zimbabwe, then called Rhodesia), give birth and have the child adopted. So she came to me, and was very brisk and brave, getting temping jobs throughout her pregnancy. I'm glad to say that all the family, even the oldest and sedatest aunts, was kind and supportive, not just me, and her mother came over to England to be with her for the birth. She was expecting the adoption agency to take the child as soon as it was born, but they said no, she must be fully aware of what she was doing, so she must keep her for a month. And that was agony. She stuck to her plan, even choosing the family to whom the child was going, but she cried for a solid month once it was gone. But then she pulled herself together, got a job as a veterinary nurse, and before a year was out had married the vet. Since when they've had four children and a good life, but she has never stopped aching deep down at having given up that baby, and has dreaded it turning up one day to blame her.

Well – last week, out of the blue, an e-mail from New Zealand, and there her daughter was – a really lovely young woman, friendly and thrilled at having traced her, telling her that she'd had a marvellous childhood with parents she dearly loves, and grandparents too, and wasn't tracing her birth mother for any other reason but natural curiosity, and was anxious not to do anything that might upset Jane or her family, but she's coming to England for a visit next week and might they perhaps meet. Jane, of course, is in raptures – all her family is thrilled – if Beth were going to be here long enough (sadly she isn't) she'd find that instead of upsetting anyone she has suddenly found a large and open-armed second family and a birth-mother quite drunk with joy at knowing at last that she didn't harm her child. She, at least, she'll have time to meet. I'd love to meet her too – after all, she spent quite a long time in this flat before she was born – and hope I will one day. And I wish my mother were still alive to know that this happy thing has happened – she was very fond of Jane.

So this family drama has rather blown everything else out of my mind at the moment – I must write to Barry and tell him all about it, because he was around, of course, and a good friend to Jane all through her pregnancy ... Everyone was, lucky little girl, and now this crowning piece of luck. Hurrah!

Let me hear your news, dear love! Diana

[My niece tells me I exaggerated her youth: she was fifteen when she fell in love and twenty-one when her child was born. She has

always been devoted to children. I asked her, when she herself was still a child, what her ambition was, and she answered, 'To be the youngest grandmother in Rhodesia'. She says now that the strongest element in her decision to have her baby adopted was dismay at the thought of giving it a miserable childhood. She envisaged how, as a single mother working full-time she would probably have to live in a town, and would certainly have often to entrust the child to minders, and that was so unlike her own very enjoyable rural childhood that it seemed to her appalling. The family she chose for her daughter lived in the country and had ponies for their children: that much she could control. It was, of course, pure luck that they turned out to be such lovable parents.]

30 OCTOBER 2007

Darling –

There are some things in my life which will remain precious until it ends, and one of them is certainly seeing the words 'for Diana Athill' at the front of *After the Fall* – not to mention the lovely handwritten message. It is *truly* a great thing to be the dedicatee of such a collection. I have just this moment got back from Norfolk and opened your parcel – done no more that weigh the book in my hands and read 'Credo'. The lugubriousness of the jacket dismayed me for a moment – it's not fair on the rich variety of mood contained within it, and I wish they'd used instead the photo of you which is on the back, looking so handsome and wise – but I think most people who read poetry think about a book's contents rather than its appearance, don't you?

I've decided what I'm going to do: make it literally my bedside book, keep it there and read not more than three or four poems every evening. Poems, like short stories, are difficult to read properly (for me, anyway) because you read one and enjoy it so you go greedily on to the next one – and the next – and the next, until you realize that your eyes have started bouncing off them without taking them in. By making myself more disciplined with yours, I'll make them a part of my life (as some are already), which poems should be. Oh dearest Edward, I do hope you are feeling as proud as you ought to feel when you see the hugeness of your achievement gathered together. And that the shenanigans of publication will be *fun*, as well as productive of handsome sales. As for me, I feel immensely proud of knowing you – and now, of people knowing that I know you! xxxxxxx Diana

3 NOVEMBER 2007

Darling –

Of course I didn't manage to stick to reading only a few poems, I read one or two and then on and on I went until I looked at the time and saw it was 3.15 in the morning! Much of it, of course, was re-reading, but the new poems do include the best thing ever, or so it strikes me – 'After the Fall'. When I finally flopped into bed my last thought before going to sleep was 'How I do love Edward!'

Yesterday I was visited by Jane's recovered daughter. Their first meeting was less easy than they expected because they were both almost unbearably nervous. I'm v. pleased with myself for playing a part in getting them over this. I'd sent a welcoming e-mail to Beth and something I said hit the right button and decided her to ask for a second meeting rather than call it a day, and that meeting went like wedding bells and climaxed in their coming here for 3–4 hours of most animated talk – really interesting and enjoyable. She's a good addition to the family. We won't be seeing much of each other because she and her partner live in New Zealand, but we'll certainly stay in touch, and enjoy doing so.

Just heard that the Hay Literary Festival (in May, and much the nicest of all the literary festivals) wants me. Both Jane and my sister live near it, in truly lovely country, so we'll have great fun. The *Guardian*'s coming to interview me soon, extracts have been sold to *Daily Telegraph* and to a v. widely circulated mag. for oldies called *Saga*, which combined with the sale to Norton has more than earned the advance, so omens are good. And my darling nephew Phil, instead of giving a large drinks party for my 90th birthday, which I forbade, is giving three big lunch parties on Dec. 14, 15, and 16, which he and his wife Annabel are going to cook for, about fifteen people at each party in their v. nice flat, which will be far more enjoyable, marred only by the absence of you and Neil. How I do wish it were possible for us to be at each other's publication celebrations! And how I do wish that

we both *astonish ourselves* by how well our life's blood
sells. Love and Love and Love xxxxxxx Diana

5 NOVEMBER 2007

Darling,

The party sounds lovely – and so many books sold! It's
amazing and delicious, isn't it, how reviving an enjoyable
occasion is – and what could be more enjoyable than an
appreciative audience! Given one about every three days,
I guess one could live for ever. Actually I find that even
enjoyable things unconnected with the nurturing of one's
ravenous ego provide a revivifying shot, if one stirs
oneself up to the point of undertaking them. The other
day I went with Clytie and Peter to an exhibition at the
Tate [*Tate Britain*], having started by saying that I wasn't
up to it because even with a door-to-door taxi it would
involve so much walking: that huge flight of steps up to
the entrance, and then such miles of marble halls to
cover ... But having dithered for a bit, I decided in a
martyred way that I ought to give it a try – after all, I
could always collapse onto a bench and let them get on
with it if it was really too much.

And when it came to it I enjoyed looking at the
paintings so much that I stopped noticing my arthritic
hips and got all the way round the exhibition very
happily – exhausted afterwards, but none the worse for
it. It was useful, too, in that I saw how many oldies were

spinning round it in wheeled chairs provided by the gallery. It seems that all the big galleries supply them nowadays, so the next time I want to go to a show I'll book one in advance – they are self-propelling, so you don't have to have a pusher – and will be able to enjoy such treats even without feeling tired afterwards. I'm sure the three consecutive days of birthday lunch-parties being organized so angelically by Phil will leave me prostrate, but while they are going on will make me forget my age [*which they did*].

Although you're a mere octo, you have a more testing time than I do now that Barry's in Jamaica. Not one single onion have I chopped or piece of pork have I grilled since he left, and my god what a relief it is!

I wonder sometimes whether living on bread and cheese, yoghurt, large quantities of fruit, occasional slices of salami or fillets of smoked mackerel – oh yes, and bowls of oatmeal porridge from time to time – may the best thing for keeping up energy, but I take a few vitamin supplements and I don't in the least *want* to eat anything else.

Probably at this stage one doesn't in fact need proper meals, and one certainly doesn't need the chore of shopping for them and preparing them. I've had people to dinner three times since he left, cooking things that could mostly be prepared a day in advance, and each time I've felt uncomfortably overfed afterwards, even though I've given myself tiny helpings. But men do need to eat more than women, so perhaps you resent regular cooking less than I did. May you have many more alert and appreciative audiences! Love and love. D

POSTSCRIPT

The collected letters go on for another year, and the correspondence still continues, as does our friendship, but it seems to me that this is the time to write FINIS. The reason is simple: we have become old. The relaxed form of the letter makes it more than just a way of keeping in touch; it is a way of sharing experience, and too often the experience old people have to share is wobbly health. One does mind a great deal about the health of a dear friend, and one wants to know about it, but the detailed swapping of symptoms does undeniably become boring, so the brisker informative style of the e-mail begins to take over from the expansiveness of the letter, and the fun goes out of the writing.

That is not to say that life after November 2007 became nothing but aches and pains. It was, in fact, very full of other matters, because both Edward and I had the luck to experience Indian Summers. He, having endured a period during which his poetry went out of fashion, is now seeing it come back again, while I . . . well, *Stet* was a success and after that book came two more, the second of which was even more of a success than *Stet;* but greatly though I enjoyed this unexpected development, the wish to write about it, strong to begin with, soon began to dwindle. I found this hard to understand at first, but now I think I know the cause. When I am doing the things entailed by success – giving talks, being interviewed, meeting well-known people and so on – I certainly enjoy it because I have discovered that I am good at it, but all the time a tiny inner voice (I think of it as the voice of my family) is whispering 'You are showing off' – and in my childhood 'showing off' was the worst thing you could do next to lying. And not only was showing off so disgraceful, but occasions favourable to showing off were 'bad for you', they were corrupting. The whisper is not loud enough to make me avoid such occasions, or to stop me having a good time at them, but it does cause me to think about them as little as possible – deliberately to avert my mind from them – so it has gradually leached away any pleasure I might take in describing them. Which leaves for letters mostly the aches and pains. I would like to end with a bang rather than a whimper, but bangs don't happen to the old (short of the last one), so please accept a quiet 'The End'.

Diana Athill,
London, March 2011